Good God

Suffering, Faith, Reason and Science

— MICHAEL BROOKS —

Sacristy Press
PO Box 612, Durham, DH1 9HT

www.sacristy.co.uk

First published in 2024 by Sacristy Press, Durham

Copyright © Michael Brooks 2024
The moral rights of the author have been asserted.

All rights reserved, no part of this publication may be reproduced or transmitted in any form or by any means, electronic, mechanical photocopying, documentary, film or in any other format without prior written permission of the publisher.

Scripture quotations, unless otherwise stated, are from the New Revised Standard Version Bible: Anglicized Edition, copyright © 1989, 1995 National Council of the Churches of Christ in the United States of America. Used by permission. All rights reserved worldwide.

Every reasonable effort has been made to trace the copyright holders of material reproduced in this book, but if any have been inadvertently overlooked the publisher would be glad to hear from them.

Sacristy Limited, registered in England & Wales, number 7565667

British Library Cataloguing-in-Publication Data
A catalogue record for the book is available from the British Library

ISBN 978-1-78959-328-0

Contents

Introduction... 1
Prologue 7

Chapter 1. The Christian hope of Heaven...................... 8

Chapter 2. Theophany: Evidence of God's love for the cosmos... 15
Science and religion... 19
Physics.. 23
Cosmology... 41
Biology 46
Theology.. 72
Philosophy of creation....................................... 78

Chapter 3. Moral evil and natural evil....................... 88
Theodicy.. 88
The Old Testament... 99
Suffering of human origin: "moral evil" 115
Suffering of natural origin................................. 128
God and suffering... 149
Summary 174

Chapter 4. How might God act in the cosmos? 176
Physics: Theological reflections 176
Theology of nature.. 185
Creativity 210

Chapter 5. Some implications of the proposed theodicy 216
The Parousia 216
The *pre-archaios* 218
A new creation... 228

Epilogue 235

Appendix. Further comparison with some other theodicies 237
Ancient 237
Modern 242

Bibliography 247

Introduction

This book is primarily written for clergy, ordinands, students of theology and lay Christian leaders. It may also be of some interest to scientists and philosophers, particularly those who are interested in the relationship between their subject and the Christian faith, whether or not the latter is held personally. The book is intended to demonstrate a defensible Christian theodicy,[1] which is compatible with the discoveries and insights of modern science. I hope that this book will stimulate a constructive dialogue between modern science and Christian theology. Although I have attempted to write this book with pastoral sensitivity (and academic rigour), the book is primarily intended to contribute to the philosophical and theological discussion of theodicy, rather than have a primary purpose to provide comfort to people who, whether they consider themselves to be Christian or otherwise, are struggling to reconcile matters of faith in the context of the current circumstances of their lives. Although pastoral matters and tragedies are not addressed directly in the main text, I hope that this book will nevertheless help to provide those who are suffering and their comforters with some ideas that may provide some consolation. Pastoral matters are mainly dealt with in the Epilogue.

Whilst reading medicine at King's College London (1975–81), my interest in theology found expression in reading for the AKC (a theology diploma), and my interest in science found expression in an intercalated year of study in 1978 in the Department of Biophysics that enabled me to obtain a degree in Cell and Molecular Biology. During this intercalated year, I wrote an essay submitted for a course on "The

---

[1] "Theodicy offers an account of why God allows suffering and evil." M. Peterson et al., *Reason and Religious Belief*, 3rd edn (Oxford: Oxford University Press, 2003), p. 137.

Social Impact of the Biosciences" titled "The conflict between science and Christianity: artefact or real?", in which I argued that any perceived conflict between science and Christianity was artefactual, i.e. of human origin. In my essay, I concluded that scientific activity could be regarded as an act of worship, i.e. acknowledging who God is and the qualities of God. Christian believers should expect Christian faith and science to be compatible. For if the cosmos is real, and the results of testing and enquiry are dependable, then any religious "truths" and scientific "truths" that we discover should be compatible, since they have their origin in the same source.

Although I had concluded that there was no *real* conflict between science and Christianity, I had not explored the question of suffering. Having qualified as a medical doctor, I was continually reminded of the suffering of humankind on a daily basis as I practised initially as a surgical trainee and then as a general medical practitioner for several decades.

Whilst undergoing theological training (South East Institute for Theological Education, 2005–8), I found no satisfactory answer to my questions regarding suffering and theodicy. The books that were recommended seemed to conclude that such matters were shrouded in "Holy Mystery". Other students seemed to have little time for apologetics, "either people have faith or they do not" being one response which I recall from a fellow student. The principal of the college wrote in my final report that I would need to wait until the next life before I could have my questions answered. Prior to commencing training, one of the answers I had received as a member of a congregation was "God is so great that God has to limit Himself",[2] which did not seem an adequate description of God deemed also to be omnipotent and loving. Another response was "God either heals people or enables them to accept their illness and both of these are miracles", which seemed pastorally insensitive and was inadequate for those who were unwilling or unable to accept their "fate". Again the description of God seemed far less than omnipotent.

---

[2] Whilst I have attempted to use inclusive language when describing God, quotes from other sources are quoted as they are without correction for the purposes of historical accuracy.

Further consideration of the interface between science and Christianity revealed that the emergence of science has questioned the need to postulate the existence of a creator god. The emergence of science has undoubtedly also diminished the authority of the Bible as a literal account; for example the narrative of Creation that took the time taken for the Earth to spin on its axis six times does not fit with the geological record. In other areas of learning, the rise of biblical criticism included the discovery of parallel ancient texts that diminished the notion that the literature in the Bible was unique and without parallel, such as the apparent influence of the Egyptian *Hymn to the Aten* on Psalm 104:20–5 when it was written, even if the theology differs.[3] Since it is no longer tenable to simply assume, as in the Bible, that suffering and death occur with no explanation apparently being required, then the Christian understanding of God who is both omniscient and omnipotent presents a considerable intellectual challenge in the face of suffering and death.

In proclaiming "one Almighty God", there is no part of the cosmos that is outside of God's knowledge and power. The consequent "sanctification of all things" results in the problem of theodicy that is confined to the monotheism of the Hebraic–Christian understanding of God: this problem would not occur with polytheist or henotheist beliefs.[4] The philosopher John Hick (1973) in his *Philosophy of Religion* has stated that the root of "the problem of evil" is that "God cannot be both omnipotent and perfectly loving".[5]

Michael Peterson, Professor of Philosophy, makes this point more starkly:

> If it should develop that a certain idea of god[6] suffers from unreconcilable internal contradictions, then with regard to that

---

[3] J. Romer, *Testament: The Bible and History* (London: Michael O'Mara Books, 1988), p. 43.

[4] John Hick, *Philosophy of Religion*, 2nd edn (Hoboken, NJ: Prentice-Hall, 1973), p. 6.

[5] Hick, *Philosophy of Religion*, p. 3.

[6] To refer to the incarnate and revealed God of the Hebraic–Christian tradition, God is spelt with an upper-case letter "G". When spelt with a lower-case letter

conception we need proceed no further: a "god" whose nature can be stated only in contradictions cannot possibly exist, and to suppose that there is such a god as that is nonsense.[7]

The proclamation of an all-loving and all-powerful God is contradicted by the level of suffering on this planet. The primary purpose of this book is an attempt to resolve this contradiction.

The book will include the understanding that whilst God is proclaimed to be omnipotent, as in all-powerful, some things, such as making an object which is both a cube and a sphere, are impossible for God to do and that God may also have good reasons to limit God's power. Critics of Christian theodicy do not appear to accept such limitations, such as the atheist philosopher Michael Tooley, who states:

> If one wants to explain the mixed state of the world by the hypothesis that the creator of the world was an omnipotent, omniscient, and morally perfect deity, one needs to postulate the existence of additional, morally significant properties that lie beyond our ken.[8]

For Tooley the omnipotence and omniscience are immutable and absolute, even to the point that any logical impossibilities could be overcome, leading to a world of fantasy, and thus for Tooley what is acceptable in morality has to be changed. This book will attempt to "explain the mixed state of the world" without resorting to redefining morality.

On a global level a constructive dialogue between science and religion is urgently required since this would help to end the conflict between ideologies that is leading to the restriction of learning and to increased suffering, and is costing human lives. The historic antipathy of the

---

"g", the word refers to other understandings of god as, for example, in the philosophical metaphysical tradition.

[7] Peterson et al., *Reason and Religious Belief*, p. 59.
[8] M. Tooley, "Theodicy and the Problem of Evil", 3.3, <http://plato.stanford.edu/entries/evil>, accessed 11 July 2023.

established Church towards science is a matter of shame and is well known. More recently some Christians have identified with the anti-vaccination movement. It is depressing to see progress being reversed; for example the divide between the West and the Islamic world increased when Turkey joined Saudi Arabia in making the teaching of evolutionary theory illegal. Yet for everyone who dies as a direct result of misguided religious extremism, perhaps many more die because of the apathy of many of those who are wealthy but do not fear that God will hold them to account for not sharing what they have more equitably. Such unjust distribution of wealth and resources causes misery and costs lives. Christian Aid estimated in 2014 that $160bn could be recovered from the abolition of tax-avoidance in the developing world,[9] and this was comparable at that time to the $150bn that the countries in sub-Saharan Africa owed to private creditors.[10] A more robust Christian apologetic, in which the two big arguments against the existence of God that are (a) the apparent explanation provided by science of "how things came to be and are now" and (b) the apparent contradiction posed by suffering that questions the existence of God as proclaimed by Christian theology, are turned against each other, could help convince people to at least live more tolerantly and more generously. Such apologetics are not provided simply to answer critics but also for "internal" use by those who have Christian faith, as in the words of St Anselm: apologetics are "faith seeking understanding".[11]

Whilst some approaches to Christian doctrine have abandoned significant and essential elements of the Christian faith in order to make a new version of Christian faith acceptable to scientists (q.v.), this book will attempt to reconcile a contemporary scientific understanding of the cosmos, and how that might inform a Christian understanding of theodicy, with traditional Christian doctrine.

---

[9] <https://www.christianaid.org.uk/resources/our-work/missing-millions-cost-tax-dodging-developing-countries>, accessed 11 July 2023.
[10] <https://www.economist.com/news/2014/11/13/the-coming-african-debt-crisis>, accessed 12 July 2023.
[11] Peterson et al., *Reason and Religious Belief*, p. 11.

I am very aware that some art historians, musicologists, physicists, biologists, medical doctors, historians, philosophers, theologians and biblical scholars may find fault with aspects of this book. I hope that such discoveries will not cloud the overall picture I have presented.

This book will argue that faith in the incarnate and revealed God of the Hebraic–Christian tradition is compatible with a contemporary scientific understanding of the cosmos, that the cosmos does indeed proclaim the greatness of God, that there is a place for faith in an age of science and reason, and that the study of the created world or "nature" provides some theological and philosophical insights. Furthermore a contemporary scientific understanding of the cosmos may help to account for a non-prejudicial distribution within the cosmos of natural evil[12] and the resultant tragedy, suffering and death.

---

[12] Natural evil refers to the harm that is caused by natural processes such as disease, natural disasters such as earthquakes, degeneration and ultimately death. The term is disliked by some since it implies a process by which all or part of the natural world is in the control of an evil power or being. I am content to use the term having witnessed the devastation and misery that such processes create.

Prologue

Here is the overall scheme that the book proposes:

- God creates the cosmos. God's love cannot be contained within the Trinity. God creates human beings who are able to exercise free will and therefore enter a loving relationship with God.
- God's holiness prevented God from being able to foresee how depraved humanity would be; nevertheless God grants humanity free will and thus the capacity to commit acts of moral evil.
- Natural evil and death are required to mitigate the effects of moral evil.
- God creates a world with a deeper physics such that natural evil (disease, disaster, degeneration and death) and the associated suffering can be distributed randomly.
- The origin of moral evil occurs in the *pre-archaios*,[1] and this explains why humanity evolved to the point of being able to exercise moral choice in a world in which animal suffering had already occurred.
- God intervenes in human history, for example the three Abrahamic covenants, and finally reconciles humanity to Godself in the salvific ministry of Jesus Christ.
- Heavenly existence will be such that complaint regarding how just or fair our mortal lives are becomes irrelevant.

---

[1] You may not find the term *pre-archaios* in any dictionary; it is a word I devised to denote a time before life existed.

1

The Christian hope of Heaven

> I consider that the sufferings of this present time are not worth comparing with the glory about to be revealed to us. (Romans 8:18)

> But, as it is written, "What no eye has seen, nor ear heard, nor the human heart conceived, what God has prepared for those who love him". (1 Corinthians 2:9)[1]

One way to come to terms with the tragic events that occur during mortal existence is the belief in an eternal life where God's goodness is so unbounded that for those who experience this eternal life, it becomes inappropriate and irrelevant to complain about any suffering or hardship that occurred during mortal life.

Theodicy as I interpret it in this book is emphatically more than the notion of "all's well that ends well", that is an "approach [that] affirms that all evils will eventually result in greater good".[2] Such "greater good" is unimaginable in some scenarios such as the stillborn child and the suffering that may be endured by those who die a protracted death; these have no seemingly greater good and to suggest otherwise suggests a lack of basic human empathy. Paul, however, proclaims the benefits of suffering in his letter to the Romans:

---

[1] The phrase is possibly a misquote of Isaiah 64:4: "From ages past no one has heard, no ear has perceived, no eye has seen any God besides you, who works for those who wait for him."

[2] M. Peterson et al., *Reason and Religious Belief*, 3rd edn (Oxford: Oxford University Press, 2003), p. 142.

> Therefore, since we are justified by faith, we have peace with God
> through our Lord Jesus Christ, through whom we have obtained
> access to this grace in which we stand; and we boast in our hope
> of sharing the glory of God. And not only that, but we also boast
> in our sufferings, knowing that suffering produces endurance,
> and endurance produces character, and character produces hope,
> and hope does not disappoint us, because God's love has been
> poured into our hearts through the Holy Spirit that has been
> given to us. (Romans 5:1–5)

Whilst suffering may have helped a remarkable person like Paul in his journey of faith as his past beliefs were discarded as he placed his trust in the New Covenant, it is hardly applicable in most cases of suffering and bereavement.

It is not the "promised bliss of heaven"[3] that *justifies* the suffering, but it is proposed that once "we" are there then the experience of Heaven will make such complaints irrelevant. We may never be able to make moral sense of the cosmos in which humanity exists at present, and this is the starting point of most philosophy and probably much theology as well. A theocentric and eschatological perspective will, however, view the unfolding of events from a different perspective and make our temporal complaints of no significance when they form an infinitesimally small part of an infinite existence. This is consonant with this expression of Paul later in his letter:

> I consider that the sufferings of this present time are not worth
> comparing with the glory about to be revealed to us. (Romans
> 8:18)

In this book, it is assumed (or rather the belief is held) that life after death is personal. "Personal life after death" requires the person to be aware of who they are (having a first person perspective) and the "presence of true memories about the previous life".[4] "The soul or re-created person is

---

[3] Peterson et al., *Reason and Religious Belief*, p. 142.
[4] Peterson et al., *Reason and Religious Belief*, p. 198.

identical to the deceased because of the basic awareness of the self".[5] The basic awareness of self may persist after death until resurrection occurs, and this delay may be between the end of a human life and the Parousia.[6] In Christian prayer, we speak of the soul "resting in peace" whilst waiting for the Parousia and resurrection to occur. Is this "resting" not a form of sleep? When we ordinarily wake after sleep, we believe we are the same person that we were when we fell asleep *because*, apart from being in a plausible location (spatially and temporally), we also have memories of being the person we believe that we are.

Christian resurrection does not mean that persons who are resurrected simply do not remember any suffering endured in a previous life. If all of life's memories are erased, this negates any reason for God to create the cosmos in which we exist. For a significant proportion of human beings the experience of mortal life is both unpleasant and short-lived. Whilst it is hoped that suffering will find recompense in eternal life, there are "resurrection" moments in this mortal life: birth, the beauty of nature, art and music, intense spiritual experience and other joys unlimited. The "life in all its fullness" that Jesus promised in John's Gospel (10:10) is not only to be experienced as an after-death benefit.

This book proposes that such memories do persist, but that any complaint is rendered irrelevant because of what the experience of living as resurrected persons in a "new Heaven and a new Earth" will be. It is hoped that the experience of heavenly life will not only consist of the re-creation of happy memories but will also include the ability to know well those who are precious to an individual even if not known well, or hardly known at all, during mortal life.

Belief in an eternal life that is "connected" to mortal life requires belief in the concept of the soul, the soul being the essence of a person that *can* exist *without* the physical body, but does so during mortal life. As per later in this book, the soul is considered to be

---

[5] Peterson et al., *Reason and Religious Belief*, p. 209.
[6] Parousia is a term for the expected return of Jesus Christ as judge of Heaven and Earth; the "second coming".

an individual essence that makes the body a human body and that diffuses, informs, animates, develops, unifies and grounds the biological functions of the body. The various chemical processes and parts (e.g. DNA) involved in morphogenesis are tools, means or instrumental causes employed by the soul as it teleologically unfolds its capacities toward the formation of a mature human body that functions as it ought to function by nature.[7]

If this definition of the soul that "inhabits" the body as much as the mind is correct, then this gives support to the Christian understanding of resurrection which is a bodily resurrection and not the continued existence of disembodied "spirits".

Atheist critics will point to a tautology in belief of life after death: the wish for certainty of belief in eternal life that generates belief in God, and then belief in God that generates hope for belief in life after death. Put more succinctly the prevalence of belief in eternal life throughout all religions suggests that the idea of god was created (by humanity) in order to "function as the purveyor of man's immortality".[8] There are, however, philosophical justifications for belief in life after death.

The justifications for belief in life after death are, briefly, several a priori arguments. These are not derived from experience but from argument or reasoning.[9]

The theologian Thomas Aquinas (1224–74) stated that "we are made for an ultimate end",[10] which is happiness that is to be found only in

---

[7] J. P. Moreland and S. B. Rae, *Body and Soul* (Downers Grove, IL: InterVarsity Press, 2000), p. 202, quoted in Peterson et al., *Reason and Religious Belief*, p. 201.

[8] C. Lamont, *The Illusion of Immortality* (New York: Philosophical Library, 1965), p. 7, quoted in Peterson et al., *Reason and Religious Belief*, p. 195.

[9] It is to be recognized that this book is not an apologetic that covers all aspects of Christian faith; it merely answers the question of how can a Christian believe in an all-powerful and loving God whilst so much suffering and death occurs?

[10] Peterson et al., *Reason and Religious Belief*, p. 213.

relation to God. This ultimate happiness cannot be achieved in mortal life and thus an eternal life is considered necessary.

The philosopher and ethicist Immanuel Kant (1724–1804), whilst considering "moral law", concluded that an eternal life was required in order that human existence could achieve moral perfection.[11]

The philosopher Plato (428–347 BC) stated that "the soul is immortal because it is imperishable". Plato considered the soul to be imperishable because it could not be divided into parts.[12] Peterson suggests the soul could be destroyed by annihilation.[13] However, this is not necessarily plausible since how can an entity such as a "soul", that is immaterial, that merely inhabits that which is material (the human body), be annihilated by any of the four forces that are manifest in the physical world?[14]

Fourthly, Augustine "came to the conclusion that that no finite end can satisfy the heart of man".[15]

Fifthly, there is an argument from the notion of divine justice: the Jewish claim that an afterlife is required for a just God to administer "final" divine justice.

Sixthly, I add my own syllogism: "There is sense in Creation."

"With no Saviour, there is no sense in Creation."

"Therefore there has to be a Saviour."

There is evidence of design and innovation that could not have happened by accident. The injustice in the world suggests that there is a need for ultimate justice and restoration. If there is a Creator, then

---

[11] Aquinas, *Summa Theologica*, Supplement to Part II Q.79 A.2, quoted in Peterson et al., *Reason and Religious Belief*, p. 213.

[12] Plato, *Phaedo*, 100b–107a, quoted in Peterson et al., *Reason and Religious Belief*, p. 213.

[13] Peterson et al., *Reason and Religious Belief*, p. 213.

[14] The "mind" is the product of the electrochemical activity of the brain and can, self-evidently, be damaged and annihilated. The mind is not to be confused with, or regarded to be the same as, the (Christian) concept of the soul that inhabits the person.

[15] Augustine, *De beat. Vit.* II; *confess.* I: I, in J. N. D. Kelly, *Early Christian Doctrines*, 5th edn (London: Continuum, 1977), p. 488.

there is (presumably) also a Saviour. If we are to be saved, then we are presumably saved to something.

There is an *a posteriori* (from experience) argument which is the resurrection of Jesus. The resurrection is to be contrasted with the account of Elijah who went straight to Heaven in a chariot of fire (2 Kings 2:11). There are, for example, the Gospel accounts of Lazarus and Jairus' daughter (John 11 and Mark 5), who were on separate occasions brought back from the dead by Jesus. Lazarus and Jairus' daughter were not resurrected into a different "form of being" such as the post-resurrection appearance of Jesus is described: having been resuscitated, Lazarus and Jairus' daughter eventually died.

The Gospels give several accounts of the post-resurrection appearances of Jesus. There is an atheist view that states that the accounts of the resurrected Jesus were an invention made by the followers of Jesus who wanted to believe that this had occurred so much that they convinced themselves that it had happened. In his book *The Resurrection of the Son of God*, the theologian and former Bishop of Durham N. T. Wright has a central argument that to regard the writings as back projections of wishful thinking creates enormous historical problems. This leads to the conclusion that the faith emerged from the accounts and not vice versa. Indeed the "birth and rapid rise of the Christian Church remain an unsolved enigma for any historian who refuses to take seriously the only explanation offered by the Church".[16]

The hope that Heaven will be the wonderful place that will render any complaint about mortal life irrelevant can only rest on the words of Jesus himself:

> Blessed are the pure in heart, for they will see God. (Matthew 5:8)

---

[16] C. F. D. Moule, *The Phenomenon of the New Testament: An Enquiry into the Implications of Certain Features of the New Testament*, SBT 2nd series, Vol. 1 (London: SCM Press, 1967), cited in N. T. Wright, *The Resurrection of the Son of God* (London: SPCK, 2002), p. 478.

> Indeed they cannot die anymore, because they are like angels and are children of God, being children of the resurrection. (Luke 20:36)
>
> Do not let your hearts be troubled. Believe in God, believe also in me. In my Father's house there are many dwelling-places. If it were not so, would I have told you that I go to prepare a place for you? (John 14:1–2)
>
> Then he [the thief] said, "Jesus, remember me when you come into your kingdom." He replied, "Truly I tell you, today you will be with me in Paradise".[17] (Luke 23:42–3)

Belief in an eternal life where God's goodness is so unbounded that it becomes inappropriate and irrelevant to complain about any suffering or hardship that occurred during mortal life can, however, imply Deism.[18] Deism is an understanding that mortal life is unimportant to God and that only the spiritual and eternal is important to God. This in turn questions why mortal existence was created at all: could God not have simply created Heaven and heavenly existence out of nothing without the "Earth" and mortal life?

---

[17] List of quotations from M. Campling, *Theological Papers* (London: Marcel Music, 2022). Michael Campling also points out that the thief quoted in Luke 23 is the only person in the Gospels to refer to Jesus by name, suggesting that Jesus and the thief had known each other perhaps since childhood.

[18] Deism: "A term used to refer to the views of a group of English writers, especially during the seventeenth century, the rationalism of which anticipated many of the ideas of the Enlightenment. The term is often used to refer to a view of God which recognises the divine creatorship, yet which rejects the notion of a continuing divine involvement with the world." A. E. McGrath, *Christian Theology: An Introduction*, 3rd edn (Oxford: Blackwell, 2001), p. 582.

2

Theophany: Evidence of God's love for the cosmos

The heavens are telling the glory of God; and the
firmament proclaims his handiwork.
Day to day pours forth speech, and night to night declares knowledge.
There is no speech, nor are there words; their voice is not heard;
yet their voice goes out through all the earth, and their
words to the end of the world. (Psalm 19:1–4)

God's love is shown in the cosmos by the very existence of the cosmos including the origin of sentient life on Earth, the ordering of the cosmos with natural laws that provide structure and predictability, the "magical" existence of four forces that have been described mathematically and others yet to be so described, and of all that is good and perceived to be beautiful in the cosmos. Such love might be likened to the affection a Creator has for what the Creator has created. God's love is shown in its fullest sense in the Incarnation and Jesus' salvific ministry. The "miracles" of creation, incarnation and Jesus' salvific ministry are pointers to God's love for the cosmos but do not explain why the cosmos exists. It may be considered, however, that love within the Trinity needed more expression, and this formed the incentive for a creation with sentient beings. Simply that God has shown evidence of God's love in the cosmos may be considered to be a sufficient reason for humanity to accept that there is a need for the cosmos to exist.

Karl Popper, the distinguished philosopher of science, stated that physical objects, knowledge and consciousness constitute the cosmos.[1] The word cosmos is used throughout this book to denote the entire continuum of time, energy, matter and space in which we have our physical existence. Whilst much theological thinking has focussed on knowledge and consciousness, this chapter mainly concerns the physical objects in the cosmos. So far, a cognitive proof that the cosmos was created has not been found. It is sufficient at this point to quote the philosopher John Hick: "there is only one universe, and it is capable of being interpreted both theistically and nontheistically".[2] The intricacies, vastness, complexities and improbabilities of the cosmos will, for some, indicate or provide confirmatory evidence of a Creator. The interpretation of such evidence, inasmuch as providing secure proof that the cosmos has a Creator, or otherwise, is nevertheless beyond scientific method as well as cognitive philosophy. This chapter is concerned with exploring descriptions of the physical cosmos to see how they might be compatible with the understanding of the incarnate and revealed God of the Hebraic–Christian tradition.

Abraham Heschel, the theologian, wrote in his book *The Prophets* (1962) that the Hebrew prophets "had no theory or 'idea' of God. What they had was an understanding".[3] Furthermore this understanding "sensed the signs of God's presence in history. Even if the prophets had affirmed the essential unknowability of God, they would still have insisted on the possibility of understanding Him by reflective intuition."[4]

In the tradition of the Hebrew prophets was John the Baptist. John's main message was one of repentance, a change of both mind and heart. His followers would have felt that they were forgiven by God because they had obeyed the Law, and that temple sacrifices had made up for their shortfalls. This was not enough for John, and he condemned this

---

[1] In A. Peacocke, *Theology for a Scientific Age: Being and Becoming—Natural, Divine, and Human* (Minneapolis, MN: Fortress Press, 1993), p. 193.

[2] J. H. Hick, *Philosophy of Religion*, 2nd edn (Hoboken, NJ: Prentice-Hall, 1973), p. 27. Philosophy of creation is discussed later.

[3] A. Heschel, *The Prophets* (New York: Harper Classics, 1962), p. 285.

[4] Heschel, *Prophets*, pp. 287–8.

complacency. John also rejected the other foundation upon which the Jews placed their hope. "Do not begin to say to yourselves, 'We have Abraham as our ancestor'; for I tell you, God is able from these stones to raise up children to Abraham" (Luke 3:8).

The ministry of John was adopted and developed by Jesus, and Christian faith is based upon the Hebrew experience of God but also, distinctively and uniquely, a revelation of God believed to be manifest in the teaching, example and ministry of Jesus that was recorded in the Gospels.

This revelation has been formed into Christian theology by a continuous process of reflection (accepting that there were periods of stagnation) that is represented by the element of "tradition" in Christian theology and the application of reason. I have taken as a benchmark for orthodox Christian theology the writing of the Anglican "divine" Richard Hooker, whose work was foundational and influential as the theology of the newly formed Church of England drew from both (Roman) Catholic and Protestant sources.

The Christian faith is not unique in claiming revelatory theology and an experience of a self-revealed God. Hick dates the emergence of revelatory (rather than natural) religion as claimed by Elijah, Amos, Hosea, Isaiah and Jeremiah to 800 BC;[5] from 800–300 BC by Zoroaster, Pythagoras, Socrates, Plato, Aristotle, Lao-Tzu, Confucius, Gotama the Buddha and Mahavira (Jainism); and later by the Bhaghavadgita, Jesus and Mohammed.[6] The scientist and theologian Arthur Peacocke describes an axial period, c.800–200 BC,[7] in which are to be found the origins of a search for god in societies that were sustained by rivers: China (Yellow River), India (Indus River) and the "Mediterranean"[8] (Tigris, Euphrates and Nile). Such revelatory religions did not always arise separately; for example the "Spirit of God" appears rarely in the Hebrew Bible, suggesting that it might be an import into Judaism after

---

[5] The use of the terms BC and AD is deliberate. The author is not inclined to diminish his public affirmation of faith by using BCE and CE.
[6] Hick, *Philosophy of Religion*, pp. 125–6.
[7] Peacocke, *Theology for a Scientific Age*, p. 259.
[8] "Near East" may be a better description than Mediterranean.

the Israelites encountered Zoroastrianism whilst in exile in Persia. The early writing of Job can be dated to the late sixth or fifth century BC and has Persian influence, and there is also parallel literature with Job in Egyptian and Mesopotamian culture.[9]

The exercise of studying the cosmos may have a dual function in that not only might it explore descriptions of the physical cosmos to see how they might be compatible with the understanding of the incarnate and revealed God of the Hebraic–Christian tradition, but also, within this framework, the exercise may help to refine this understanding of God by reflecting on or emphasizing some of the qualities of God. Since the revelation of God to humanity has to be perceived, heard or otherwise experienced by humankind, it is proposed that the understanding of the incarnate and revealed God of the Hebraic–Christian tradition is amenable to the influence that arises from the examination and interpretation of the cosmos. The Psalmist was inspired to declare "the heavens are telling the glory of God; and the firmament (Earth) proclaims his handiwork" (Psalm 19:1), and for others, for example, the natural beauty of Galilee renders it to be a "fifth Gospel". In contrast, the mental constructs of god as in the philosophical or metaphysical traditions have tended to set absolute and immutable descriptions of god. For example, for the theologian Jürgen Moltmann (1967) having Christology grounded in the god of metaphysics is problematic, because the eschatological promises do not fit well with god as an unchangeable, immutable and impassible unity.[10] For Moltmann, it was YHWH who raised Jesus, who was a Jew, from the dead. The Hebraic–Christian God (YHWH) is thus neither Parmenides' "eternal present of Being", nor Plato's "highest idea" nor Aristotle's "un-moved mover".[11]

---

[9] J. L. Crenshaw, in *New Revised Standard Version HarperCollins Study Bible* (2006), p. 693.

[10] J. Moltmann, *Theology of Hope: On the Ground and the Implications of a Christian Eschatology*, tr. James W. Leitch (London: SCM Press, 1967), p. 127.

[11] Moltmann, *Theology of Hope*, p. 128.

Theophany is defined as "a visible manifestation to humankind of God or a god".[12] It is similar to epiphany that is (also) used in secular language in which there is an element of an abrupt change: "a moment of sudden and great revelation or realization". In this chapter, I will attempt to demonstrate that belief in God as Creator is not only possible in an age of science and reason, but that the natural world proclaims the greatness of God to the extent that we are so immersed within this revelation that the suddenness of this revelation is often lost.

The next part of this chapter examines the physical cosmos to try and determine if events happen as time passes in a predetermined manner, or whether there is an element of randomness, or an intrinsic unpredictability, which results in events happening as time passes in a non-predetermined manner. The result of this question has theological implications for those who believe that the sustenance, as well as the Creation, of the cosmos is a product of the will of the Creator, and to what extent the sustenance of the cosmos is predetermined.

Science and religion

Whilst "hostility towards religion in favour of science is declining . . . the public perception of a conflict between science and religion remains, however: more than 80 per cent of people in the survey (2022) said that the two were incompatible".[13] Furthermore there is antipathy towards religion that persists:

> Sixteen years ago, at about the time of the publication of Richard Dawkins' *The God Delusion*, ComRes found that 42 per cent of UK adults polled agreed with the statement: "Faith is one of the world's great evils, comparable to the smallpox virus but harder

---

[12] Word definitions in this book are from the *Oxford English Dictionary* (OED).
[13] H. Williams, "Young choose not to fight the old science v. religion battle, research suggests", <https://www.churchtimes.co.uk/articles/2022/29-april/news/uk/young-choose-not-to-fight-the-old-science-v-religion-battle-research-suggests>, accessed 12 July 2023.

to eradicate." The new research tested the same proposition. The proportion now agreeing is 21 per cent.

One of the aspirations of this book is that science and religion may be seen to be compatible, and that the pursuit of scientific truth will not only be regarded, as per my hopes in my dissertation of 1978, as for the material benefit of humankind and the planet on which we live, but also form part of the process in which the wonders of God's creation will be better known.

The relationship between science and religion has been, and remains, both complex and controversial. Whilst "the attempt to define, distinguish and interrelate the activities of theology and natural science is a philosophical undertaking",[14] the conflict between religion and science, particularly scientific materialism versus biblical literalism,[15] is very much in the public domain.

Ancient "science" was of a different form altogether and was merged with philosophy. Plato and Aristotle "both believed that the true nature of things is to be found in their *form* and not in their *matter*". "Ancient Greek science assumed we could know the properties of a thing from a definition of its essence, and without having to study it empirically."[16]

In the mediaeval period, the relationship between science and religion had been that of independence; mediaeval dualistic metaphysics had contrasted and separated the supernatural and the natural,[17] although the mediaeval tradition of natural theology (teleology) had sought to use the natural world as an opportunity to learn about the nature of God.

In the early twentieth century, the philosophy of logical positivism was developed that "exemplified" scientific materialism, but "collapsed" "as philosophers began to realize that sensory input does not even provide an indubitable starting point for science".[18] Logical positivists had been

---

[14] M. Peterson et al., *Reason and Religious Belief*, 3rd edn (Oxford: Oxford University Press, 2003), p. 247.
[15] Peterson et al., *Reason and Religious Belief*, pp. 248–9.
[16] Peterson et al., *Reason and Religious Belief*, p. 254.
[17] Peterson et al., *Reason and Religious Belief*, p. 251.
[18] Peterson et al., *Reason and Religious Belief*, pp. 248–9.

unable to expand their claim that statements had to be verifiable to have cognitive meaning beyond the assessment of scientific statements, since there are many areas such as religion and ethics where related statements do not have a sensory component or "input".[19] There is also an epistemological question when scientific "truth" and religious "truth" are compared. This was noted by Augustine of Hippo (354–430), who wrote "when some passage in the Bible appears to conflict with established scientific thought, that passage should probably be interpreted metaphorically".[20]

The Judeo-Christian doctrine of creation enabled modern science with the assumptions that God, being both good and ordered, makes the operations of the creation contingent and "thus amenable to inductive and empirical methods", and that "creation is good and therefore worthy of study".[21] It is therefore somewhat ironic, and a little ungracious of those scientists that are most antagonistic towards religion, that science is now regarded to have superseded religion and/or somehow rendered the Christian faith to be an unnecessary or even harmful illusion.

More recently there has been dialogue that can occur at the boundaries of science and religion, most famously the discussion between Stephen Hawking and the pope about the start of the "Big Bang", where the laws of physics were suspended, and then "science took over", the nature of the cosmos before the "Big Bang" being considered to be a question of theology. Theology, however, is not there to fill gaps but to "make sense of the contingency and general order that science discovers in the universe".[22]

There are contemporary attempts at integration in which traditional natural theology seeks evidence of God's existence from design and the existence of the cosmos itself.[23] Other attempts at integration include

---

[19] Peterson et al., *Reason and Religious Belief*, pp. 248–9.

[20] Peterson et al., *Reason and Religious Belief*, pp. 248–9. It is lamentable that when Christian authorities sought to attack scientists, those responsible did not first look further into their past.

[21] Peterson et al., *Reason and Religious Belief*, p. 254.

[22] Peterson et al., *Reason and Religious Belief*, p. 255.

[23] Peterson et al., *Reason and Religious Belief*, p. 260.

those by Arthur Peacocke, whose theology of nature "uses the content of science to tutor, reformulate, and reinterpret traditional theological doctrines, rather than to argue for the existence of God".[24] Doctrines that are such affected include those of creation, providence and human nature; these are replaced by the interplay of chance and law. Peacocke will be critiqued in more depth in later chapters of this book that attempts to integrate science and the Christian faith *without* dispensing with much traditional doctrine.

A systematic synthesis was proposed by Alfred North Whitehead, who provided a "comprehensive metaphysical system".[25] Whitehead rejected the mediaeval view of nature that is "fixed and hierarchical" and operates teleologically "directed towards rational ends". Mediaeval dualism of spirit and matter is rejected. Whitehead rejected the Newtonian view of nature, a "continual rearrangement of unchanging components of the universe" that in turn leads to atomism: "the belief that reality operates by strict causal necessity". Whitehead accepted chance, randomness, "even chaos"; nature is understood as being rational, ecological and interdependent. Reality is "constituted by events and relationships"; the mediaeval model of the cosmos as a kingdom is rejected; the Newtonian machine model is rejected; the cosmos is a community. According to Whitehead, "a holistic conception of reality invalidates virtually all forms of dualism".[26] A hierarchy of organization is described. Whitehead's god is not in monarchical control of the universe conceived as a kingdom; rather god "'persuades' and 'influences' at a very deep level".[27] Bearing in mind how almighty "Almighty God" is, then being persuaded and influenced would probably feel the same as being controlled. As with Peacocke's attempt at integration, Whitehead's systematic synthesis will be critiqued later in this book.

---

[24] Peterson et al., *Reason and Religious Belief*, p. 260.
[25] The process theism and process theodicy of Alfred North Whitehead are both discussed later in this book.
[26] Peterson et al., *Reason and Religious Belief*, p. 261.
[27] Peterson et al., *Reason and Religious Belief*, p. 262.

Physics

Classical physics

In 1687, Isaac Newton published *Philosophiæ Naturalis Principia Mathematica* and laid the foundation for what is termed classical physics; indeed such was the magnitude of Newton's contribution that classical physics is also referred to as Newtonian physics. In the classical description of the cosmos, it is proposed that matter interacts in a precise and fully predictable manner, and Newton was able to describe such interactions with mathematical formulae that could also be used to predict outcomes. Inherent in this physics was and is a supposition that natural phenomena had been "explained". It is, however, perhaps more accurate to state that natural phenomena had been described, albeit in much greater detail.

Newton famously deduced that there was a force between objects, named gravitational force, which draws objects closer together. The apple falls as the Earth attracts the apple and vice versa, except the effect of gravity on the Earth moving towards the apple is minimal. The moon, however, as it orbits the Earth, exerts a gravitational force that is responsible for tidal activity in the oceans and seas.

Whilst the theory could predict the path of planets, it did not explain gravitational attraction itself. Nevertheless "science" triumphed as the theological view that the Creator Spirit "interpenetrates, quickens and animates the world" was "pushed out" by the modern mechanistic world picture.[28] The question is still unanswered: put simply, why should two objects attract each other? Furthermore, if the notion of a Creator God is rejected, there is a need to explain not only the origin of matter but also the source of the mathematical relationships and physical constants that govern matter, and how forces such as gravity exist.

---

[28] J. Moltmann, *God in Creation*, tr. Margaret Kohl (London: SCM Press, 1985), p. 98, quoted in D. Atkinson, *Renewing the Face of the Earth: A Theological and Pastoral Response to Climate Change* (Norwich: Canterbury Press, 2008), p. 74.

The mathematics of Newtonian gravitation is relatively simple. Imagine two objects of mass[29] M (large) and m (small) separated by a distance r. The gravitational force attracting them could be considered intuitively to be proportionate to the magnitude of each of the masses: the greater either mass, the greater the force. As the surface area of a sphere ($4\pi r^2$) is proportionate to the square of its size or radius (r), so gravitational force would be expected to be inversely proportionate to the square of the radius, as the force is "spread out" over the hypothetical sphere of influence of gravitational force: the further apart, the smaller the force. Hence the gravitational force between objects (Fg) is proportionate to the mass of each object (M and m) and inversely proportional to the square of the distance between them (r^2). Postulating a gravitational constant (G), turns the proportionality (α) Fg α Mm/r^2 into the equation Fg = GMm/r^2. The gravitational constant is calculated from observation to be 6.67408×10^{-11} m^3 kg^{-1} s^{-2}, but, as stated above, the force it represents is not explained. Such gravitational force is insignificant unless one of the objects, such as a planet or a star, is massive. Gravitational force also becomes significant and the effects observable as it places a celestial body into an orbital path around another celestial body, or a satellite around the Earth. The effect of gravity induces a curve in the path of an object that would otherwise travel in a straight line. There is a belief from antiquity that a deity or deities were responsible for moving the celestial bodies. Whilst we now have a theory and mathematics that describe gravitation, we are left to ponder the source of the force that moves objects together and can thus hold a moving object in an orbital path.

Newton recognized that his physics produced a mathematical description but did not explain why gravitational force existed:

> that gravity should be innate, inherent and essential to matter, so that one body may act upon another at a distance ... is to me an absurdity ... Gravity must be caused by an Agent acting constantly according to certain Laws, but whether this Agent be

---

[29] Mass is a property of matter. It only has weight when subject to a gravitational force.

material or immaterial, I have left it to the Consideration of my Readers.[30]

The theory of gravitational force and other principles of motion could be used to predict planetary orbit. At the time of Newton, the predictions did not fit exactly the observed orbit of Mercury. Such observations were deemed to be "anomalous", and thus the reputation of Newton's *Principia* was preserved. The necessary refinement was provided by Einstein in his theory of relativity that modified Newton's equations. A corrective factor, the square root of $1-v^2/c^2$, where v = velocity of the object under consideration and c = the speed of light, is applied, and this only becomes of any practical significance as the velocity of the object being observed (v) approaches the speed of light (c) which is approximately 300,000 kilometres per second.[31] For the corrective factor to be as little as 0.1 per cent, the velocity of the object being observed needs to be 13,413 km/sec. The Earth orbits the Sun at 30 km/sec, and the surface at the equator spins round the Earth's axis at 0.465 km/sec.[32]

Another consequence of the theory of relativity was the challenge that Einstein proposed: whilst Newton had time and space to be absolute and the speed of light relative, Einstein proposed that the speed of light was absolute and space and time intervals were relative. "Einstein's contribution (the theory of relativity) was dramatic because it so fundamentally challenged the framework of classical physics that had

---

[30] C. Rovelli, *Reality is not what it seems* (London: Allen Lane, 2014), pp. 41–2, quoting I. Newton, *Letters to Bentley* (Whitefish, MO: Kessinger, 2010). In H. S. Thayer, *Newton's Philosophy of Nature* (New York: Hafner, 1953), p. 54.

[31] Special relativity is derived from the speed of light "c" being constant; it leads to the observation that clocks do not run at the same speed, being affected by gravitational fields; from S. Hawking and L. Mlodinow, *The Grand Design* (London: Bantam Books, 2010), p. 127.

[32] The theory added considerable layers of complexity as (massive) objects distort the time and space in which they are placed. See Einstein's Field Equations in, e.g., <https://en.wikipedia.org/wiki/General_relativity>, accessed 12 July 2023.

been accepted for the previous 200 years."[33] Time becomes relative and dependent upon matter and its ability to distort time. "We must think of time instead as a localized phenomenon: every object in the cosmos has its own time running, at a pace determined by the local gravitational field."[34]

Einstein declared that space was curved, that massive objects distorted the space-time continuum: "The Earth turns around the Sun because spacetime around the Sun is curved, rather like a bead that rolls on the curved wall of a funnel."[35] Imagine that the funnel is inverted, and the analogy no longer works. There is an irony in the tautology of using the image of an object rolling either down or alongside an incline to try to explain gravity: space does not have a right or wrong side up.[36]

More complex equations quantify and describe the other forces of nature that are the strong nuclear force, the weak nuclear force and the electromagnetic force.[37] James Clerk Maxwell (1865) published a paper entitled *A Dynamical Theory of the Electromagnetic Field* that described the mathematics of electromagnetism, but did not explain why magnetic attraction occurred.[38] I have stressed this point of science providing a description rather than an explanation for two reasons. Firstly because it is possible to hold a number of contradictory descriptions of the physical cosmos that may be in tension whereas pursuing one fully encompassing explanation may not be achievable; and secondly, perhaps more significantly, this does render the cosmos more mysterious than the scientific descriptions may imply.

The scientist Carlo Rovelli (2014) in *Reality is not what it seems* attempts to use field theory to explain the problem of action at a distance,

---

[33] J. Schwartz and M. McGuinness, *Introducing Einstein* (Cambridge: Icon Books, 1992), p. 118.
[34] Rovelli, *Reality is not what it seems*, p. 153.
[35] Rovelli, *Reality is not what it seems*, p. 66, Figure 3.6.
[36] See <http://www.esa.int/spaceinimages/Images/2015/09/Spacetime_curvature>, accessed 12 July 2023, and imagine the image inverted.
[37] There may be other forces, for example the dark forces that are pulling the cosmos apart (Rovelli, *Reality is not what it seems*, p. 72).
[38] Schwartz and McGuinness, *Introducing Einstein*, p. 38.

the tendency of one object to move another where there is no physical material connection. Yet there is a flaw in using field theory to explain action at a distance. To suggest that objects move according to the forces in a field is merely an acknowledgement of the apparent absurdity, viz.

Q   Why does gravity make (A) a small object move closer to (B) a massive object?

A   Because A is in a force field created by the gravitational attraction of B and as such A is obliged to move along the lines of force.

Q   What creates the force field?

A   Gravity does.

Q   Are you saying that gravity, by creating a force field, makes A move to be closer to B?

A   Yes, I am.

Q   So it is gravity that makes A move to be closer to B?

A   Yes, it is gravity that makes A move to be closer to B!

Q   Why does gravity make (A) a small object move closer to (B) a massive object?

In the above illustration of a circular argument, magnetism can be substituted for gravity; (A) becomes an iron filing and (B) a magnet.

Magnetic lines of force may be clearly demonstrable, as in the pattern of iron filings produced by the magnetic field of a magnet, but the underlying question of why such forces should arise is not answered.

"Magnetic field lines don't exist physically—they're a mathematical construct to help us visualize how magnets work. However, iron filings around a magnet will line themselves up along the field lines, so we can then see how the magnetic field 'looks.'"[39] A force field is a "mathematical construct" but might also, less respectfully, be regarded as a cloaking device that disguises the current situation in which there is no explanation as to why or how the force that it represents exists.

This distinction between description and explanation was made by the physicist Niels Bohr, who used Quantum Theory to develop the atomic model that is in use today. Bohr stated:

---

[39] <https://www.scienceworld.ca/resources/units/magnets>, accessed 12 July 2023. Science World is based at the Telus World of Science in Vancouver, British Columbia.

> There is no quantum world. There is only abstract quantum physical description. It is wrong to think that the task of physics is to find out how nature is. Physics is concerned with what we can say about nature.[40]

The abstract qualities of quantum physical description are well exemplified with the apparent contradiction that electrons both "occupy" the discrete quantized electron shells of the Bohr atomic model yet exist with a spatial distribution such that each electron *might* exist literally anywhere within the cosmos.

Quantum physics

The theories of electromagnetism had provided a challenge to classical physics. August Tuschmid, who was Einstein's physics teacher at the cantonal school in Aarau that Einstein attended in 1895–6, wrote referring to James Maxwell's equations published in 1865:

> The central problem in physics today is the resolution of Newton's mechanical world view with the new equations of electro-magnetism.[41]

At the turn of the twentieth century, contemporary physics emerged as phenomena were observed that could not be explained by classical physics. One of the first of these phenomena related to the radiation produced by a hypothetical thermally hot "black" body and was called the "ultraviolet catastrophe". Classical physics had suggested that the energy radiated by such a "black" body should increase to infinite levels as the wavelength of the emitted radiation decreased, and this would lead to an energy imbalance between the energy absorbed by such a body as it was heated and the energy that it would emit. Stephen Hawking described the problem in his book *A Brief History of Time* (1988):

---

[40] J. Polkinghorne, *Quantum Theory: A Very Short Introduction* (Oxford: Oxford University Press, 2002), p. 83.

[41] Schwartz and McGuinness, *Introducing Einstein*, p. 38.

> According to the laws we believed at the time, a hot body ought to give off electromagnetic waves (such as radio waves, visible light, or X rays) equally at all frequencies . . . Now since the number of waves per second (frequencies) is unlimited, this would mean that the total energy radiated would be infinite . . . an obviously ridiculous result.[42]

The mathematical and physical concepts that Max Planck used to solve this problem are complex. In order to achieve a solution, Planck suggested in 1900 that waves "could not be emitted at an arbitrary rate, but only in certain packets that he called quanta."[43]

The photoelectric effect was discovered that demonstrated that light waves could affect electrical charge, i.e. the light waves could move electrical charge; however, a minimum wavelength of visible light was required to produce this effect. Red light has a longer wavelength than violet light, yet however intense the red light beamed at the detecting apparatus, there was no demonstrable photoelectric effect, whereas weak violet light was effective. According to classical physics an intense wave of longer wavelength (red) ought to be able to have an effect if a less intense wave of shorter wavelength (violet) could do so. At a time when the dominant theory was that light was in the form of a wave, rather than a stream of particles, Einstein had proposed that light could be considered as a stream of particles and that each particle contained a "quantum" of energy. The failure of red light to produce this effect was explained on account of the quanta of energy in each red light particle not having sufficient energy to shift an electron. As an analogy consider trying to knock over a cup of coffee by throwing table-tennis balls at the cup rather than golf balls. The analogy is made more realistic if the speed for each type of ball is limited to a maximum.

---

[42] S. Hawking, *A Brief History of Time* (London: Bantam Books, 1988), p. 62.
[43] Hawking, *A Brief History of Time*, p. 62. For further description of Planck's solution see <http://hyperphysics.phy-astr.gsu.edu/hbase/mod6.html> and <http://www.webassign.net/question_assets/buelemphys1/chapter27/section27dash1.pdf>, both accessed 12 July 2023.

Quantum theory has described, with much experimental proof, that the cosmos is not a mechanical system with predictable interactions and outcomes. It is important to recognize that quantum theory is not to be dismissed; it can explain why the sun shines whereas classical physics cannot.[44] Quantum researchers "went so far as to throw out the rules of cause and effect": it was noted that when an electron was subject to an interaction only the probabilities of the outcomes could be calculated.[45] Quantum theory developed and it became one of the history of science's many ironies that Einstein, who first used the term "quantum", would later reject quantum theory on account of the inability to predict outcomes, being able only to quantify the probability of a number of outcomes, to state the much-quoted "God does not play dice".[46]

An essential part of quantum theory is unpredictability. An example of this unpredictability is the behaviour of radioactive substances that over a period of time will transform (called decay) as radiation in the form of either particles or energy is emitted, effecting a change in the nature of the particular atomic nucleus from which the radiation was emitted. It is not currently possible to predict which atom will decay when, but it is possible to measure how long it takes for half the remaining undecayed atoms to emit radiation (the half-life). It is noteworthy that Einstein eventually conceded that there was quantum unpredictability, declaring in 1916 that there was "no direct causality in radioactive decay and atomic (electron shell) transitions".[47]

Superposition

Experiments with beams of particles, initially small particles such as photons and electrons, demonstrated how they coexist as wave forms, and that such wave-particles can exist simultaneously in two places. This is the origin of the diffraction patterns in the double-slit experiment. In the double-slit experiment, particles travel one at a time through the

---

[44] J. Gribbin, *In Search of Schrödinger's Cat* (London: Transworld Publishers, 1984), p. 175.

[45] Schwartz and McGuinness, *Introducing Einstein*, p. 168.

[46] Hawking, *Brief History of Time*, p. 64.

[47] Gribbin, *In Search of Schrödinger's Cat*, p. 94.

apparatus but are able to produce a diffraction pattern that can *only* be produced if each individual particle (with its associated wave function) passes through both of the two slits *simultaneously*. As the wave-particles arrive at the detector screen, the wave-function "collapses" and the particle leaves its mark as a single point.[48] In addition, if detectors are placed to determine through which of the two slits the particle passes, the wave-functions collapse and then the effect does not happen. This superposition principle, in which objects can be shown to exist in two places at the same time, is demonstrated by this double-slit experiment, and has been described as the "death of classical physics".

It may be just possible to imagine that sub-atomic particles such as electrons or photons, that are already mysterious in nature, can exhibit the phenomenon of superposition. Professor Anton Zeilinger at the University of Zurich, however, has used the double-slit experiment to demonstrate that whole molecules, containing as many as 60 carbon atoms, also "exist" as probability fields and can thus exist in two places simultaneously. As an indication of relative size, a molecule of glucose has 6 carbon atoms, whilst cholesterol has 27. The molecule with 60 carbon atoms used was Buckminsterfullerene, named after the architect Buckminster Fuller who designed geodesic dome structures that look similar to C_{60}.[49]

Later experiments (2019) have demonstrated that such phenomena can occur with molecules having 2,000 atoms.[50] The fundamental

---

[48] It should be noted that the collapse of the wave-function is not explicable by quantum theory, and this has led to the multiverse (multiple cosmos) theory to provide an explanation.

[49] M. Arndt et al., "Wave–particle duality of C_{60}," *Nature* 401 (1999), pp. 680–2. The discovery of Buckminsterfullerene was published by H. W. Kroto et al., "C_{60}: Buckminsterfullerene", *Nature* 318 (1985), pp. 162–3. These molecules are the "buckyballs" described in Hawking and Mlodinow, *The Grand Design*, pp. 83–4. They are created by applying a laser beam to sheets of carbon atoms in the form of graphene. For an illustration see <http://www.godunov.com/bucky/fullerene.html>, accessed 12 July 2023.

[50] Y. Fein et al., "Quantum superposition of molecules beyond 25kDa", *Nature Physics* 15:12 (2019), pp. 1242–5.

indeterminacy of the cosmos is founded upon the superposition principle which is clearly demonstrable by experiment. Richard Feynman, one of the pioneers of quantum theory, stated:

> In reality it [the double-slit experiment] contains the only reality. We cannot make the mystery go away by "explaining" how it works. We will just tell you how it works. In telling you how it works we will have told you about the basic peculiarities of all quantum mechanics.[51]

Richard Feynman also remarked, more succinctly: "I think I can state that nobody really understands quantum mechanics".[52] We are trying to comprehend the cosmos using a tool that is not understood. It is somewhat akin to studying a novel in a language that nobody, including the author, understands.

Hence within the quantum cosmos there is uncertainty or unpredictability of both place and time. The physicist John Gribbin (1984) was more forthright in his summary of the mysteries of nature revealed by quantum physics: "In the quantum world ... the best you can hope for is a set of delusions that agree with one another."[53]

Determinism or non-determinism

The division between a predictable "classical" cosmos and a random "quantum" cosmos is not, however, either clearly defined or exclusive. Consider a game of billiards. To determine the pattern of collisions that will follow on from the first interaction, the precise direction of the first ball to be moved is critical. It is assumed that the first ball starts its course in a perfect line but then deviates having been attracted by the gravitational pull of other objects. The calculations were done by the mathematician Sir Michael Berry in *The Black Swan* (1978):

---

[51] Polkinghorne, *Quantum Theory*, pp. 21–2.
[52] Rovelli, *Reality is not what it seems*, p. 119.
[53] Gribbin, *In Search of Schrödinger's Cat*, p. 214.

If you know a set of basic parameters concerning the ball at rest, can compute the resistance of the table, and can gauge the strength of the impact, then it is rather easy to predict what would happen at the first hit. The second impact becomes more complicated, but possible; and more precision is called for. The problem is that to correctly compute the ninth impact, you need to take into account the gravitational pull of someone standing next to the table. And to compute the fifty-sixth impact, every single elementary particle in the universe needs to be present in your assumptions! An electron at the edge of the universe, separated from us by 10 billion[54] light years, must figure in the calculations, since it exerts a meaningful effect on the outcome.[55]

This calculation illustrates the magnitude of the task of devising a cosmos in which all will follow inexorably according to plan following a "Big Bang" or other initialization event. Berry's calculations apply to the initialization of a simple system of billiard balls on a table; a cosmos of matter would add the complexity of a multitude of other celestial bodies, smaller objects, atoms and sub-atomic particles that would all mutually interact in three, rather than only two, dimensions. Hawking was clear on the near impossibility of the hope of a predictable cosmos: "we cannot even solve exactly for the motion of *three* bodies in Newton's theory of gravity, and the difficulty increases with the number of bodies and the complexity of the theory".[56] Whereas Newton's theory of gravity yields this equation that describes the gravitational force between two objects, $Fg = GMm/r^2$, Einstein's theory of general relativity[57] yields this equation that describes the force between two objects as one (m) orbits the other (M): $Ff(r) = -GMm/r^2 + L^2/mr^3 - 3GML^2/mc^2r^4$. "The first

---

[54] In this book, the short-scale billion is used to represent 10^9 or 1,000,000,000 that is equivalent to the prefix Giga or G.

[55] <http://www.anecdote.com/2007/10/the-billiard-ball-example/>, accessed 13 July 2023.

[56] Hawking, *A Brief History of Time*, p. 204.

[57] General relativity is a new theory of gravity, curved space and geodesics. Hawking and Mlodinow, *The Grand Design*, p. 128.

term represents the Newton's force of gravity, which is described by the inverse-square law. The second term represents the centrifugal force in the circular motion. The third term represents the relativistic effect."[58] Further elaboration is outside the scope of this book; the point is made that the mathematics of the theory and the factors that are required have both become more complex.

Free will

Human beings have affected the course of history such that it is proposed that this geological age is called the Anthropocene. Any discussion of whether events in the cosmos follow a predetermined path must include consideration of whether human beings possess free will. Hawking stated: "the reason we say that humans have free will is because we can't predict what they will do."[59] It is, however, possible to restate this subjectively: "I say that I have free will because I can't (always) predict what I will do." Hawking, in *The Grand Design* (2010), further appears to attempt to dismiss the concept of human free will with the claim that knowing the position of all the atoms in a person's body could lead to a prediction of how the person would behave.[60] This statement, coming from a "book (that) is rooted in scientific determinism"[61] seems to ignore the uncertainty of where the atoms might be and the consequent effects. Rovelli argued: "this *indeterminacy* is the third cornerstone of quantum mechanics: the discovery that chance operates at the atomic level".[62]

Jim Al-Khalili, a Professor of Theoretical Physics, in a book co-authored with the biologist Johnjoe McFadden (2014), *Life on the Edge: A Coming of Age of Quantum Biology,* notes that "quantum events taking place within individual molecules can have consequences for an entire organism".[63] Such quantum events are considered indeterminate unless

---

[58] <https://en.wikipedia.org/wiki/General_relativity>, accessed 13 July 2023.
[59] Hawking, *A Brief History of Time*, p. 183.
[60] Hawking and Mlodinow, *The Grand Design*, p. 46.
[61] Hawking and Mlodinow, *The Grand Design*, p. 48.
[62] Rovelli, *Reality is not what it seems*, p. 103 (Rovelli's italics).
[63] J. Al-Khalili and J. McFadden, *Life on the Edge: A Coming of Age of Quantum Biology* (London: Black Swan, 2014), p. 388.

the whole of quantum mechanics is considered to be superdeterministic. Al-Khalili also states that "consciousness, or free will, just doesn't figure in an entirely deterministic universe".[64] If the cosmos is non-deterministic, and this view is supported by quantum physics, then a corollary is that free will (and consciousness) may exist in the cosmos.

Hawking stated that "recent experiments in neuro-science support the view that it is our physical brain, following the known laws of science, that determines our actions, and not some agency that exists outside of these laws".[65] Hawking did not cite what equipment was used to detect any "agency that exists outside of these laws", and it is possible that no such equipment exists.[66] The physicality of the brain is certainly true and a part of established neurosurgical practice: for example, movement of a muscle can be produced by the electrical stimulation of the motor cortex of a brain; however, the conscious physiological *initiation* of movement by the brain normally depends on the global function of a complex and interrelated network of neurons. If the brain is considered to be a network of physical processes, then Hawking has provided his own answer to whether our thoughts and actions can be predicted: "according to quantum physics, no matter how much information we obtain or how powerful our computing abilities, the outcomes of physical processes cannot be predicted with certainty because they are not *determined* with certainty [Hawking's italic emphasis]".[67] The scientific determinism that was stated as the root of *The Grand Design*, that has dismissed human free will, appears to have undermined itself.

In neurobiology, whether an atom is positioned inside or outside of a cell is of great importance, since neural impulses flow as sodium and potassium ions pass through cell walls.[68] Cell membranes are typically

---

[64] Al-Khalili and McFadden, *Life on the Edge*, p. 322.
[65] Hawking and Mlodinow, *The Grand Design*, p. 45.
[66] Consciousness is thought to be regarded either as non-physical in which the biochemical and electrical activity of the brain is inhabited by a non-physical entity, or as physical consciousness in which consciousness is the biochemical and electrical activity of the brain.
[67] Hawking and Mlodinow, *The Grand Design*, p. 92.
[68] <https://en.wikipedia.org/wiki/Action_potential>, accessed 13 July 2023.

10 nanometres thick;[69] the double slits in the superposition experiment are typically placed 0.1mm apart,[70] and this is 10,000 times wider than a cell membrane. Could superposition, with its inherent unpredictability, affect what is in and what is out of a nerve cell, and hence be an unpredictable influence in the neurobiological function that drives our higher intellectual processes? There is research that is supportive of this theoretical prediction; quantum phenomena have been shown to be important in the ion channels that are important in neurotransmission.[71] Thus the dismissal of the notion that humans possess free will based on the argument in the above paragraph would seem to be an arbitrary choice.

A robot may appear to exhibit free will; however, we could not be certain if it had self-awareness. If self-awareness and free will are uniquely human then they may not be explicable by the complexity of the human brain, or any advanced biochemical or electrical function, and so there must be a non-physical constituent responsible for this property, something transcendental, a soul perhaps? If human beings are considered not to be unique in this respect, we do not have to reject the idea of a human soul, and we could alternatively credit other creatures with having souls too.

If it is accepted that human beings can exercise free will, then if the cosmos is to be measured and adjusted by a divine being to ensure that events unfold in a predetermined manner, then presumably some form of interaction with the matter that constitutes the cosmos would be required. In quantum mechanics, the Heisenberg Uncertainty Principle has demonstrated that observing a sub-atomic particle influences its "behaviour". Heisenberg's Uncertainty Principle is based upon wave–particle complementarity: waves have momentum, and

---

[69] <https://en.wikipedia.org/wiki/Cell_membrane>, accessed 13 July 2023.

[70] <https://en.wikipedia.org/wiki/Double-slit_experiment>, accessed 13 July 2023.

[71] G. Bernroider and J. Summhammer, "Can quantum entanglement between ion transition states effect action potential initiation?", *Cognitive Computation* 4 (2012), pp. 29–37, cited in Al-Khalili and McFadden, *Life on the Edge*, p. 347.

particles have position; momentum and position cannot be determined simultaneously.[72] The double-slit experiment, for example, will not work if you place a sensor to try and find which slit the electron is passing through. Thus in human terms it is a completely overwhelming and unimaginable task to determine the state of each particle, let alone to compute and intervene within the entire cosmos to render it effectively completely deterministic in nature: what you were trying to measure would change as it was being measured. Thus the acceptance of human free will counters the assumption that we live in a predetermined cosmos.

There is another approach to the question of free will using theocentric theology. If it is accepted that the cosmos was created, why should such a creator fill the cosmos only with events that the creator could foretell would happen? The divine creation of human "conscience", by which I mean an inherited and innate tendency to do that which is morally correct, may be regarded as a limitation of free will that God has ordained for the increase of "goodness" in human behaviour.

Quantum gravitation

Since the emergence of quantum mechanics, the complex mathematical and physical concepts that have been devised to describe the cosmos in all magnitudes have revealed some incompatibilities. A unifying theory, titled "Quantum Gravitation", has been proposed. It is hoped that this theory will deal with the incompatibilities between Quantum Theory, which describes the sub-atomic world, and that of Gravitation, which describes the "normal" world, including massive objects such as planets and stars.

"Quantum mechanics does not describe objects: it describes processes and events which are junction points between processes." Whilst quantum mechanics "teaches us not to think about the world in terms of things but in terms of processes instead",[73] this does not prove that things do not possess existence beyond our mental constructs. Perhaps quantum mechanics that describes processes is complemented by the theory of gravity that describes the character of matter?

---

[72] Gribbin, *In Search of Schrödinger's Cat*, pp. 161–2.
[73] Rovelli, *Reality is not what it seems*, p. 116.

Whilst this theory is being sought, dark matter, which eludes direct observation, has been inferred to form a major part of the cosmos:[74] it is estimated that "between 90 per cent and 99 per cent of the matter in the universe is dark: unseen and of unknown composition".[75] Dark energy has been proposed to explain why the cosmos continues to accelerate as it moves apart following the "Big Bang".[76] From Newton onwards, there is an increasing complexity of the description of cosmos, and then, according to Hawking, "quantum uncertainty, curved space, quarks, strings and extra dimensions, and the net result is 10^{500} universes, each with a different set of laws".[77]

The underlying indeterminacy of quantum mechanics may underlie the behaviour of small things but does not explain the behaviour of larger things such as a planet, a turnip or a grain of rice. The cosmos is clearly not purely chaotic or there would be neither objects to observe nor observers to consider the meaning of their observations. The mixed model of the cosmos, that of laws and chaos, may be underpinned by the dual effects of quantum mechanics and general relativity (gravitational theory); and the incompatibility of these two theories may be not only the root cause of the mixed model but also a necessary incompatibility in order for the cosmos, as we know it, to exist at all. If a theory of quantum gravitation is formulated and found to be provable, this argument is not invalid, for even if one Grand Unified Theory (GUT) combines quantum mechanics and gravity it is our common experience that gravity has a dominant effect on large objects and in the laboratory the effects of quantum mechanics occur on the minutely small, and in this way the two aspects of any GUT will be experientially distinct.

Since the discovery of dark matter and dark forces, the quest for a unifying theory now seems even more distant and elusive, although it

---

[74] <http://hyperphysics.phy-astr.gsu.edu/hbase/Astro/darmat.html>, accessed 13 July 2023.

[75] F. Pirani and C. Roche, *The Universe for Beginners* (Cambridge: Icon Books, 1993), p. 148.

[76] <http://hyperphysics.phy-astr.gsu.edu/hbase/Astro/dareng.html>, accessed 13 July 2023.

[77] Hawking and Mlodinow, *The Grand Design*, p. 52.

holds grandiose hopes within the scientific community: the Professor of Rational Mechanics Felix Pirani claims that "a single theory, that describes the whole universe ... [if discovered] we shall all be able to take part in the discussion of why it is that we and the universe exist ... it would be the ultimate triumph of human reason—for then we would know the mind of God".[78] Whilst we might be able to conjecture *how* the cosmos came into existence, we could not determine from this *why* God had chosen to be a Creator.

Superdeterminism

Quantum physics has demonstrated the EPR effect, also known as "spooky action at a distance". EPR is an ironic acronym for Einstein, Podolsky and Rosen, who had published a paper in 1935 that questioned if the quantum mechanical description of reality was complete. To produce the effect, pairs of electrons produced by a single event are sent in different directions. When apparently random characteristics are measured, the behaviour of one appears to instantaneously affect the other one of the pair. It is as if pairs of coins are left to spin, and if the first produces a "head", then the second is more likely to do so. It was originally suggested that there was some communication between the particles that travelled faster than the speed of light, something that is deemed impossible by the theory of relativity that is the most refined "classical" physics of all. The other explanation is that the particles were somehow entangled at the point of production. Rather confusingly, this characteristic of entanglement is used to describe either the mutual "imprint" that each particle left upon the other as both were created,[79] or the apparent ability to communicate instantaneously.[80] That an electron, recently separated from the other one in the pair, could carry with it a propensity to behave in a predetermined manner has been described as an extreme form of determinism: namely superdeterminism.

---

[78] Pirani and Roche, *The Universe for Beginners*, p. 162.
[79] As in the quote from John Bell below.
[80] "Measuring (the spin of) just one of an entangled pair immediately collapses the superposition of the other, irrespective of how far away it is". See Al-Khalili and McFadden, *Life on the Edge*, p. 252.

This entanglement phenomenon has supported the idea that there is a deterministic interpretation of all quantum phenomena, although this is not yet verifiable experimentally.[81] John Bell, who provided the mathematics to interpret the EPR effect, stated:

> There is a way to escape the inference of superluminal speeds and spooky action at a distance. But it involves absolute determinism in the universe, the complete absence of free will. Suppose the universe is superdeterministic, with not just inanimate nature running on behind-the-scenes clockwork, but with our behaviour, including our belief that we are free to choose to do one experiment rather than another, absolutely predetermined, including the "decision" by the experimenter to carry out one set of measurements rather than another, the difficulty disappears. There is no need for a faster-than-light signal to tell particle A what measurement has been carried out on particle B, because the universe, including particle A, already "knows" what that measurement, and its outcome, will be.[82]

I have included a long quotation here because there is a notion that the EPR effect somehow "disproved" Einstein.

Al-Khalili, in describing the results of an experiment that tested the EPR effect, declared that the data provided "absolute proof that Albert Einstein (who regarded quantum theory to be incomplete) was wrong and Niels Bohr (an advocate of quantum theory) was right".[83] Al-Khalili

---

[81] Polkinghorne, *Quantum Theory*, pp. 53–5.
[82] The quotation is from the edited transcript of a BBC Radio interview with John Bell from 1985, cited in P. C. W. Davies and J. R. Brown, *The Ghost in the Atom: A Discussion of the Mysteries of Quantum Physics* (Cambridge: Cambridge University Press, 1986/1993), pp. 45–6.
[83] J. Al-Khalili, *The Secrets of Quantum Physics* (Furnace Ltd., 2014), at <https://www.dailymotion.com/video/x37sq23>, accessed 19 July 2023. Al-Khalili and McFadden, *Life on the Edge*, p. 253, state that whilst measurement forces the electron to "choose" its spin direction (from two superimposed states), this choice forces the other to adopt the complementary state however far

continues: "the two entangled photons' properties could not have been set from the beginning but are summoned into existence when we measure them", and concludes that the experiment had proved Einstein wrong and that there was no objective reality. The difference between Al-Khalili and Bell's interpretations of the evidence could not be further apart on the spectrum of quantum uncertainty and superdeterminism. The point being made is that even when scientific experiments have been created to investigate phenomena the evidence may still be subject to (human) judgement and interpretation as to what the data obtained actually means or proves.

Cosmology

In this chapter, I have critiqued cosmology since some will regard cosmological theory as having undermined the need to postulate a Creator, and so undermined the argument that God has shown God's love through the universe that God created.

In 1929, the astronomer Edwin Hubble provided the origins of the proof that the cosmos had a beginning by demonstrating that galaxies were moving away from each other. It was calculated that 10–20 thousand million years earlier the galaxies would have been together, and prior to the assumed "Big Bang" the cosmos would have been very small and very dense.[84] If it is assumed, and there is much proof, that the cosmos had a beginning rather than having existed in perpetuity, then a temporal boundary might be drawn between when the cosmos existed, and when it did not. The idea of a boundary had existed in philosophical thought long before Edwin Hubble used his observations to predict the "Big Bang": St Augustine of Hippo had stated that "time was a property of the universe that God had created, and that time did not exist before the beginning of the universe". In 1988, in *A Brief History of Time*, Stephen Hawking stated "the concept of time has no meaning before the beginning of

---

apart, i.e. such that any "message" between them would have to travel in excess of the speed of light.

[84] Hawking, *A Brief History of Time*, p. 10.

the universe".[85] Hawking appears to accept the possibility that a creator existed at the beginning, prior to the "Big Bang": "an expanding universe does not preclude a creator, but it does place limits on when he might have carried out his job!"[86] Other physicists such as Pirani concede that the start of the "Big Bang" is not within scientific description: "present day physics has nothing to say about how the expansion started ... current physical theory cannot deal with 'a beginning'".[87] There is also the question of how, when or where did the matter that created the "Big Bang" exist when neither time nor space existed? Another corollary of this boundary between what science can and cannot explain is shown by Hawking, perhaps with a sense of intellectual frustration: "if he (god) had started it off in such an incomprehensible way, why did he choose to let it evolve according to laws we could understand?"[88]

The Deists understood God to have intervened sparsely in the cosmos. Hawking took this further to concede that god may have created the cosmos, but no longer intervenes:

> Science seems to have uncovered a set of laws that, within the limits set by the uncertainty principle, tell us how the universe will develop with time, if we know its state at any one time. These laws may have originally been decreed by god, but it appears that he has since left the universe to evolve according to them and does not now intervene in it.[89]

For Hawking, the uncertainty principle does no more than create a limited range of possible outcomes. Such unpredictability might also be considered to be an opportunity for God to act imperceptibly (see Chapter 4).

One way of dismissing the boundary between the "before" that science cannot explain and the "after" that science purports to "explain" is to

---

[85] Hawking, *A Brief History of Time*, pp. 9–10.
[86] Hawking, *A Brief History of Time*, p. 11.
[87] Pirani and Roche, *The Universe for Beginners*, p. 55.
[88] Hawking, *A Brief History of Time*, p. 139.
[89] Hawking, *A Brief History of Time*, p. 138.

dismiss the concept of a boundary, and this could lead to the dismissal of the idea of a creator:

> The idea that space and time may form a closed surface without boundary also has profound implications for the role of god in the affairs of the universes.... So long as the universe had a beginning we could suppose it had a creator. But if the universe is really completely self-contained, having no boundary or edge, it would have neither beginning nor end: it would simply be. What place, then, for a creator?[90]

Apart from the obvious tautology of a "closed surface without a boundary", it might be argued that a cosmos that simply was, always had been and always would be, would only appear to be so when observed, or experienced from within itself, for the whole crux of the theory is that there is no "outside"; this would apply whether such observations were made in what is believed to be real time or through the mathematical device of "imaginary" time that is used to construct a model of the cosmos that lacks such boundaries. Such a boundless model does not disprove the possibility that the temporality in which we exist nevertheless had its origins in a different mode of existence, for example in the *pre-archaios*, and such a mode might contain an infinite past. If the cosmos is indeed proven to be a "closed surface without boundary", this could imply that the Creator not only created time itself (cf. e.g. Augustine of Hippo) but also is in possession of a greater infinity.

Hawking and Mlodinow state that time is curved, like the surface of a sphere, and therefore there is no need to consider the beginning of time.[91] Even if time is curved thus, there is still the problem of the unmoved mover that enabled time to start flowing. Time would also seemingly need to start in the "correct" direction, with an increase in disorder in accordance with the second law of thermo-dynamics.

Later in *The Grand Design* there is an attempt to overcome the difficulty of excluding the possibility of a creator god by citing that there

---

[90] Hawking, *A Brief History of Time*, pp. 160–1.
[91] Hawking and Mlodinow, *The Grand Design*, pp. 172–3.

is more than one universe.[92] M-theory is described as a whole family of different theories, which are still part of a greater whole (unified) theory that can "all be regarded as aspects of a greater theory":[93]

> M-theory predicts that a great many universes were created out of nothing. Their creation does not require the intervention of some supernatural being or god. Rather, these multiple universes arise naturally from physical law.[94]

The hope provided by the expectation of a grand unified theory is almost reminiscent of religious belief of what the future might hold; however, the more important challenge comes from Karl Popper's philosophy of science that states that a good scientific theory will include a means of it being disproved. An observer cannot disprove the possibility of another universe if by definition they are constrained to live in only their own universe. If another universe were to be observed or experienced in some way whilst in one universe, then it would become part of the universe in which it was observed or otherwise experienced. It does not seem to answer the problem of how a single universe might exist by postulating a multi-universe theory.

Following the "Big Bang" it is proposed that quantum fluctuations[95] were necessary to produce a cosmos that, after the "Big Bang", was not homogenous and so galaxies, stars and planets would coalesce. "The fluctuations correspond to temperature differences of less than a thousandth of a degree of the Centigrade scale. Yet they were the seeds

---

[92] The word "universe" has assumed another meaning in cosmology: "it refers to the spacetime continuum that we see directly around us, filled with galaxies the geometries and history of which we observe. There is no reason to be certain that, in *this* sense, this cosmos is the only one in existence." (Author's italics) Rovelli, *Reality is not what it seems*, p. 181.

[93] Hawking and Mlodinow, *The Grand Design*, p. 17.

[94] Hawking and Mlodinow, *The Grand Design*, p. 18.

[95] Hawking and Mlodinow, *The Grand Design*, p. 175.

that grew to become the galaxies."[96] Hawking and Mlodinow concluded: "If one were religious, one could say that god really does play dice."[97] It would appear that the "Big Bang" theory is incomplete; quantum fluctuations of no apparent origin were required for the process that led to the cosmos as we know it.

Hawking stated that matter can arise spontaneously because the "positive energy of matter" is balanced by "negative gravitational energy".[98] It is to be noted that matter and energy are interchangeable as per Einstein's famous equation $E = mc^2$, but even if we accept that Hawking's assertion "because there is a law like gravity, the universe can and will create itself from nothing . . ."[99] is correct, then there would be no way of knowing if such an event had happened or whether it had been created deliberately *ex nihilo*. It is also to be noted that gravitational law provides a mathematical description but, as Newton himself remarked, offers no explanation as to why "action at a distance" should occur. Newton wrote that why gravity "should occur is to me an absurdity".

The Standard Model describes the sub-atomic particles created during the "Big Bang": "If the rate of expansion one second after the "Big Bang" had been smaller than even one part in a hundred thousand million million, the universe would have recollapsed before it ever reached its present size."[100] From such sub-atomic particles, elements would eventually form. These elements would then form chemical bonds resulting in biochemical structures such as the enzyme ATPase with its remarkable revolving mechanism, and such molecules became the building blocks from which questioning creatures are made. It would

---

[96] Hawking and Mlodinow, *The Grand Design*, p. 176; see also <https://map.gsfc.nasa.gov/media/121238/index.html> and <https://map.gsfc.nasa.gov/media/121238/ilc_9yr_moll2048BW.png> (accessed 13 July 2023), which has an illustration from the NASA Wilkinson Microwave Anisotropy Probe showing minute fluctuations in the temperature of the universe dating back 13.7 billion years.

[97] Hawking and Mlodinow, *The Grand Design*, p. 177.

[98] Hawking and Mlodinow, *The Grand Design*, p. 227.

[99] Hawking and Mlodinow, *The Grand Design*, p. 227.

[100] Hawking, *A Brief History of Time*, p. 138.

seem that having a planet on which life could develop is as remarkable as there being a planet in the first place and furthermore there appears to be no explanation offered by the study of either physics or biology that explains why or how sentient creatures have self-awareness: an understanding that they exist.

A universe that appeared *de novo* is miraculous: it is outside our experience that something exists where nothing had once existed. A universe that has always existed is also miraculous; it is outside our experience of living life normally that an object, person or animal has always existed.

Biology

To provide an account of the cosmos, having only attempted to describe the physical properties of matter, would be inadequate since human beings do not generally consider themselves to be exclusively electrochemical in nature but living beings. A Christian theological description of the cosmos would be incomplete without some reference to the biological sciences since it is within the biosphere, the living matter in this planet, that, according to all major religions, sentient creatures live; it also is within this biosphere that suffering is confined.

From within the biological sciences has arisen a substantial element of the driver for dispensing with the need to postulate a Creator that is derived from the assertions such as Peacocke's that there is a "staggering new understanding"[101] that science has afforded the cosmos. The theologian Wolfhart Pannenberg stated that there is a "self-sufficient and overwhelmingly successful scientific description of nature".[102] Such authors have failed to see the limit of scientific description. Farmers from ancient until pre-Enlightenment times knew that putting a bull and cow together might produce a calf; today we only have a more detailed

---

[101] A. Peacocke, *Theology for a Scientific Age: Being and Becoming—Natural, Divine, and Human* (Minneapolis, MN: Fortress Press, 1993), p. 28.

[102] W. Pannenberg, *An Introduction to Systematic Theology* (Grand Rapids, MI: Eerdmans, 1991), p. 38.

description of the processes involved. Many of the reproductive processes are remarkable. For example, the periodicity in the menstrual cycle arises as a hormonal control mechanism flips from one of negative feedback to positive feedback above a certain threshold.[103] Secondly, the apparent ability for a special type of cellular division (meiosis versus mitosis) to create gametes (ova and spermatozoa) that effectively sets the biological clock back to zero, untarnished by the effects of ageing, would, like gravity itself, astonish and astound us except that it is commonplace.[104]

Whilst evolutionary theory is not totally derived from historical enquiry, for some processes are demonstrable and observable, it is still questionable whether the theory of evolution and the discovery of DNA fully explain how life originated from the primaeval soup of the simple chemical compounds from which organisms are constituted. It is not only those with faith in a Creator who may have difficulty in accepting that life may have arisen through "spontaneous" means; Gribbin stated that "the puzzle is why a world ideal for life should have appeared out of the Big Bang".[105] For example, the Carboniferous Era (359mya to 299mya)[106] was the time during which the carbon reserves that are now available to humankind in this Anthropocene Era were deposited in the Earth's crust. This deposition could only have happened in the manner in which it did because plants had developed lignin to prevent the rotting process and thus "dead plants did not completely decay".[107] It took the 60 million years of the Carboniferous Era for fungi to develop the enzymes[108] needed to

---

[103] This dual-mode feedback mechanism provides the efficacy of the oral contraceptive pill that, by providing an external source of oestrogen, renders ineffective the hormonal feedback loop that controls egg release.

[104] I have to acknowledge some bias since the "miraculous" nature of conception and childbirth never ceased to astonish me as I practised as a medical doctor for several decades.

[105] Gribbin, *In Search of Schrödinger's Cat*, p. 320.

[106] mya is an abbreviation for "million years ago".

[107] <http://www.ucmp.berkeley.edu/carboniferous/carboniferous.php>, accessed 13 July 2023.

[108] <https://en.wikipedia.org/wiki/Lignin-modifying_enzyme>, accessed 13 July 2023.

degrade the lignin in the wood. If the other millions of enzymes[109] present in the natural world had taken similar amounts of time to come into existence then life as we know it today could not have been developed during the 3,800 million years since life first appeared in the Archean Eon.[110] The biologist Simon Conway Morris, in his book *Life's Solution: Inevitable Humans in a Lonely Universe* (2003), states that "99.9 per cent recurring of biological space (is) where things don't work" and therefore there seems to have been little time for evolution to have occurred in gentle stages. "Life, it is claimed, is simply too complex to be assembled on any believable timescale" is countered by "evolution's uncanny ability to find the short cuts across the multidimensional hyperspace of biological reality".[111] Even ignoring the anthropomorphic language in this quote there is still a suggestion that something other than evolutionary drivers and inevitabilities are required for humanity to be as it is now.

Such observations do not of course prove that a Creator is necessary; however, they point to the improbability of life appearing on Earth through random and spontaneous means. Demonstrating that evolutionary theory is not sufficient to explain the existence of living organisms (let alone those that question why they exist) will be for some a pointer to a Creator; for others it will be an incentive for further enquiry, and for others both responses will be elicited.

Evolution

The concept of evolution is not new. In the sixth century BC in Miletus, a culturally Greek settlement on the west coast of modern Turkey, the philosopher-scientists Thales, Hecataeus and Anaximander questioned creation mythologies and sought a rational world view.[112] Anaximander

---

[109] "(Collagenase) is just one of millions of enzymes on which all animals, microbes and plants depend to perform nearly all the vital activities of life." Al-Khalili and McFadden, *Life on the Edge*, p. 142.

[110] <http://www.ucmp.berkeley.edu/precambrian/archean_hadean.php>, accessed 13 July 2023.

[111] S. Conway Morris, *Life's Solution: Inevitable Humans in a Lonely Universe* (Cambridge: Cambridge University Press, 2003), p. 309.

[112] Rovelli, *Reality is not what it seems*, p. 4.

stated that, "plants and animals evolve to adapt to changes in their environment... man must have evolved from other animals".[113] What was achieved in the nineteenth century was a theory that described how evolution occurred. The main driver for natural evolution (as opposed to selective breeding) is that natural variance within a species occurs, and the better adapted an individual is to the environment in which they live then the greater the chance that their genetic factors will be continued within the species as they procreate.

When Darwin published his theory, there was opposition from the Church (of England), and such opposition from the Church to such theories of the natural world was not new. Leucippus and Democritus had founded the atomist school in Abdera *c.*450 BC,[114] the purposelessness of the cosmos as described by Atomism was challenged by Plato and Aristotle, who sought meaning in the cosmos.[115] Lucretius expresses Democritus' world view in poetry that was rediscovered by Poggio Bracciolini in 1417 and then prohibited from being read in schools in 1516 by the Florentine Synod and finally banned in 1551 by the (Roman Catholic) Church at the Council of Trent.[116] It is interesting that the Atomist School, with its purposelessness, should have been banned by the Church, since it accords with a resigned attitude to the presence of evil in Scripture.[117] The Bible does not seek an explanation of why there is evil in the world, accepting that it exists: the Serpent participates in the Genesis creation mythology without justification or explanation. This is similar to the atomism of Democritus in which atoms simply do what they do, and that is all there is to the world order. Rovelli describes how "the mediaeval cosmos so marvellously sung by Dante was interpreted on the basis of a hierarchical organization of the universe which reflected

---

[113] Rovelli, *Reality is not what it seems*, p. 6.

[114] Rovelli, *Reality is not what it seems*, pp. 7-8. Abdera was a culturally Greek city in the Eastern Mediterranean.

[115] Rovelli, *Reality is not what it seems*, p. 10.

[116] Rovelli, *Reality is not what it seems*, pp. 20-4.

[117] I have used a capital S to denote Scripture to denote my personal belief that Scripture is inspired by God and given to us to fulfil God's purposes.

the hierarchical organization of European society",[118] and it would seem that the neo-Platonic cosmos with its hierarchical organization was more palatable to the Roman Catholic Church. It was difficult to imagine, in an ordered hierarchy in which humans were regarded as the supreme and unique beings, that humans could have evolved from lesser creatures.

There are a number of inconsistencies within evolutionary theory that certainly do not disprove the theory, but suggest that it is currently incomplete.

Diversity versus constancy

Evolution has produced several types of eye: the mammalian eye that has the retinal vasculature overlying the neural receptors, the cephalopod (e.g. octopus) eye that has the neural network of the retina in front of the retinal vasculature, and the compound insect eye. These creatures all use rhodopsin to convert light energy into the electrical signals that the brain interprets, and whilst it is accepted that the similarity arises because of common ancestry, the unaltered use of rhodopsin contrasts with the considerable variation of form and other features of the creatures being compared.[119] Rhodopsin is just one example of a biochemical product that is distributed across many phyla (forms of life) but its ubiquitous nature is far from unique: the four bases that form DNA, the 20 amino acids that form proteins,[120] and the enzymes facilitating the Krebs cycle in which glucose is metabolized to create energy (via the formation of ATP)[121] are common (although not necessarily universal) throughout animal, fungal, bacterial and plant life.

---

[118] Rovelli, *Reality is not what it seems*, p. 25.

[119] Rhodopsin is present in bacteria and functions in some unicellular organisms; it is an example of convergence (q.v.), Conway Morris, *Life's Solution*, pp. 170–1.

[120] Two base pairs and 20 amino acids are "found in all terrestrial life". Conway Morris, *Life's Solution*, p. 15.

[121] "ATP is central to the storage and transfer of energy within the cell." Conway Morris, *Life's Solution*, p. 25.

ATPase is now known to have a rotatory component and is a more foundational and ubiquitously essential metabolic and cellular constituent:

> All of the ATPases share a common basic structure. Each rotary ATPase is composed of two major components: F0/A0/V0 and F1/A1/V1. They are connected by 1–3 stalks to maintain stability, control rotation, and prevent them from rotating in the other direction. One stalk is utilized to transmit torque.[122]

If the four bases, the Krebs cycle and the 20 amino acids occur without variation because they are the only ones that result in viability, this could infer that life had to first occur *de novo* with all such systems up and running. This constancy could be considered to be contrary to the spontaneous occurrence of diversity which is one of the main drivers of evolutionary change.

Excess baggage versus sleek machine
Many mechanisms used by organisms are very complex. At one end of the evolutionary scale is the flagellum (external "paddle") of a unicellular organism that is powered by an internal molecular motor that spins it, thus enabling it to move through water and reach food:

> Whilst we should not underestimate the difficulty in explaining how such a flagellar motor might have evolved ... the question as to how the flagellar motor was assembled is still unsolved.[123]

In some creatures, such as bats and toothed whales, there is an echolocation system requiring apparatus to produce ultrasonic sound waves, a receiving apparatus that converts the reflected sound into information with a spatial element plus a cerebral cortex equipped to interpret the neural impulses. Such creatures would be disadvantaged until the entire system was up and running. It is similarly conceptually

---

[122] In <https://en.wikipedia.org/wiki/ATPase>, accessed 13 July 2023.
[123] Conway Morris, *Life's Solution*, p. 111.

difficult to imagine how a cyclical phenomenon such as the menstrual cycle evolved, since the necessary molecules would have been without purpose until the whole system was in place. It is also difficult to imagine how the thoracic wall mechanism that allows lungs to function evolved, since the mechanism depends upon the use of geometry, and structures that evolved before the whole system was in place would have been without purpose and therefore, according to the rules of evolutionary theory, would have led to disadvantage and extinction. In the thoracic wall mechanism, the *contraction* of (external intercostal) muscles causes the thoracic cage to which they are attached to *enlarge*.

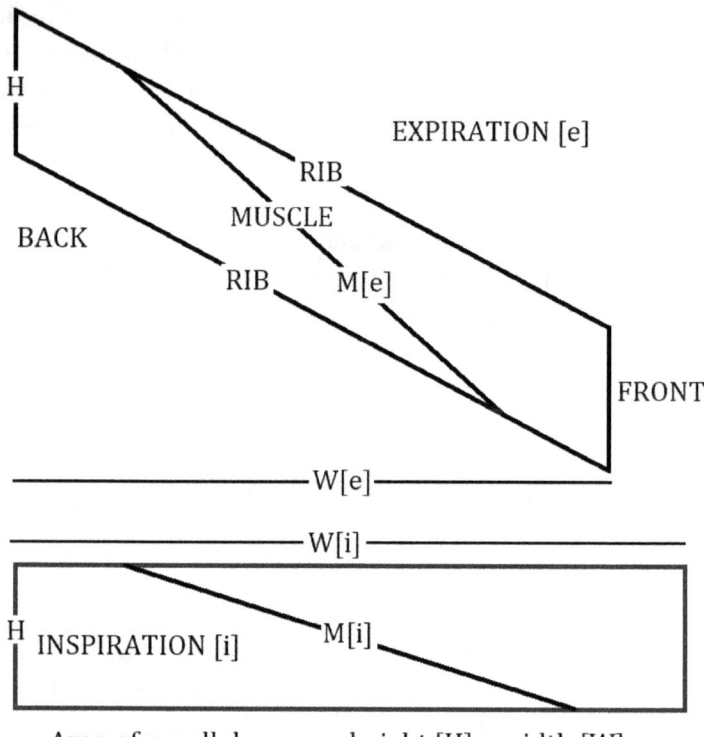

Area of parallelogram = height [H] x width [W]

The illustration above shows ribs that are connected to the thoracic vertebral column (back) via the costovertebral joints and to the sternum (front) via the costochondral joints. Intercostal muscles are connected obliquely between the ribs. During inspiration, the (external) intercostal muscles contract: M(i) is shorter than M(e), and this increases the area of the parallelogram formed by the ribs, sternum and thoracic vertebral column by changing it into a more rectangular form, thus increasing the surface area: W(i) is longer than W(e), and thus the volume of the thorax increases. Hence, as the external intercostal muscles contract the thoracic cage to which they are attached enlarges. The process works laterally as well as front to back.[124]

The evolutionary problem is that of irreducible complexity: one step is missing and the whole enterprise fails.[125] It is tempting to invoke the "intelligent design" argument. However, if an intelligent designer is rejected, then there is no alternative except to acknowledge that the building blocks of matter, and here I mean the atoms themselves, do appear to possess a remarkable propensity to organize themselves into complex structures.

The theory of evolution would suggest that organisms with only a part of these complex systems would be selected out since the incomplete system would offer no competitive advantage, but by expending energy and resources into characteristics that did not improve their chances of surviving to reproduce, they would be disadvantaged. Therefore only the simultaneous occurrence of an organism with a complete system would have an evolutionary advantage.

The "principle of inherency . . . is widely recognized",[126] in which unicellular organisms have the property to synthesize complex enzymes and proteins such as neuropeptides, chlorophyll, crystallins, haemoglobin and sodium channels that apparently have limited usefulness. Whilst the "principle" of excess baggage would suggest that such properties would be lost as evolution progressed, if the property only had the form of stored information, then this would have little demand on the unicellular

---

[124] Illustration from M. Brooks, "The Mechanics of Breathing", *The Trombonist* 1 (1996), pp. 28–9. Internal intercostal muscles are placed with their fibres at right angles to the external ones and produce forced expiration.

[125] A more elaborated critique of irreducible complexity by Michael Behe (b. 1952) is in Peterson et al., *Reason and Religious Belief*, p. 95.

[126] Conway Morris, *Life's Solution*, p. 237.

organism, although it is fascinating to consider why such abilities evolved in the first instance. Whilst there are counter-arguments within evolutionary theory to explain the sequential occurrence of all of the parts that make up the sum necessary to convey an advantage, such as a propensity to sexual selection, of the random genetic drift that can occur in small populations or of the coincidental conference of fitness of an intermediate form, the total effect of all such proposed mechanisms has to be weighed against the supreme driver of evolution; it is the sleek organism that does not carry excess baggage that is the one that is more likely to breed and over generations such uncluttered forms will dominate.

Altruism versus selfishness

The essence of evolutionary theory is that the strong survive to breed and the weak do not. Altruism would be expected to be bred out of a species and yet an extraordinary capacity to forgive is observable in humans and occasionally other animals as well. Whilst altruism may convey an advantage of a group of organisms, evolutionary theory triumphs the survival of the fittest (individual), and that the strongest of the breed produce the next generation and so "selfish" genes inexorably increase their occurrence in the gene pool. The persistence of altruism, therefore, can only be seen as anomalous in evolutionary theory since it seems to be counter to the key evolutionary driver.

Diversity versus species

Whilst it is tempting to reduce evolutionary theory to a two-word summary, "organisms change", it is to be recognized that the change from one species to another is considerable. Whilst the commonality of DNA can be measured, for example the much-quoted chimpanzee that shares 98.5 per cent of its DNA with humans and the genetic differences between chimpanzees and humans have been described as "negligible",[127]

---

[127] Conway Morris, *Life's Solution*, p. 242, quoting from V. M. Sarich and A. C. Wilson, "Immunological time scale for hominid evolution", *Science* 158 (1967), pp. 1200–3, and M. C. King and A. C. Wilson, "Evolution at two levels in humans and chimpanzees", *Science* 188 (1975), pp. 107–16.

there is, however, a markedly different genetic constitution. For example, humans have 23 pairs of chromosomes while chimpanzees have 24. At the end of each chromosome is a repeating DNA sequence called a telomere. Chimpanzees and other apes have about 23kb[128] of repeats; humans are *unique* among primates with telomeres of only 10kb. Chimpanzee and human chromosomes differ; chromosomes 4, 9 and 12 show evidence of being "remodelled". The Y chromosome in particular is of a different size and has many markers that do not line up between the human and chimpanzee. The clone map of chromosome 21 has "large, non-random regions of difference between the two genomes".[129] In human medical genetics, the addition or absence of large pieces of genetic material or entire chromosomes frequently leads to unviability (from spontaneous abortion to neo-natal death),[130] and minor genetic and metabolic anomalies often cause severe disease. An example of a metabolic anomaly is found in the Lesch-Nyhan syndrome which is an "inborn error of purine metabolism characterized by the absence or deficiency of the activity of the enzyme hypoxanthine-guanine phosphoribosyltransferase (HPRT)... Lesch-Nyhan syndrome is inherited as an X-linked recessive genetic disorder that most often affects males. The symptoms of Lesch-Nyhan syndrome include impaired kidney function, acute gouty arthritis, and self-mutilating behaviours such as lip and finger biting and head banging. Additional symptoms include involuntary muscle movements and neurological impairment."[131] Thus one error of significant variation in the metabolism of purines (that are found in many nitrogen-containing foods) has far-reaching consequences, so to transition from one species

---

[128] kb refers to one thousand base pairs; each pair is the basic unit of the genetic code.

[129] <https://creation.com/greater-than-98-chimp-human-dna-similarity-not-any-more>, accessed 13 July 2023. Although this website has an overt creationist bias, the article is referenced from respectable peer-reviewed sources such as *Chromosoma, Proceedings of the National Academy of Sciences* and *Science*.

[130] There are exceptions such as the Turner syndrome and Down's syndrome.

[131] <https://rarediseases.org/rare-diseases/lesch-nyhan-syndrome/>, accessed 19 July 2023.

to another, with the required change having to occur in much genetic material, involving thousands of such "small" steps, must surely be a most hazardous and unlikely process.

The process of change is driven by changes in the DNA sequence that "codes" for the form and function of the organism. "High-fidelity copying is crucial for life because the extraordinary complexity of living tissue requires an equally complicated instruction set, in which a single error could be fatal."[132] This suggests that the intermediates between chimpanzees and humans were unlikely to have survived, suggesting at least one more evolutionary mechanism is required other than the combination of chance mutations.[133] Thus the transition from the common ancestor of the chimpanzee and human to either of today's species is remarkable. For the purposes of clarity: I am not proposing that evolution does not and did not happen; what I am proposing is that when a complete explanation is provided then the complexity and detail, together with the improbability of such processes happening at all, will be such that it will require an enormous leap of faith to believe that life in all of its forms developed on planet Earth somehow by itself.

Spontaneous mutations were once thought to be largely caused by "rogue" radiation. A quantum phenomenon called tunnelling, however, moves the protons to create tautomeric forms of the DNA bases and so alters the pattern of hydrogen bonds leading to mutations via incorrect pairings in the reading of the genetic code.[134] Such tautomeric forms that potentially lead to errors in reading the genetic code account for 0.01 per cent of all natural DNA bases, 100,000 times higher than the "one in a billion rate of mutation found in the natural world", so "most of the resulting errors must be removed by the various error correction (proofreading) processes that help to ensure the high fidelity of DNA

---

[132] Al-Khalili and McFadden, *Life on the Edge*, p. 273.
[133] Luria and Delbrück, who won the Nobel Prize in 1969, "established the principle of the randomness of mutation as a cornerstone of modern evolutionary biology". Cf. Al-Khalili and McFadden, *Life on the Edge*, p. 288.
[134] Al-Khalili and McFadden, *Life on the Edge*, pp. 290–3.

replication".[135] But what (and where) is the indestructible reference source that the proofreading mechanisms refer to? The theologian Christopher Southgate states that "evolutionary self-transcendence is dramatically illustrated in such cruxes as the symbioses that gave rise to the first eukaryotic cells,[136] or the Middle to Upper Palaeolithic 'transition' in Homo Sapiens".[137] When organisms as a whole are considered, the change from chimpanzee to human may seem small (for example consider otherwise the change from a chimpanzee to an octopus), but paradoxically when the intricacies of cellular biology are viewed at a molecular level, the transition seems to be immense. Had such evolution from one species to another (to be contrasted with selective breeding within a species), that requires perhaps thousands of genetic mutations, been gradual, it might have been expected that the fossil record would reveal a continuum of biological forms and it would not be possible to classify creatures of the past (and present) into identifiable species. If "evolution proceeds by the preservation and accumulation of infinitesimally small inherited modifications",[138] where are the creatures within the fossil record that are not clearly identifiable as belonging to one particular species? Furthermore, the absence of such intermediates today is remarkable. The fossil record that occurs in geological layers overturns the "classical" doctrine of creation that states that all life forms appeared at the same time.[139] The counter-argument that successful specific combinations of genes lead to a successful organism that proliferates and dominates the fossil record is currently conjecture. The process through which a sub-population of a species with a natural variant may come to dominate that population has been

---

[135] Al-Khalili and McFadden, *Life on the Edge*, p. 293.

[136] Eukaryotic cells are characterized by the inclusion of structures such as mitochondria that have a genetic system based on RNA rather than DNA.

[137] C. Southgate, *The Groaning of Creation* (Louisville, KY: Westminster John Knox Press, 2008), p. 65.

[138] Al-Khalili and McFadden, *Life on the Edge*, p. 276.

[139] For some, fossils are deemed to have been placed there by God in order to test faith; this is another example of how evidence is open to interpretation.

observed and is the basis of selective breeding; an origin of a species has not yet been observed.

Diversity versus convergence
In the preface to his book *Life's Solution*, Conway Morris states:

> There is, however, a paradox. If we, in a sense, are evolutionarily inevitable ... then where are our equivalents, out there, across the galaxy? So in Enrico Fermi's famous words concerning putative extra-terrestrials: "Where are they?" "Either we are a cosmic accident, without either meaning or purpose, or alternatively ... "[140]

The expectation that life may be "out there, across the galaxy" is because "life on earth" has some of its origins in organic chemicals found in interstellar space and the organic compounds found in meteorites; therefore the whole cosmos is the "space" or "laboratory" in which life originated.[141]

Conway Morris describes the "inevitable emergence of sentience"[142] which is ascribed in part to the phenomena of evolutionary convergence:

> These complex systems (e.g. echolocation) can arise from very different starting positions, but again and again converge on the same evolutionary solution.

Whilst evolutionary mechanisms may suggest an inevitability of the emergence of the level of biological complexity that is required for sentience to exist, this does not prove that the sentience itself, however, is inevitable. A consciousness of being may elude the most complex biological (or electronic) system. Conway Morris gives a description of

---

[140] Conway Morris, *Life's Solution*, p. xiii. The indeterminate ending of this particular sentence is by Conway Morris.
[141] Conway Morris, *Life's Solution*, pp. 32–43.
[142] Conway Morris, *Life's Solution*, p. xiv.

a world controlled by leaf-cutter ants[143] that are highly socially organized and able to communicate with each other. The ants also demonstrate intelligent behaviour and practice agriculture. Would such abilities, however, prove that they had a conscience? Would they have "souls"? Would they feel guilt and other emotions and have an understanding that they exist, as most humans do?

There is another paradox: the divergence or natural variation which drives the evolutionary process versus the convergence that Conway Morris describes in detail with numerous examples. It is conceded by Conway Morris that "evolution is both riven with ambiguities and, paradoxically, is also rich in implications". Such implications are from "deeper structures and potentialities, if not inevitabilities" that organic evolution contains.[144] Furthermore, evolutionary convergence is not easily explicable by the rules of the "Game of Life" that are used to describe evolutionary trends.[145]

Conway Morris states: "The topic of convergence is very far from being just another example of the frustrating imprecisions of biology where apparent rules and laws melt into exceptions and counter-examples",[146] and "if we humans had not evolved then something more-or-less identical would have emerged sooner or later".[147]

The extensively documented phenomenon of evolutionary convergence is analogous to the physical laws that constrain non-living matter; it is a counter to the randomness of the evolutionary diversity that itself is analogous to quantum events. Biological processes therefore function in a mixed causal nexus although they are subject to physical phenomena. Massive events such as the impact of the K/T asteroid in what is now the Yucatan peninsula ended the dominance of dinosaurs on this planet, and at the other end of the spectrum there is the "rogue" gamma ray, a single quantum of radiation that might result in the development of a lethal cancer.

---

[143] Conway Morris, *Life's Solution*, p. 197.
[144] Conway Morris, *Life's Solution*, p. 2.
[145] Conway Morris, *Life's Solution*, p. 12.
[146] Conway Morris, *Life's Solution*, p. 127.
[147] Conway Morris, *Life's Solution*, p. 196.

Evolutionary theory challenged the established beliefs about the origin of life, and the study of the genetic basis of evolutionary development led to the idea of the gene being the absolute origin of living things and their diversity; the "selfish" gene that was not controlled by other factors that would perpetuate itself if the organism that it served was able to reproduce in its environment. Such a rule of genetic dictatorship is analogous to the classical notion of the inevitability of objects following a path that is fully predictable.

Whilst such "evolutionary theory was expanded with the insights of genetics, which gave further support for a scientific and secular view of how humans evolved" to the extent that "developing technologies such as genetic engineering and human enhancement may end up giving another important boost to the belief that science has (or eventually will have) the answers to life's mysteries",[148] there is a counter-argument with the recognition that there are environmental "epigenetic"[149] factors that create a mixed picture in which the acceptance of the environmental factors that affect gene expression are in tension with a reductive approach that proclaims an "absolute" role of the gene.

The findings of Cairns (1998) "appeared to contradict the central dogma of molecular biology: the principle that information flows only one way during transcription, from DNA out to proteins to the environment of a cell or organism".[150] This is in accord with the notion of epigenetic factors affecting mutations in DNA, at a macroscopic level

---

[148] T. Heneghan (2017) commenting on a conference hosted by the Ian Ramsey Centre, University of Oxford. <http://religionnews.com/2017/07/28/scientists-theologians-ponder-if-latest-biological-findings-are-more-compatible-with-religion/>, accessed 13 July 2023. No proceedings were published. For further reading see <http://onlinelibrary.wiley.com/doi/10.1111/zygo.2017.52.issue-2/issuetoc>, accessed 13 July 2023.

[149] Epigenetic from the Greek *epi* "upon, near to, in addition" (OED).

[150] J. Cairns, J. Overbaugh and S. Millar, "The origin of mutants", *Nature* 335 (1988), pp. 142–5, in Al-Khalili and McFadden, *Life on the Edge*, p. 298. Although controversial, such a contradiction to the dogma of molecular biology has been curiously absent from public debate in which the selfish gene was held to be supreme.

with the Lamarckian concept of the environment moulding the creatures to fit it; Al-Khalili leaves an open question as to whether this is a quantum phenomenon or if it may be explained by classical physical bio-chemistry. In this context, "environmental factors" does not only mean factors external to the organism's whole body but also the organism's internal environment; not the *milieu intérieur* proposed by early physiologists such as Claude Bernard, but effectively any part of the organism that is not genetic material, for example the cytoplasm that surrounds the nucleus in most cells.

There is thus within the biological sciences the emergence of a more holistic biology that is not genetically dominated, and in this mixed model the product of biological processes is not predetermined. Environmental factors are considered to be a part of evolutionary progression, and a mixed model of genetic law and environmental chaos could be the means for a Creator God to act imperceptibly.

It is suggested that God does not effect change only through chaotic environmental factors, from events such as the aforementioned K/T asteroid to the "rogue" gamma ray, but also through subtler, and even preventative, ways that would pass unnoticed. In a fully deterministic biology in which the effects of genetic factors were unopposed, such "acts of God" would be more apparent.

Evolutionary theory would therefore exist as a paradigm, a collection of statements with internal tension between constancy and diversity, between excess baggage and sleek machine, between altruism and selfishness and between diversity and species being four examples. Since it is currently indiscernible as to which of any of the four pairs of the protagonists listed in the previous sentence would dominate at any particular time, evolutionary theory seems to provide a mixed model of the predictable and unpredictable, i.e. similar to the mixed model of law and chaos that physics provides. If it is accepted that God might be active yet unnoticeable in the physical world, there is no reason why this might not also be the case in biological systems, in life itself. If a dogmatic approach to evolutionary theory is taken, with a belief that it either has explained or in due course will fully explain all biological phenomena, it is to be noted that living matter is grounded in the physical world, and subjected to the effects of such phenomena as epigenetic factors, radiation and meteor strike, and that the cosmos described by physics is a mixed model of law and chaos.

The origin of life

Conway Morris describes a "yawning gulf"[151] between having the basic building blocks of life and life itself. Furthermore:

> The second problem is that while life must have originated in a series of step-like processes, as one moves to even simpler compounds, so the real difficulty, that of bridging the gap between complex organic chemistry and any sort of functioning system we choose to call living, actually grows.[152]

To synthesize a protein chain with the specific amino acid sequence that will enable the protein chain to function, a number of amino acids (usually 20) and DNA are required. But much more is also needed. The required DNA code is (somehow) selected, unravelled and a template made from the correct side that is called messenger RNA (mRNA). The mRNA is transcribed into a protein chain at a ribosome, a structure that contains its own ribosomal RNA (rRNA). At the ribosome, 20 types of transfer RNA (tRNA) molecules are required that each have a base triplet at one end and can bond, temporarily, *with only one* of the "coded for" amino acids at the other.[153] Having synthesized the amino acids in their required sequence, enzymes are then required to modify the transcribed protein chain into its final form. Proteins are used in the cell to provide structure and form the enzymes that enable biochemical reactions. Protein synthesis is one of many processes required by a unicellular organism; a multicellular organism such as a human being requires a genetic code and the mechanism of expression to enable growth and development from a single cell into the final morphology

---

[151] Conway Morris, *Life's Solution*, p. 27.
[152] Conway Morris, *Life's Solution*, p. 53.
[153] A selection of three bases, each of which may be of four types of nucleic acid (or "base"), creates 64 possible combinations. There is some duplication of triplet codes for each type of amino acid.

(the phenotype), physiological control mechanisms, special senses and a highly developed nervous system; this list is not exhaustive. The origin of Ribose, a constituent of RNA and DNA in its deoxy form, cannot be synthesized in a pure form from formaldehyde even in laboratory conditions that attempt synthesis in "primordial" conditions via an abiotic (non-biological) pathway.[154] Similar experiments by Miller and Urey in the early 1950s that were popularly proclaimed to have produced "life" in the chemistry laboratory, succeeded in synthesizing amino acids with racemic equivalence, that is with equal numbers of the left-handed and right-handed forms that compounds with the same molecular formulae can adopt. Natural amino acids, however, are left-handed. [155]

The atheist biologist and Nobel Laureate, Sir Francis Crick, who jointly won the Nobel Prize for discovering the structure of DNA, conceded:

> An honest man, armed with all the knowledge available to us now, could only state that in some sense, the origin of life appears at the moment to be almost a miracle, so many are the conditions that would have had to have been satisfied to get it going.[156]

Stephen Hawking in *A Brief History of Time* (1988) wrote:

> The laws of science, as we know them at present, contain many fundamental numbers, like the size of the charge of the electron

---

[154] Formaldehyde is a simple molecule that can be made via an abiotic process that contains carbon, hydrogen and oxygen, the constituent atoms of many organic compounds including sugars such as ribose. Conway Morris, *Life's Solution*, pp. 50-1.

[155] Conway Morris, *Life's Solution*, p. 60, also quoting S. Miller and H. Urey, "Production of Amino Acids Under Possible Primitive Earth Conditions", *Science* 117 (1953), pp. 528-9 and "Production of Some Organic Compounds under Possible Primitive Earth Conditions", *Journal of the American Chemical Society* 77 (1955), pp. 2351-61.

[156] Francis Crick (1982), *Life itself: Its Origin and Nature* (London: MacDonald, 1982), p. 38, cited in Conway Morris, *Life's Solution*, p. 67.

> ... the remarkable fact is that the values of these numbers seems to have been very finely adjusted to make possible the development of life.[157]

Another amusing illustration has been provided by Al-Khalili: the emergence of life being likened to pouring a can of chicken soup into a pot, heating and stirring it to make a chicken. Sir Fred Hoyle, who coined the term "The Big Bang", likened the emergence of life to having a tornado blow through a junkyard that resulted in the assembly of a fully functioning jumbo jet. It is assumed that "cellular life must have been preceded by simpler self-replicators".[158]

The complexity of and improbability of (even) RNA-based self-replicators is immense; the existence of RNA with enzyme-like qualities (ribozymes) avoids the question of whether enzymes or RNA chains arose first.[159]

If it is assumed that a piece of RNA with 100 bases could self-replicate, then 4^{100} "attempts" might be needed for the required sequence to arise by chance; 4^{100} (10^{60}) of such chains would weigh 10^{50} kilogrammes, 10^8 times greater than the entire mass of the Milky Way, which is 10^{42} kilogrammes; put another way, there is a chance of 1 in 100,000,000 that this short piece of RNA consisting of 100 bases could have arisen by chance before exhausting the material resources of the entire Milky Way. It is to be noted that self-replicating RNA, DNA or protein has neither been made in a laboratory nor discovered in nature.[160] It is also to be noted that the human genome contains 6.3 billion base pairs.[161]

---

[157] Hawking, *A Brief History of Time*, pp. 141–2.
[158] Al-Khalili and McFadden, *Life on the Edge*, pp. 366–7.
[159] Al-Khalili and McFadden, *Life on the Edge*, pp. 368–73.
[160] Al-Khalili and McFadden, *Life on the Edge*, p. 374.
[161] The human male genome has 6.27 billion base pairs, and the female human genome has 6.37 billion base pairs; the greater number of base pairs is because the X chromosome is larger than the Y chromosome. Males have one X and one Y chromosome, and females two X chromosomes. <https://bmcresnotes.biomedcentral.com/articles/10.1186/s13104-019-4137-z>, accessed 13 July 2023.

It is suggested that variants may be produced in the primordial "soup" by quantum processes: "the proto-enzyme (ribozyme) can exist in all its possible configurations simultaneously as a quantum superposition".[162] However, this simultaneous existence in all forms undermines the necessity for genetic material (or its self-replicator equivalent) to have the property of accurate reproduction that is an essential characteristic for evolution to occur.

The "enemy" of superposition is decoherence, and it is suggested that if decoherence alternately collapses the superposition this may explain the ability of the (theoretical) self-replicator to grow in number.[163] As the complexity of the system increases, however, from the 100 pairs that the self-replicator contains to the 6.3 billion pairs found in the human genome, then the phenomena of decoherence would soon overwhelm the probability of superposition enabling the process overall.

Quantum biology

It is to be noted that quantum phenomena do not impact upon living systems exclusively through the random effects of radiation and "stray" sub-atomic particles. In their book *Life on the Edge: A Coming of Age of Quantum Biology* (2014), the physicist Jim Al-Khalili and molecular biologist Johnjoe McFadden state: "Life appears to have one foot in the classical world of everyday objects and the other planted in the strange and peculiar depths of the quantum world. Life, we will argue, lives on the quantum edge."[164] Stephen Hawking had stated in 1988 that quantum mechanics "is the basis of modern chemistry and biology".[165] If quantum mechanics with its inherent unpredictability does underpin biological processes then this surely means that any form of genetic determinism cannot provide a complete description and explanation of how life has evolved or will evolve.

---

[162] Al-Khalili and McFadden, *Life on the Edge*, p. 380.
[163] Al-Khalili and McFadden, *Life on the Edge*, p. 381.
[164] Al-Khalili and McFadden, *Life on the Edge*, p. 46.
[165] Hawking, *A Brief History of Time*, p. 64.

Demonstrating the vital necessity of quantum phenomena in living systems demonstrates the remarkable qualities of the cosmos at its smallest level.

Biochemical respiration is the process through which carbon atoms in carbohydrates are combined with oxygen molecules to create carbon dioxide and energy. When carbon-laden fuel is combined with oxygen in a conventional "fire", the temperatures attained are too high for biological systems: a more subtle stepwise process is required. Biochemical respiration requires quantum tunnelling,[166] the "quantum edge" that is necessary for the existence of living creatures. Al-Khalili continues: "few scientists now doubt that electrons travel along respiratory chains via quantum tunnelling. This places the most important energy-harnessing reactions in animal and (non-photosynthetic) microbial cells firmly within the sphere of quantum biology."[167] Electrons travelling along respiratory chains provide the subtle stepwise process. At a simplistic level quantum tunnelling may be regarded as the property of an electron to travel as a wave or "cloud of probability".[168] There was resistance to the acceptance of a quantum phenomenon being part of a biological process since a form of stability called quantum coherence is required to emulate such phenomena in laboratory conditions and these are absent within a living cell:

> Quantum coherence would not be expected to survive within this molecular turbulence (as inside a living cell), so the discovery that quantum effects, such as tunnelling, manage to persist in the sea of molecular agitation that is a living cell is very surprising.[169]

This is a significant surprise that demonstrates how improbable life is.

The "flip-side" of biochemical respiration that is necessary in an ecosystem that has both plant and animal life is photosynthesis, in which carbon dioxide is converted into carbon atoms that may become

---

[166] Al-Khalili and McFadden, *Life on the Edge*, p. 126.
[167] Al-Khalili and McFadden, *Life on the Edge*, p. 130.
[168] Al-Khalili and McFadden, *Life on the Edge*, p. 131.
[169] Al-Khalili and McFadden, *Life on the Edge*, p. 138.

incorporated into energy sources such as carbohydrates and fats (via sugar molecules) whilst releasing oxygen. The superposition principle is required to explain the energetics of photosynthesis. Experiments show that the exciton, produced when a light particle collides with part of a chlorophyll molecule, does not take "a single route through the chlorophyll maze but instead follows *multiple routes simultaneously*".[170]

Thus two quantum phenomena, superposition and quantum tunnelling, are essential for plant and animal life; yet the incoherence of living tissue suggests that such quantum phenomena could not happen. This is far from "surprising"; it is currently a significant paradox. The physical world exists because of the mysterious action of four or more forces; the biological world appears to be even more remarkable.

The emergence of human beings

A world dominated by leaf-cutter ants has been described. New Caledonian crows both make and use tools, and so can even a species of parasitic wasp. The use of tools by chimpanzees is well known; indeed a chimpanzee has been observed to perform primitive dentistry on another chimpanzee. "Giant brains, tool use, bipedality, and even a precision grip are not (therefore) specific to humans."[171] One conclusion is that early human societies that were highly organized, who practised tool-making and agriculture, could have done so without necessarily having need of or been in possession of the "higher cortical" function that is necessary for abstract thought, emotion or consciousness as in the awareness of being.

The use of fire and care for the sick dates from 400,000 years ago in the emergence of *Homo sapiens* even though modern humans themselves did not appear until 125,000 years ago.[172] The production of fire is still exclusively human, and evidence of care for the sick comes from the discovery of human remains which exhibit healed fractures that could not have occurred unless the injured person had been helped to recover. Ornaments, beads and perhaps musical instruments appear 50,000 years

---

[170] Al-Khalili and McFadden, *Life on the Edge*, p. 174.
[171] Conway Morris, *Life's Solution*, p. 271.
[172] Conway Morris, *Life's Solution*, pp. 261–4.

ago, whilst "cave paintings, figurines and other sculptures [appear] from about 35,000 years ago".[173]

The question of when *human* beings arose is complicated. The provision of care for the sick, from 400,000 years ago, is surely evidence of emotional development and empathy. In the animal kingdom parents care for their young in a myriad of ways. This might be dismissed as evolutionary necessity: inherent behaviour that provides a pro-creative advantage. The sight of animals, however, providing what little care they can to their injured or dying offspring makes it difficult to assume that humans are completely set apart from the rest of the animal kingdom in terms of emotion and empathy. Could human beings, in the fullest sense of a creature that is self-aware, empathetic and inclined to ask metaphysical questions, date from the time when there was the emergence of culture that produced art and music, which occurred circa 40,000 years ago? Had Conway Morris' leaf-cutter ants built (and visited) art galleries and concert halls in order to freely express themselves (rather than having created such institutions in a dispassionate manner solely for the purpose of social control) would we be persuaded that they had our human qualities? Rather than deciding criteria to determine when our ancestors became human in our understanding of what being human is, it is perhaps better to view the members of the entire animal kingdom as being somewhere in the spectrum of sentience.

Theophany of nature

"Darwinian theory plays a role in evolutionary biology that is analogous to the one Newtonian theory plays in celestial mechanics. It provides the mechanism of change; it specifies the law-governed processes that determine how species develop and adapt in a possibly changing environment."[174]

---

[173] Conway Morris, *Life's Solution*, pp. 274–5.

[174] M. Carrier, "Evolutionary Change and Lawlikeness: Beatty on Biological Generalization", in G. Wolters and J. G. Lennox (eds), *Concepts, theories and rationality in the biological sciences* (Konstanz and Pittsburgh, PA: Universitätsverlag Konstanz and University of Pittsburgh Press, 1995), pp. 83–97, cited in Conway Morris, *Life's Solution*, p. 312.

There is another similarity, for whilst Newtonian theory can predict trajectories, it does not explain why celestial bodies are attracted to each other. Similarly Darwin's theory does not give a full or satisfactory answer to how the living arose from the inanimate, but given that creatures live at all, Darwin's theory explains how they adapt.

In *The Grand Design*, Hawking and Mlodinow stated that: "very little in physical law can be altered without destroying the development of life as we know it".[175] Later in the same book, Hawking conceded that we have a *choice* in accepting a Creator or that science provides an atheist explanation.[176]

The weak anthropic principle: "our location in the universe is necessarily privileged to the extent of being compatible with our existence as observers", and the strong anthropic principle: "the universe (and hence the fundamental parameters on which it depends) must be such as to admit the creation of observers within it at some stage", which were first described by the physicist Brandon Carter in 1974,[177] suggest that the universe in which we exist was made for humanity.[178] Peterson describes the anthropic teleological principle, the exact conditions necessary for sentient life. "How does one best explain why these conditions have precisely the life-engendering or life-fostering values they have?"[179]

The cosmological argument postulates a necessary being (a creator) for the cosmos to exist, and this has been explored in previous chapters. The teleological argument, that such a Creator being creates the conditions for life, has been described.[180]

---

[175] Hawking and Mlodinow, *The Grand Design*, p. 205.
[176] Hawking and Mlodinow, *The Grand Design*, p. 215.
[177] Pirani and Roche, *The Universe for Beginners*, p. 160 are also discussed in Hawking, *A Brief History of Time*, pp. 140–1.
[178] Rovelli, *Reality is not what it seems*, p. 112.
[179] Peterson et al., *Reason and Religious Belief*, p. 93.
[180] Peterson et al., *Reason and Religious Belief*, p. 100. Peterson also describes a moral argument as evidence for God's existence since living (human) beings have a moral dimension; this is as described in C. S. Lewis' *Mere Christianity* (Glasgow: Collins Fontana Religious, 1952), p. 16.

Michael Martin stated that negative atheism finds weakness in the theistic argument, whilst positive atheism finds reasons for unbelief; negative atheism states that God does not provide evidence of God's existence, and positive atheism cites the presence of evil.[181] The importance of confronting the question of evil is thus:

> We estimate, on the one hand, the combined strength of the various arguments for God's existence, and, on the other hand, the strength of the argument from evil as well as other arguments against theism.[182]

It is the intention of this book to supply necessary evidence to make the cosmological and teleological theistic arguments strong rather than weak, and, in response to the objection of positive atheism, to assert necessary reasons for the presence of moral evil and natural evil. There may thus be a theistic principle in the cosmos in which we exist, a cosmos in which God included the conditions of a mixed model of order and chaos such that God could intervene without denying humanity the freedom to either reject or accept God without coercion.

If, in the aftermath of the "Big Bang", matter was somehow able to organize itself into the rich palette of elements that form the building blocks of everything that we see, that form the mechanisms that create our ability not only to see the cosmos but also a desire to observe the cosmos, that create a being that can possess both the ability and desire to question how and why it all happened, then it is still a wonderful act of Creation that occurred.

Conway Morris concludes the final section of *Life's Solution*, "Towards a Theology of Evolution", with:

> The complexity and beauty of "Life's Solution" can never cease to astound. None of it presupposes, let alone proves, the existence of

---

[181] Peterson et al., *Reason and Religious Belief*, p. 101, from M. Martin, *Atheism: Philosophical Justification* (Philadelphia: Templeton University Press, 1990), pp. 97, 100, 152.

[182] Peterson et al., *Reason and Religious Belief*, p. 108.

God, but all is congruent. For some it will remain as the pointless activity of the Blind Watchmaker, but others may prefer to remove their dark glasses. The choice, of course, is yours.

The beauty or awesomeness of the cosmos does not only apply to living creatures but also to the physical world in its greatest manifestations. Richard Dawkins (1998) in *Unweaving the Rainbow* states that science itself, properly understood, leads to a sense of wonder and delight. Keats held that Newton's physics had "destroyed all the poetry of the rainbow";[183] Dawkins argues that "a Keats and a Newton listening to each other might hear the galaxies sing".[184]

A restatement of the theophany of nature is required on account of the failure of Christians to engage with the theology of the created world, and the science that provides another description of this created world. This failure has come from the idea that "the non-human creation (is) merely a stage on which the drama of God and humans is being played out—and a temporary stage at that" and also that the dualism and Gnosticism of John and others who considered "human embeddedness in nature as a fate from which humans need to be liberated".[185] Such dualism and Gnosticism are countered by the *bodily* resurrection of Jesus.[186]

It could be argued that the very existence of sentient life on just one planet, given the enormous odds that are stacked against such an occurrence, is evidence of the hand of a Creator. The cosmos is immense in size, but it does not necessarily contain the infinite number of potentially habitable planets that would mean that all infinitesimally small possibilities were inevitable.

---

[183] R. Dawkins, *Unweaving the Rainbow: Science, Delusion and the Appetite for Wonder* (London: Penguin, 2006), p. 39.

[184] Dawkins, *Unweaving the Rainbow*, p. 313. Both Dawkins quotes are from Atkinson, *Renewing the Face of the Earth*, pp. 47–8.

[185] R. Bauckham, *Bible and Ecology: Rediscovering the Community of Creation* (London: Darton, Longman & Todd, 2010), p. 145.

[186] Bauckham, *Bible and Ecology*, p. 148.

The starting point for this book is theocentric and it is apt to close this part of this chapter with a supposed view of human scientific activity from God's perspective:

> You sought order and pattern in the cosmos and when you found it you were surprised by the unfathomable complexity and interdependence in what you had discovered. Yet somehow many of you chose to believe that it all just happened, all by itself.

Theology

God's love for the cosmos has been demonstrated through the self-revelation of God, particularly through the incarnation of Jesus Christ.[187] The salvific ministry of Jesus Christ who redeemed a fallen creation will be discussed in Chapter 3.

God's self-revelation

The self-revelation of God can inform Christian faith through the three sources of Hooker's (1597) understanding of the basis of Christian Faith, namely Scripture, reason and tradition.[188] The self-revelation of God is considered to be the source and inspiration of *Scripture* as it was written and then examined both historically and currently to describe and explain God's interaction with humankind in the Jewish and Christian journeys of faith. The self-revelation of God might be considered by some to be

---

[187] It is to be recognized that this book is not an apologetic that covers all aspects of Christian faith; it merely answers the question of how can a Christian believe in an all-powerful and loving God whilst so much suffering and death occurs?

[188] This is discussed in M. Brooks, "The Church's One Foundation: 'Why Christians in the Church of England may disagree on matters of faith with each other and others, and an approach to resolving such disagreements'". Dissertation submitted in part fulfilment of the requirements for the Degree of Master of Arts in Ministerial Theology of the University of Canterbury Christ Church, 2013.

the source and inspiration of the development of *reason* as applied to the examination of the constituents of the cosmos, i.e. Popper's physical objects, knowledge and consciousness.[189] The self-revelation of God might be considered by some to be both the source and the inspiration for the examination of the *tradition* of the Church, tradition being the specific contribution made to the development of the faith of the Church by examining its history. Later interpretations of Hooker's writing have implied an equality of these three sources.[190] Hooker, however, placed the three in a distinct hierarchy.

> What Scripture doth plainly deliver to that the first place both of credit and obedience is due; the next whereunto is whatsoever any man can necessarily conclude by force of reason; after these the voice of the Church (tradition) succeedeth.[191]

Note that in all three sources, Scripture, reason and tradition, the self-revelation of God works through the human mind either intellectually or transcendentally (spiritually) or both. There is presently no specific monument, creature or other object that declares the existence of God with cognitive certainty.

Jesus Christ: The Incarnation

I wish to describe the extraordinary nature of Jesus Christ, a special gift to humankind that demonstrates *above all else* God's love for the cosmos. In John's Gospel, Jesus declares:

> For God so loved the world that he gave his only Son, so that everyone who believes in him may not perish but may have eternal life. (John 3:16)

---

[189] In Peacocke, *Theology for a Scientific Age*, p. 193.

[190] The "three legs of a stool" analogy is misleading, since it implies equality in the height of leg.

[191] R. Hooker (1597), *Of the Laws of Ecclesiastical Polity*, Book V viii 2.

A more literal translation would be: "For (thus) God so loved the system (universe) that he gave his only Son, so that everyone who believes in him should not be perishing but may be having eternal life."[192] The NT Greek word often translated as "world" is κόσμον (*kosmon*), from which cosmos is derived.[193] The Gospel declares a cosmic role for Jesus, a role that is not limited to humanity.[194]

It may be argued that for Christians there was a specific "creature" who declared the existence of God with cognitive certainty, namely the person of Jesus Christ. The Incarnation is much more than the "mechanics of Jesus' conception",[195] and the consideration of Jesus' conception has led to the denial of the "Virgin birth" as some theologians have attempted to make Christian faith more acceptable to a sceptical scientific community. Denial of such a "Virgin birth" does create a contrast between the view of Peacocke, for example, and a more orthodox view of Christian theology. Peacocke is simply wrong to suggest that a fertilized ovum (zygote), created *de novo,* would not have reflected Jesus' ancestry.[196] Such a bespoke and unique zygote could have been endowed with the genetic code to share our evolved humankind and Jesus' origins in particular; that is after all an important function of the genetic code that is reproduced by DNA: inherited factors are passed on via such genetic material or substance. There is also the intriguing question as to whether there is a *theological* difference between God creating *de novo* the DNA

---

[192] <https://www.scripture4all.org/OnlineInterlinear/NTpdf/joh3.pdf>, accessed 13 July 2023.

[193] According to Bauckham, these translations of New Testament words may be made: *kosmos* = human world, *pasa ktisis* = whole creation, *panta* = all things, "heaven and earth". The NT often includes the natural world when terms are used. The NT writers assumed their writing would be added to the OT. Bauckham, *Bible and Ecology,* p. 142.

[194] The "Cosmic Christ" is described by Paul in Colossians 1:15-20, who inserted a hymn into the letter; Part 1 concerns creation by the pre-existent Christ and Part 2 is the reconciliation by the crucified Christ; the whole of creation is emphasized, see Bauckham, *Bible and Ecology,* pp. 151-2.

[195] R. Williams, *On Christian Theology* (Oxford: Blackwell, 2000), p. 82.

[196] Peacocke, *Theology for a Scientific Age,* p. 277.

that was the origin of Jesus' human body and the DNA that is the genetic code for any other person or creature; they are all manifestations of the Creator's will. To suggest that divine conception does not produce a fully human Jesus requires a limited view of what God can do.

If it is accepted that God created the cosmos, then creating *de novo* a zygote with appropriate genetic material would not have been impossible for God. To suggest that divine conception is not believable also requires a very limited view of God's capabilities; reflecting on the complexity of the cosmos or the vastness of the cosmos would seem to disperse such doubts. With the help of the Hubble telescope, we now have a better image, literally a bigger picture, of the cosmos in which we exist. It is accepted that the vastness of the cosmos only adds a little weight to belief in the existence of a Creator via an essentially emotional appeal; indeed the vastness increases the possibility that a planet such as Earth may have been formed upon which life may have arisen spontaneously. The point being made, however, is that if a Creator can create all of this, then why is it difficult to believe that God created *de novo* the zygote from which Jesus was begotten?

As well as suggesting that a zygote created *de novo* would not have reflected Jesus' ancestry, Peacocke also casts doubt on the creation of Jesus *de novo* on the grounds that God has to be consistent; another interpretation is that there may be a need to consider that God does not have to be consistent. The Hebrew Bible has several covenants, the Noahide, Abrahamic and Mosaic, whilst the New Testament has the New Covenant. These covenants are inconsistent in that they are not restatements of each other, emphatically so in the case of the New Covenant. It would seem that Peacocke is taking attributes of the classical metaphysical concept of god that insisted that God is consistent and applying them to the God of the Hebraic–Christian tradition.

The Nicene Creed (AD 325) gives an indication of the special nature of Jesus' origin: Jesus was not made or born: Jesus was "begotten". The Nicene Creed was modified by the First Council of Constantinople (AD 381), and the word "begotten" was retained. John Robinson, theologian and former Bishop of Woolwich, stated how the Definition of Chalcedon, formulated in AD 451 to resolve the doctrine of the Incarnation and Divinity of Christ, had retained the word "begotten", and that "properly speaking it is not a solution but a statement of the problem".[197] Understanding the origin of Jesus is one of the mysteries of the Holy Trinity, how one part, the "Father", can create another, the "Son", when both are equal (with the Holy Spirit) and also indivisible. It would seem that inventing a special word was a convenient way of dealing with the mystery.

Peacocke has a further objection to the Virgin birth.[198] He states that the birth narratives are the sole evidence for the virgin conception, and this may be contrasted with the Christ-event, the Resurrection, which had a "seismological effect"[199] upon Jesus' early followers, and subsequent human history. This objection in which the narratives are rejected denies the authenticity of the written narrative since the Gospel writers had to write that which would have been acceptable to the earliest members of the early Church, some of whom would have known Mary the mother of Jesus, Jesus' brothers and sisters, and their descendants.[200] In passing, it is interesting that the first-order relatives of Jesus have little mention in the Gospels, possibly because they detracted from the "special nature" of Jesus. One rare example of Jesus' siblings being referred to is in Mark 6:3: "Is not this the carpenter, the son of Mary and brother of James and Joses and Judas and Simon, and are not his sisters here with us"?

It is to be conceded that the necessity for a *Virgin* birth itself is not securely rooted in Scripture. It is not mentioned in either the Gospel according to Mark or to John, and the "Q" material used in both Matthew and Luke's Gospels is considered to have relied upon the Septuagint, a Greek translation of the Hebrew Bible. In the Hebrew version of Isaiah (7:14), the word הָעַלְמָה (*eolme*) is translated as a damsel.[201] In the Septuagint, this word is translated to παρθένος (*parthenos*) meaning virgin. Hence, while the NRSV translation of Isaiah 7:14 is "Therefore the

---

[197] J. Robinson, *Honest to God* (London: SCM Press, 1963), p. 65.
[198] Peacocke, *Theology for a Scientific Age*, p. 279.
[199] Peacocke, *Theology for a Scientific Age*, p. 293.
[200] Mark's Gospel may have been written no later than AD 70. C. Clifton Black, in *New Revised Standard Version HarperCollins Study Bible* (2006), pp. 1722–3. Mark's Gospel was the starting point for the Gospels of Matthew and Luke.
[201] <http://www.scripture4all.org/OnlineInterlinear/OTpdf/isa7.pdf>, accessed 13 July 2023, p. 2.

Lord himself will give you a sign. Look, the young woman is with child and shall bear a son, and shall name him Immanuel", Matthew 1:23 has "Look, the virgin shall conceive and bear a son, and they shall name him Emmanuel." Thus the original prophecy in the Hebrew Bible spoke of a young woman or damsel, the Greek translation that Luke and Matthew used spoke of a virgin.

That Jesus' DNA may not have been created entirely *de novo* does not necessarily detract from the special nature of Jesus' conception since all conception can be regarded as special and indeed miraculous. Jesus can still be regarded as in the Nicene Creed; the "Son of God . . . , begotten, not made, of one Being with the Father",[202] even if the Father did permit Jesus' DNA to form in one of Mary's ovaries and one of Joseph's testes rather than *de novo* in Mary's womb. When Jesus took on flesh, he took on lungs and sputum, ears and wax, eyes and "sleepy-men", guts, vomit and faeces, muscles, skin and stinking sweat-sodden clothes, so why should God regard an "ordinary" human egg and spermatozoa to be unacceptable if God had created all of the other aspects of human biological existence?

The point that I am making, in this combination of cell biology and astronomy, is that if it is believed that the cosmos was created by God, then there is no need to reject statements contained in the Nicene Creed on account of humankind, with an imagination that is too small to understand what God can do, by deeming such actions not to be "provable" in scientific terms. Near the start of this part of this chapter, I quoted from John Hick's *Philosophy of Religion*: "There is only one universe, and it is capable of being interpreted both theistically and nontheistically."[203]

---

[202] The Archbishops' Council, *Common Worship* (London: Church House Publishing, 2000), p. 173.

[203] Hick, *Philosophy of Religion*, p. 27.

Philosophy of creation

In this part of the chapter, I wish to introduce and explore some ideas that may inform further development in the book and add support to the view that the cosmos is the work of a Creator.

Hick makes the point that whilst the philosophy of religion was once seen as the test of "revealed" theology against "natural", i.e. metaphysical (classical) theology that "prepared the way for the claims of revelation", it is now seen as philosophical thinking about religion. Such use of philosophy to defend religious beliefs is termed apologetics.[204] Religion always relates to persons and personal experience, and since existential philosophy implies personal involvement in philosophical thought, so it would seem inevitable that there is an existential element in the philosophical approaches to religion.

The concerns of human existence as it is experienced do not readily resolve with experience and, particularly as a person ages, increasing amounts of thought about human existence may be concerned with negative preoccupations, those of "finitude, anxiety, guilt, dread of death, loneliness", all in all "the language of the soul's distress".[205] It has also been stated that "Christian apologetics are derived from the problem of evil".[206] If it is agreed that a cognitive approach to or logical "proof" of the existence of God yields no defining answer, then an empirical approach is required.

In "empiricist philosophy, matters of fact are not susceptible to logical proof, a weight of evidence is desired",[207] and it is possible to develop this further by stating (again) that it is the interpretation of evidence that is required,[208] not the evidence itself since empiricism is that which is known by experience; it is rationalism, the application of rational

---

[204] Hick, *Philosophy of Religion*, p. 1.
[205] Hick, *Philosophy of Religion*, p. 2.
[206] Hick, *Philosophy of Religion*, pp. 60–1.
[207] Hick, *Philosophy of Religion*, p. 95.
[208] As in Hick, *Philosophy of Religion*, p. 62, faith and evidence for God is a matter of the interpretation of the evidence.

thought,[209] that interprets evidence. Interpretation of evidence is required although it is recognized that the outcome of this process is not "proof". Peterson states: "Critical rationalism is committed to the analysis and evaluation of religious beliefs but does not maintain that these beliefs are subject to conclusive proof or disproof."[210]

In the philosophy of logical positivism, then, to be true a statement has to also make a difference that can be experienced.[211] All human experience is subjective, and those people who claim to have religious experience frequently describe that it makes a difference to their lives:

> We can experience God like we experience bread. We don't need a philosopher to prove that a loaf of bread exists before I can enjoy eating it, I don't need a philosopher to prove that God exists before I can experience God in my life.[212]

This "religious truth" would seem to fulfil the logical positivist criteria. Those who have religious experience will also claim that it does not "feel" as if their convictions have arisen from sociological pressure or internal psychological drivers. The atheist physicist Francis Crick spent much time in his later life trying to prove that religious activity in the human brain was the function of a religious centre in the brain and thus used the normal apparatus, stating that "we are nothing but a bundle of neurones".[213] According to Peterson, the theologian and philosopher Alvin Plantinga "holds that there is a component in the cognitive equipment of each one of us that is specifically designed to produce belief in God, given certain 'inputs' that are commonly available in our ordinary environment". Such "inputs" can be a sense of awe, guilt or

---

[209] Hick, *Philosophy of Religion*, p. 48.

[210] Peterson et al., *Reason and Religious Belief*, p. 3.

[211] Hick, *Philosophy of Religion*, pp. 85–6.

[212] This is my paraphrase of an exposition of the "nevertheless" argument by Simone Weil; in Peterson et al., *Reason and Religious Belief*, pp. 107–8.

[213] In F. Watts, R. Nye and S. Savage, *Psychology for Christian Ministry* (London: Routledge, 2002), p. 277.

forgiveness. This is similar to John Calvin's *sensus divinitatis* ("sense of divinity").[214]

Higher intellectual function is thought to be a global function of the cerebral cortex and so to propose a "religious centre" does, somewhat paradoxically, suggest that religious activity has a foundational function such as speech that does appear to be located in defined cortical areas. The designation of the brain into centres, however, may not be as defined as Crick thought. In the mid-nineteenth century, Wernicke and Broca deduced from pathological specimens that specific areas of the cortex were important for the comprehension and production of speech respectively. Recent research has cast doubt on this and suggested that language function is more diffusely spread in the cortex and also involves sub-cortical structures.[215]

Bearing in mind that such "centres" of higher intellectual function are more diffuse than once thought, if such a religious centre were to be found within the human brain (the most likely positions being either the cerebral cortex in which higher intellectual function is located or the limbic system in which emotion, motivation and mood are located), then it would be open to interpretation whether this had evolved because creatures survived better if a proportion of them had a sense of the transcendental, or eternal, or was simply more altruistic, or whether God had put it there for God to use. For, as in Watts et al., if God had created such a centre, then there is no reason why God would expect God's creatures not to use what God had made.[216]

Tooley states:

> in the case of religious experiences it might be argued that personal contact with a being may provide additional evidence concerning the person's character, it is clear that the primary

---

[214] Peterson et al., *Reason and Religious Belief*, p. 121.

[215] P. Tremblay and A. S. Dick, "Broca and Wernicke are dead, or moving past the classic model of language neurobiology", *Brain and Language* 162 (2016), pp. 60–71, at <https://www.sciencedirect.com/science/article/pii/S0093934X16300475?via%3Dihub>, accessed 14 July 2016.

[216] Watts et al., *Psychology for Christian Ministry*, p. 277.

evidence concerning a person's character must consist of information concerning what the person does and does not do.²¹⁷

Although cited as evidence against the existence of God and the authenticity of religious experience, this apparent receptiveness to God that is not consistently reflected in behaviour or character may be explicable by some form of religious centre, or at least subjective religious influence within the brain. This, in turn, might explain why some research has made the intuitively surprising discovery that undesirable characteristics such as racism have been found to be more prevalent in churchgoers than non-believers;²¹⁸ perhaps this "religious centre" is triggered by an innate sense of guilt, and the Church is truly a group of sinners calling for help. Were a religious centre to be discovered, it should not cause alarm amongst those who have faith in God, for such a centre would be evidence to indicate that God had intentionally created a facility in the human brain for this purpose.

Hick conveniently lists "Grounds for Belief in God",²¹⁹ and the understanding of the cosmos afforded by contemporary science permeates each of these grounds. Whilst contemporary science may not have any direct relevance to the ontological argument (an historic "proof" of the existence of God), Kant's counter, that there is "no self-contradiction in rejecting the concept of an absolutely necessary being"²²⁰ implies that there is complete acceptance that the cosmos (somehow) created itself. Kant's counter does seem, from an empiricist aspect, to recede into obscurity as the sheer complexity of the created world is discovered. In this, I am particularly minded of the apparent use of geometry in the thoracic cage mechanism and the beautiful symmetry of the table of Standard Model of Elementary Particles that shows the

---

[217] M. Tooley, "Theodicy and the Problem of Evil", 3.3, <http://plato.stanford.edu/entries/evil>, accessed 11 July 2023, 6.1. Tooley's probabilistic mathematical attempt to prove, or otherwise, the existence of God is discussed in "Theodicy".
[218] Watts et al., *Psychology for Christian Ministry*, p. 43.
[219] Hick, *Philosophy of Religion*, p. 16.
[220] Hick, *Philosophy of Religion*, p. 18.

interrelations of the quarks that are the constituents of atomic nuclear particles (protons and neutrons), the leptons that are the constituents of the electrons that orbit the atomic nucleus, and other particles. The Standard Model does not, however, include the constituents of "dark" matter,[221] and neither does the Standard Model include the Higgs boson, the so-called "god" particle that has been claimed to "explain mass". It has been noted that such a claim does not explain the mass of the Higgs boson.[222]

The Standard Model is a simplification. For example, a quark has one of three "colours" (These colours are not represented in the diagram[223] in which colour is used to differentiate between quarks, leptons and gauge bosons). A proton or neutron is made of three quarks; two "up" and one "down" forms a proton, and two "down" and one "up" forms a neutron.[224] That the cosmos exists at all is due to the fact that whilst particles and their equivalent antiparticles usually behave symmetrically, they do not always do so,[225] and thus the equal mixture of matter and anti-matter that might have been expected to have been produced by the "Big Bang" did not self-annihilate in what might have subsequently been an even bigger "flash", when as particles collide and mutually annihilate, their corresponding anti-particle radiation is emitted.[226]

For Karl Barth, the Reformed Church pastor and theologian, the ontological argument was "an unfolding of the significance of God's revelation of Godself", leading to "an already formed deeper understanding of its object".[227] This unfolding of the self-revelation of God may include increasing realization of the complexity of the cosmos. The ancients probably imagined the smallest possible fragments of matter to be vastly greater in size than they actually are, and quantum

---

[221] Rovelli, *Reality is not what it seems*, p. 108, footnote.
[222] Rovelli, *Reality is not what it seems*, p. 109, footnote.
[223] <https://en.m.wikipedia.org/wiki/File:Standard_Model_of_Elementary_Particles.svg>, accessed 5 January 2024.
[224] Hawking, *A Brief History of Time*, p. 74.
[225] Hawking, *A Brief History of Time*, pp. 87–8.
[226] Hawking, *A Brief History of Time*, p. 87.
[227] Hick, *Philosophy of Religion*, p. 20.

mechanics has shown that such particles also exist as a wave form that collapses when detected. The discovery of DNA has merely scratched the surface of the complexities of the genetic code and how this is translated via molecular structures far more complex and less probable than the relatively simple helix of DNA, such as transfer RNA and ribosomes.

Such complexity may encourage humankind to accept that the cosmos *is* created; the humility becomes necessary as a corollary of a created cosmos in that humans are to be regarded as creatures, and therefore not "self-made".

Since the central argument of this part of the chapter is the re-commendation of the divine designer argument, some counters to the criticisms of the philosopher David Hume (1711–76) are required. Hick states that it has "seemed to most philosophers that the design argument, considered as proof of the existence of God, is fatally weakened by Hume's criticisms".[228] Hick's *Philosophy of Religion* was written in 1973, and it could be argued that the expectations and optimism regarding an exclusively science-based explanation of everything was at its zenith. In biological studies, there was optimism that with the discovery of gene-sequencing technology all disease would soon be eradicated and that immortality itself was a real prospect during the next few decades. Stephen Hawking was considered to be the person who could create a unifying theory that would resolve the incompatibilities of quantum theory and gravitational theory. In 1988, Hawking described "a glimpse of the shape of a quantum theory of gravity yet to come".[229] The two theories are, however, still considered to be incompatible. Whilst the discovery of black holes posed little threat to the emergence of such a unifying theory, the discovery, by inference, of dark matter and dark forces[230] that defy description have complicated any attempt to reduce the understanding of the physical world to one monolithic theory.

---

[228] Hick, *Philosophy of Religion*, p. 25.

[229] Hawking, *Brief History of Time*, p. 90.

[230] Dark forces are not to be confused with the paranormal that is not otherwise discussed in this book. For further information and validation of such phenomena, please refer to the work of Bishop Dominic Walker, a former

Stephen Hawking seems to concede that the unifying theory may not be possible:

> In physics it may be necessary to use different formulations in different situations, but two different formulations would agree in situations where they both can be applied. The whole collection of different formulations could be regarded as a complete unified theory, though one that could not be expressed in terms of a single set of postulates.[231]

I am not using the current state of ignorance to promote a "God-of-the-gaps" argument, in which all that is unexplained has to be attributed to the work of a Creator god. When the mechanisms used by the genetic code are fully described, and the unifying theory of quantum-gravitation that encompasses the "dark" aspects of the cosmos is fully refined, then for some this will be a pointer to the greater glory of God, and for others a reason to reject the idea of the cosmos requiring a creator.

David Hume
The first objection made by the philosopher David Hume to the acceptance of the divine designer is based in the notion that "any universe is bound to have the appearance of being designed".[232] This statement, in itself, would appear to be of neutral status in the quest to determine if there is a divine designer; a cosmos created by a divine designer is bound to appear created unless such a divine designer were deliberately perverse, for why should a divine designer hide what had been created? The objection could also be countered by the question "What sort of cosmos would not appear designed, and could such a cosmos contain sentient creatures in what might appear to be an irrational cosmos?" Contemporary science diminishes Hume's argument in his counter

---

Diocesan Exorcist, <https://en.wikipedia.org/wiki/Dominic_Walker_(bishop)>, accessed 14 July 2023.

[231] Hawking, *Brief History of Time*, pp. 200–1.

[232] D. Hume (1779), *Dialogues Concerning Natural Religion* Part VIII, quoted in Hick, *Philosophy of Religion*, p. 25.

claim, namely the Epicurean hypothesis in which random processes will eventually create a self-perpetuating stable order. Thus the Epicurean hypothesis proposes that the *particles* that constitute the cosmos will eventually become organized in a self-perpetuating manner. The Laws of Thermodynamics, which were developed in the century after Hume, that pervade all areas of physics, state clearly (Law II) that the disorganization of matter (entropy) always increases; indeed energy is required to reverse this process.[233] This suggests that a cosmos created by Epicurean randomness is thermodynamically impossible. Biological systems are, however, examples of a reversal of this process of disorganization; organisms are considerably more complex than the molecules from which they are synthesized.

Hume also rejects the argument from design on the grounds that the analogy between the cosmos and a complex machine such as a watch "is rather weak".[234] For Hume, to make the analogy that God created the cosmos as a human makes a watch falls down since the cosmos does not resemble a watch: "Only if the world is shown to be rather strikingly analogous to a human artefact, is there any proper basis for the inference to an intelligent designer."[235] This would suggest that in Hume's time the paucity of known detail about the cosmos, that contemporary science has subsequently uncovered, together with an anthropocentric view of

---

[233] Gribbin, *In Search of Schrödinger's Cat*, p. 63.

[234] Hick, *Philosophy of Religion*, p. 26.

[235] Hick, *Philosophy of Religion*, p. 26. There is one phenomenon that occurs in the natural world that is claimed to point to an intelligent designer, and that is the observation in nature of the numbers in the Fibonacci sequence. These numbers occur more often than might be expected either through random processes or biological processes such as binary division. The Fibonacci numbers are found in, for example, the number of petals in a flower. The numbers in the Fibonacci sequence consist of the sum of the two previous numbers, e.g. 0, 1, 1, 2, 3, 5, 8, 13, 21, 34, 55, etc. Furthermore, when this series is continued the ratio of the last two numbers converges to 1.6180, which is known as the golden ratio. This ratio is aesthetically pleasing and is found in human artefacts such as architecture. See <http://www.livescience.com/37704-phi-golden-ratio.html>, accessed 13 July 2023.

Creation in which humans were considered to be God's equal, led Hume to conclude that a cosmos created by God would resemble something that humans had made. We could be generous to Hume and infer that perhaps he was describing the "better" artefact that humans would attempt to create: a world with either less suffering or no suffering at all. The complexity of Creation suggests that the analogy of the divine watchmaker can exist since there is a vast chasm between the creative abilities of humans and God.

Hume's third grounds for the rejection of the design argument is although the design argument may infer a divine designer, it does not prove that the designer has the characteristics that Christians claim. In this, Hume appears to be considering a metaphysical classical god, and then judging what he has decided god is like according to the claims of the Hebraic–Christian tradition. The Hebraic–Christian tradition does not make claims about the wisdom and goodness of God through metaphysics; it is the essence of this tradition that God has revealed and does reveal Godself to humankind. The claimed qualities of God in the Hebraic–Christian tradition do not have their basis in either the design argument or any other "natural theology": the claims are derived from the history and experience of people who believed that they had been sought by the one God, and then more latterly in the Christian tradition through the experience and understanding of the person of Jesus Christ.

One objection to the design argument that is particularly significant if an all-powerful and benevolent God as in the Hebraic–Christian tradition is proposed is the question of why God allows suffering and evil. When the Free Will Defence proposed by Alvin Plantinga and others prevailed to explain the presence of moral evil in the cosmos and was able to 'prove that the logical argument does not show theism to be inconsistent', this led to the emergence of the evidential approach (that rejects belief in god) in the 1980s. Peterson summarized the challenge to theists:

> If (these) theists can convincingly argue that there is a place for pointless evils within a theistic conception of the world, then they stop the evidential argument from going through.[236]

---

[236] Peterson et al., *Reason and Religious Belief*, p. 137.

Whilst the evidential approach of Michael Tooley is critiqued in the next chapter, such a "weight of evidence" approach does, intuitively, have some merit when used to proclaim the notion of a Creator. When Al-Khalili's *Life on the Edge* is read, the *pages* of description of the intermolecular and electronic interdependence that underpin even the most basic essential processes of life, coupled with their reliance on quantum processes, adds evidence to the proposition that the cosmos, and the life within it, was *created*. If no Creator is accepted, then it would appear to be an enormous act of faith to believe that life somehow created itself.

God's love is shown in the cosmos because we may, by both personal devotion and scientific enquiry, be led to the view that the cosmos has a Creator, and the creation of the cosmos occurred because the Creator had a reason to do so, and the sustenance of the cosmos occurs because the Creator has a reason to do so. This alone renders God worthy of praise and worship, and our response to God's salvific ministry through the life, death and resurrection of Jesus Christ should render such praise and worship imperative.

3

Moral evil and natural evil

> Those eighteen who were killed when the tower of Siloam fell on them—do you think that they were worse offenders than all the others living in Jerusalem? (Jesus, quoted in Luke 13:4)

The cosmos was created by God as a place in which sentient beings capable of rejecting Godself could live, there being no possibility of valid love without the option of rejection. The potential for the expression of the free will that human beings possess may lead to authentic love for God but also the existence of moral evil. It will be demonstrated that there is a necessity for natural evil in the world if moral evil exists in the world. The physical limitations of our planet and the imperfect (sinful) nature of humanity create a necessity for human beings (and other creatures) to be mortal.

Theodicy

Theodicy, from the Greek θεός (*theos*) God and δίκη (*dike*) justice or righteousness, is broadly defined in this book as the justification of God's goodness in the face of the fact of evil.[1] In this book, it will be assumed that human or "moral" evil is perpetuated as a result of an intentional

---

[1] J. H. Hick, *Philosophy of Religion*, 2nd edn (Hoboken, NJ: Prentice-Hall, 1973), p. 37 footnote.

process. For human beings to be held "morally accountable" for moral evil,[2] a cosmos in which human freedom of choice is real is required.

It will be assumed that phenomena such as earthquakes and resultant tsunamis, for example, are natural evil and are not the *direct* consequence of moral evil. The theological relationship between moral evil and natural evil will be discussed later in the book. Writing at a time when the Covid pandemic draws to a close and as extreme weather events become more common, I am minded of the impact of human activity on what would have formerly been described as "pure" natural evil.

Theodicy is not just about the forms of evil but is also a question of justice. Since both humans and God are believed to be moral creatures, it is not sufficient to only consider how God's goodness might be justified in the face of the suffering that natural evil and moral evil might produce, but it is also necessary to consider how the (human) perpetrators of moral evil might be dealt with justly. It is also to be considered how God, as the omnipotent Creator, might be regarded "justly" as the ultimate cause of natural evil.

Whilst "the heavens are telling the glory of God; and the firmament proclaims his handiwork" (Psalm 19:1), when this glory is both proclaimed and ascribed to a creator God who, as in the Christian understanding of God, is believed to be benevolent, this is often followed by the recognition and reminder of the harmful aspects of the cosmos such as the effects of human evil and the occurrence of natural disaster and disease, to the extent that belief in a Creator, let alone a benevolent Creator, is dismissed.

When suffering occurs, it would appear to be a natural response to ask, "Why does this happen?", and when a person is affected, they may ask more poignantly, "Why is this happening to me?"[3] Such questions seem to be less overt in artistic endeavours. Literature, music and visual art seem to have many examples that show the effects of suffering but often

---

[2] M. Peterson et al., *Reason and Religious Belief*, 3rd edn (Oxford: Oxford University Press, 2003), p. 129.

[3] Here I draw on both personal experience and 30 years of experience as a medical doctor and 15 years as an ordained minister in the Church of England.

seem to avoid the question of why suffering should happen at all. It is either ascribed to evil of human origin, with the "mad" or "bad" question sometimes being asked, or an apparent acceptance that natural disasters do happen. Among non-biblical literature, *The Brothers Karamazov* (1879) by Dostoyevsky is so frequently quoted that this suggests that there are few other sources of literature that question why God allows suffering to happen.

In the Bible, there seems to be an acceptance that evil and death exist, with little or no explanation offered as to why they exist. Richard Bauckham, referring to Colossians 1, has stated that "about the origins of evil, the Bible is characteristically reticent".[4] In the Hebrew Bible, there are a few exceptions, for examples the book of Job, Lamentations and the Psalms. In the Hebrew Bible, the book of Job is from an Edomite source, almost to imply that writing about such questions was not a "proper" activity for a Hebrew writer.

In the New Testament, the devil and demonic forces are sometimes cited as the cause of natural and moral evil:

> When he came to the other side, to the country of the Gadarenes, two demoniacs coming out of the tombs met him. They were so fierce that no one could pass that way. Suddenly they shouted, "What have you to do with us, Son of God? Have you come here to torment us before the time?" (Matthew 8:28–9)

> The devil had already put it into the heart of Judas son of Simon Iscariot to betray him. (John 13:2)

Passing the blame on to such entities of course begs the question of why God should allow such entities to exist. The words of Jesus, however, seem to accord with this view:

> You are from your father the devil, and you choose to do your father's desires. He was a murderer from the beginning and does

---

[4] R. Bauckham, *Bible and Ecology: Rediscovering the Community of Creation* (London: Darton, Longman & Todd, 2010), p. 155.

not stand in the truth, because there is no truth in him. When he lies, he speaks according to his own nature, for he is a liar and the father of lies. (John 8:44)

It may be considered that it was sufficient for Jesus' ministry to deal with the "Problem of Evil" on a cosmic scale rather than instigating a philosophical and theological revolution. The principle of *kenosis*[5] might also indicate that belief that the devil was the source of all evil was, for Jesus, a sufficient explanation.

The presence of suffering in the world calls many to reject the belief that the world was created at all, and more so by a God who is proclaimed to be both all-loving and all-powerful. It has been stated that the Enlightenment, that included a strong critique of Christian and other theology from a philosophical perspective, as it pursued "the critical pursuit of truth"[6] was in part provoked by the earthquake in Lisbon on All Saints' Day in 1755 that, together with the subsequent tsunami and fires, led to substantial loss of life in "Christendom".[7] It is difficult to believe that there would be atheism in a world devoid of any form of suffering and death, although, as Hick points out, survival after death may not lead an atheist to believe in God if the "afterlife" is (also) religiously ambiguous.[8]

Christian theology is not unique in claiming the goodness of God. Hick questions whether the qualities of God define goodness, or whether

---

[5] The principle of kenosis is that Jesus was voluntarily self-limited.

[6] A. Peacocke, *Theology for a Scientific Age: Being and Becoming—Natural, Divine, and Human* (Minneapolis, MN: Fortress Press, 1993), p. 260.

[7] The *Poème sur le désastre de Lisbonne* (English title: *Poem on the Lisbon Disaster*) is a poem in French composed by Voltaire as a response to the 1755 Lisbon earthquake. It is widely regarded as an introduction to Voltaire's 1759 acclaimed novel *Candide* and his view on the problem of evil. The 180-line poem was composed in December 1755 and published in 1756. It is considered one of the "most savage literary attacks on optimism". <https://en.wikipedia.org/wiki/Po%C3%A8me_sur_le_d%C3%A9sastre_de_Lisbonne>, accessed 14 July 2023. See also <https://www.uh.edu/engines/epi1964.htm>, accessed 14 July 2023.

[8] Hick, *Philosophy of Religion*, p. 92.

God is to be judged against an external standard.[9] Immanuel Kant stated that "the Holy One of the Gospel (Jesus) must first be compared with our ideal of moral perfection".[10] This quote, from Kant's *Religion within the Limits of Reason Alone*, is not only anthropocentric in that it places humankind to be Jesus' judge, but also makes the assumption that somehow humankind is equipped to judge their creator, as if they have been able to develop a sense of morality beyond that which their creator had provided for them. In the Hebraic–Christian tradition, God does define goodness, since God is believed to be the ultimate reality. God is also believed to be the ultimate creator of everything; to assume that humankind could judge God therefore makes the assumption that God could be responsible for the awareness of a higher moral standard than one which God is committed to follow, and this would not be compatible with God's "ultimate" goodness.

A more pertinent question is does God *choose* to be good? This does open the question of whether God is by nature loving and unable to exist in any other way, or whether the exercise of true love involves the possibility of it being withdrawn. The supreme example of God's love being withdrawn in Christian theology is expressed in Jesus' words on the cross, "My God, my God, why have you forsaken me?", that imply a time when God the Father's love was temporarily withheld. It would seem to be instinctively correct that God could only makes creatures that can exercise the choice to love or otherwise if God is also at least aware of the option to choose to love or otherwise.

During the period of Enlightenment, Deism became a popular apologetic, which taught that whilst God had created the world, God was unconcerned with suffering, and that God's goodness was available in an eternal life, as if God was only "interested" in our immortal souls. This Deism fitted with the deterministic ("clockwork") view of the cosmos

---

[9] Hick, *Philosophy of Religion*, p. 12.

[10] The use of the capital G in Gospel is an alteration from the lower case used by Kant. I. Kant, *Religion within the Limits of Reason Alone*, quoted in J. Moltmann, *The Crucified God: The Cross of Christ as the Foundation and Criticism of Christian Theology*, tr. R. A. Wilson and John Bowden (London: SCM Press, 1974), p. 93.

supported by Newtonian mechanics in which all proceeds according to a predetermined script. The "clock" had been made, and God was allowing it to run its course. Interestingly such Deism also fits with a completely *non*-deterministic ("random") model of the cosmos: the universe had been made, and God was allowing it to run its unknown course. In either case, Deism would appear to describe a god who is detached from mortal human experience, and liable to the accusation that such a god also lacks empathy. Such theology of detachment or temporal indifference, of course, denies the continuing presence or immanence of God within Creation expressed via, for example, the Incarnation, the transcendental, and the belief that prayer does sometimes affect material outcomes. It also has Ebionite overtones, in which Jesus is a "purely human figure",[11] since it is difficult to imagine Jesus being anything other than a creature or God's agent in this scheme.

Whilst suffering, accidents and evil may lead to an unresolved metaphysical, philosophical or otherwise "natural" understanding of god, a Christian theodicy is concerned about the reconciliation of the dreadful things that have happened, and continue to happen, in the world in which Godself became incarnate. God became a person in human history, a person of human flesh whose flesh was crucified. The eternal significance of the cosmos in which we exist beyond death was demonstrated in Jesus' resurrection body that was reported to be neither ghostly nor ethereal: Jesus ate with his disciples after he was resurrected:

> "Look at my hands and my feet; see that it is I myself. Touch me and see; for a ghost does not have flesh and bones as you see that I have." And when he had said this, he showed them his hands and his feet. While in their joy they were disbelieving and still wondering, he said to them, "Have you anything here to eat?" They gave him a piece of broiled fish, and he took it and ate in their presence. (Luke 24:39–43)

---

[11] A. E. McGrath, *The Christian Theology Reader*, 2nd edn (Oxford: Blackwell, 2001), p. 699.

In Christian theology, this suggests that the cosmos continues in some form into eternity, and that the cosmos is not a temporary structure that is discarded after the mortal death of all humanity. The cosmos provides the fabric in which Christ, and those who place their trust in Him, are resurrected; the implication is that God is not separable from God's Creation.

The causal nexus

Most physical events that are (humanly) observable appear to be deterministic or predictable, yet as described in the first chapter both classical physics and contemporary science support both deterministic and non-deterministic models of the cosmos. The implication is that the cosmos functions as a causal nexus that combines these descriptions; there is an apparently random element functioning alongside an ordered framework.[12]

The ordered element gives the cosmos structure. Were the cosmos to consist of entirely random processes it is difficult to imagine a "real" world in which any form of consciousness would be more than illusory. It is suggested that there is a chaotic, violent, natural world contained by God that might be totally unproductive without the continuous interventions of God.[13] The random element in the cosmos does not necessarily only lead to a *mild* degree of uncertainty of a precise outcome; through the mechanisms described in chaos theory, namely exponential increase and sensitive dependence, random actions may have a global impact. At the atomic level, nuclear activity, a ubiquitous part of the fabric of the cosmos (termed background radiation), can produce mortal effects in living creatures.

---

[12] Current physical explanations may be mapped along a (one-dimensional) line, with Newtonian physics at one end of the spectrum and the random aspects of quantum physics at the other. In due course, the theories that will explain dark matter or dark forces may require that physical theories are mapped using a two-dimensional diagram or even a multi-dimensional model.

[13] Bauckham, *Bible and Ecology*, p. 169.

It is tempting to ascribe order in creation to that of a benevolent demi-god, and the random and chaotic to a malign demi-god. The random element may, however, be part of the process of creativity and thus a source of joy for both God and sentient creatures made by God.

It is, nevertheless, the random element that may be responsible for how a great deal of misfortune is distributed via natural evil in all of its forms. If such misfortune is the result of a random process, this might explain how God is able to distribute such misfortune in a non-prejudicial manner, affecting "good" and "bad" people similarly.

It is recognized that letting a person know that their misfortune or disease may be wholly "bad luck" will often be pastorally insensitive, but this is close to the response that Jesus gave about two examples of suffering, that of the Galileans as an example of human evil, that of those killed when the tower of Siloam fell as an example of a natural accident:

> At that very time there were some present who told him about the Galileans whose blood Pilate had mingled with their sacrifices.[14] He asked them, "Do you think that because these Galileans suffered in this way they were worse sinners than all other Galileans? No, I tell you; but unless you repent, you will all perish as they did. Or those eighteen who were killed when the tower of Siloam fell on them—do you think that they were worse offenders than all the others living in Jerusalem?" (Luke 13:1–4)

Jesus seems to be making the point that those who died were no worse than others, and therefore there was no particular reason why it was they, and not others, who had died. If the "bad luck" explanation for the occurrence of suffering due to a natural cause is rejected, for Theists the only alternative is that God for whatever reason intended that the suffering should happen, and the former may be easier to accept.

---

[14] Making animal (blood) sacrifices was part of Jewish Temple ritual of the time; the implication is that the Galileans were killed whilst offering such sacrifices. The self-defilement that the unfortunate Galileans may have undergone might have been such that they were also considered to be unforgivable by God.

Sometimes it can be seen how illness can have benefits; for example it may provide the catalyst that enables reconciliation between two people when one becomes terminally ill, but such benefits tend to be "fringe" benefits and rarely occur.

In *The Gospel of Luke*, the theologian and biblical scholar Joel Green states that there was a "widely held convention that drew a direct line from iniquity to judgement".[15] In Luke 12:49–56, Jesus had been describing the final judgement, and Jesus is clear that the misfortune of the Galileans and Jerusalemites who died in the tower collapse had *not* suffered on account of such a "direct line"; Jesus, however, uses the narrative to confirm the universality of the need for repentance. Charles Talbert's *Reading Luke* summarizes the passage thus:

> Tragedy, says Jesus, is not the measure of one's sinfulness and of one's need to repent. Those whose lives are tranquil likewise need to repent. All need to repent or all will perish.[16]

The theologian and biblical scholar Leon Morris in *Luke* titles the passage 13:1–9 "Repentance" and the unpredictability of the timing of one's death is used to exhort all to repentance immediately, the "urgency of repenting".[17]

Thus the three commentaries point out how Jesus disassociates the link between iniquity and judgement, and point to Jesus using the examples to encourage repentance. It is remarkable that none of these commentaries speculate on why Jesus responded in this way. For example, Jesus, having rejected the notion that the Galileans and Jerusalemites had deserved their respective fates on account of their sinful choices, as was the "widely held convention", could have stated that the death of these people was part of a greater plan. Jesus (or the commentators)

---

[15] J. B. Green, *The Gospel of Luke*, The New International Commentary on the New Testament (Grand Rapids, MI: Eerdmans, 1997), p. 513.

[16] C. H. Talbert, *Reading Luke: A Literary and Theological Commentary on the Third Gospel* (Macon, GA: Smyth & Helwys, 2002), p. 161.

[17] L. Morris, *Luke*, Tyndale New Testament Commentaries (Leicester: InterVarsity Press, 1988), p. 242.

could have emphasized that since there was, however, seemingly nothing special about those unfortunate Galileans and inhabitants of Jerusalem who suffered and died, there was an implication that their deaths were a random act of "bad luck". To ascribe the fate of human persons to such random events does undermine an understanding of the omnipotence of God that is fulfilled through a predetermined plan, rather than an understanding of a "greater" omnipotence in which God will achieve God's will despite the occurrence of such random acts. The Tower of Siloam suggests that God allows misfortune to affect people by random processes rather than God deliberately allowing misfortune to happen to particular people at particular times.

If the distribution of natural evil occurs through the random, non-deterministic properties of the cosmos, the question of how God might ensure that God's purposes are fulfilled arises. Whilst chaos theory has demonstrated the convergence of systems characterized by natural distribution (stochastic) which might serve as a model as to how God achieves God's purposes through generalities rather than a specific "script and stage directions" that humans are obliged to follow, the core proposal is that God generally acts through the causal nexus of the deterministic and the non-deterministic and as such may act imperceptibly. There are exceptions that are far from being imperceptible, most notably the resurrection, but there are other episodes of a gentler theophany in Scripture, for example the account of Moses and the burning bush in Exodus 3. The need or otherwise of a specific "script and stage directions" may be illustrated by the sequence of events that led to the crucifixion of Jesus. This was a likely outcome for Jesus who preached a potentially revolutionary message in a military dictatorship in which the death penalty was also used to settle religious arguments. The crucifixion of Jesus was a probable outcome that could have occurred without the betrayal of Judas that required that "the devil had already put it into the heart of Judas son of Simon Iscariot to betray him" (John 13:2). It may be considered, therefore, that the events leading to the cross in their exact detail did not need to be predetermined; there was neither need nor inevitability that Judas (and Jesus) would "follow the script". Jesus expressed his doubts with the words "Father, if you are willing, remove this cup from me; yet, not my will but yours be done" (Luke 22:42).

The words imply a lack of inevitability of what would happen to Jesus and that it was Jesus' willing to do the Father's will that resulted in Jesus' crucifixion. For some Christians, the narrative of the Christian faith is diminished if it is regarded to be less than the working out of God's detailed plan; for others the ultimate triumph of God will be seen to be greater if God achieves God's purposes through a myriad of possibilities that the cosmos, and human free will, create.

Why is there suffering?
The "mixed-model" description of the cosmos in which deterministic and non-deterministic phenomena coexist may answer the question of how suffering is distributed, but it does not answer the question as to why suffering is an apparently necessary part of the universe that humanity inhabits. A response might be to ask if the question "Why is there suffering" should be asked at all: should we (Christians) simply accept that that is how God has decided things should be? In a post-Enlightenment world, it would seem to be a source of contempt for those who believe in an all-powerful and loving God to accept suffering with complete passivity and offer no attempt at an explanation.

Atheists do not have to answer this question since they can take the view that all of life's events are accidents, happy or otherwise. This fatalistic outlook, with an acceptance of evil that lacks protest, also existed in Christendom, at least officially, as late as the times of the Puritans. The will of God was not to be questioned by Christian believers and public grieving was to be avoided as it was evidence of faithlessness. In Islam, the will of the Almighty is not to be questioned. Current "Christian" theodicies, such as that of John Piper, blame the evils of the world on Satan but proclaim that we should nevertheless always rejoice as God will emerge the final victor,[18] as if we should enjoy observing the world whilst a cosmic tale of vengeance was being performed. The theodicy offers no explanation as to why Satan is permitted by God to act; for Piper it is sufficient to accept this view as it was held by some of the writers in the Bible. Thus for Piper God can be regarded as the ultimate creator

---

[18] <https://www.desiringgod.org/messages/ten-aspects-of-gods-sovereignty-over-suffering-and-satans-hand-in-it>, accessed 15 July 2023.

of both good and evil acts and whilst this may explain suffering itself, there is no answer to the question of the justice of God in this, the δίκη (*dike*), i.e. righteousness of God, or indeed any real love, empathy and other expressions of benevolence.

Other Christian theologians have rejected the question of "Why is there suffering?" on the grounds that, since the cosmos is broken or "fallen", then it is not possible to provide an objective perspective from which the question could be answered. Such a lack of objectivity could lead to the rejection of any moral question, and this would, if taken to an absurd degree, lead to the abdication of all moral questions by persons of faith. Any resulting moral philosophy would be atheistic, i.e. the "greatest good for the greatest number" arbiter for deciding what is wrong and what is right. Whilst it is accepted that our imperfect nature and imperfect minds can only ever lead to imperfect understanding, there is a Dominical[19] imperative to attempt to answer such questions; Christians were commanded by Jesus to "love the Lord your God with all your mind (intellect)"[20] (Mark 12:30) and therefore making an attempt to understand fully the world in which humankind is placed may be regarded as a core activity of being a follower of Jesus rather than an option. It is therefore proper for a Christian, i.e. a follower of Jesus who accepts Jesus' authority, to ask the question, why is there suffering?

The Old Testament

The book of Job

An ancient attempt at an answer to the problem of suffering is to be found in the Hebrew Scriptures in the book of Job. The Old Testament scholar James Crenshaw states that Job, the central character of the book, is an Edomite who existed before the Israelites, i.e. in the prepatriarchal

---

[19] Dominical meaning an imperative ordered by Jesus as Lord and Master.

[20] The word διάνοια (dianoia) is often translated as "mind"; however, this is to mean "comprehension" or "intellect" rather than being minded as in being resolute. <https://www.scripture4all.org/OnlineInterlinear/NTpdf/mar12.pdf>, accessed 15 July 2023.

period. The Edomites were known for their wisdom. Job was written in the late sixth or fifth century BC with Persian influence. Similar literature arose from the Egyptian and Mesopotamian cultures at that time.[21]

In his book *Man's Anger and God's Silence: The Book of Job* (1990), the theologian and Old Testament scholar Dermot Cox states that:

> the prevailing understanding at the time of writing was 'cosmic order' (Egyptian ma'at, Mesopotamian ME) to which even the gods were subordinate; contradictions in this order, such as the experience of suffering or absurdity led to intellectual exploration and scepticism or open contestation.[22]

"Suffering and absurdity" were seen to create "contradictions" in the understanding of how the "cosmic order" *should* be. Such innate expectations are discussed later.

The book of Exodus, however, asserts a Hebrew revelation of God, the "I AM" of Exodus 3:14, and this implies belief in a God who was not, as in the above quotation, "subordinate", the "I AM" implying domain over all that is. The events described in Exodus 3 date to the fifteenth century BC, and this suggests that the Hebrew understanding of God derived from or expressed in the account of Exodus 3 was not part of the prevailing understanding of god in the Edomite culture in the sixth and fifth centuries BC in which Job was written. It is fascinating to consider why the Hebrews included a Persian-influenced Edomite treatise on theodicy in their Scriptures. Could this be due to an unwillingness to express scepticism or openly contest Yahweh? The priest and theologian Gustavo Gutiérrez, in his book (1986) *On Job: God-Talk and the Suffering of the Innocent*, however, quotes similar complaints in Psalm 73:2–14 and Lamentations 3:1–9.[23] In Psalm 73:2–14, the complaint is less vehement

---

[21] Commentary in the *New Revised Standard Version (2006) HarperCollins Study Bible*, p. 693.

[22] D. Cox, *Man's Anger and God's Silence: The Book of Job* (Slough: St Paul Publications, 1990), pp. 13–14.

[23] G. Gutiérrez, *On Job: God-Talk and the Suffering of the Innocent* (Maryknoll, NY: Orbis Books, 1986), pp. 57–8.

than Job. Lamentations was written after the destruction of Israel by the Babylonians,[24] and has a "nevertheless" quality, with a sudden change of attitude marking an acceptance of affliction:

> The thought of my affliction and my homelessness
>   is wormwood and gall!
> My soul continually thinks of it and is bowed down within me.
> But this I call to mind, and therefore I have hope:
> The steadfast love of the Lord never ceases, his mercies never come
>   to an end; they are new every morning; great is your faithfulness.
> "The Lord is my portion," says my soul, "therefore I
>   will hope in him." (Lamentations 3:19–24)

Christian theology might regard the Edomite "cosmic order" as having resonance with the concept of the *logos,* and particularly explicit in the Gospel of John is the affirmation that the *logos* IS God. Whilst the I AM of Exodus is maintained within Christian theology as the doctrine of omnipotence, i.e. belief in one all-powerful God who is by definition not obliged to be subordinate to anything, there are examples of belief in the voluntary "subordination" of God. Firstly a belief that the example of the ministry of Jesus in which such "subordination" led to self-limitation (*kenosis*) may now be interpreted not to have been an inevitable condition caused through powerlessness but through voluntary choice, the ultimate example of voluntary powerlessness being the crucifixion that Jesus endured. Secondly there is the belief that the self-limitation that God enforces for God's purposes in order to preserve human free will is voluntary.

Job is not so much about "innocent suffering" as "divine culpability".[25] Job suffers the loss of loved ones and property, and is afflicted by severe physical disease. The protest of Job is severe; he curses the day he was born (3:1), regrets being born alive (3:11) and even wishes he had been

---

[24] Commentary by W. E. Lemke, revised by Kathleen O'Connor in the NRSV (2006), p. 1086.
[25] Cox, *Man's Anger and God's Silence,* p. 23.

buried as "an abortion" or stillborn child (3:16).[26] Job does not suffer alone; indeed it is noted that there is a random distribution of suffering in that all humankind "has been arbitrarily cast into life by a God who equally arbitrarily causes suffering from which there is no escape".[27] In Genesis 6:5–6, God expresses regret about what God has created:

> The Lord saw that the wickedness of humankind was great in the earth, and that every inclination of the thoughts of their hearts was only evil continually. And the Lord was sorry that he had made humankind on the earth, and it grieved him to his heart.[28]

This regret contrasts with Job in which the implied lack of God's foreknowledge is suspended and a more sinister accusation is made: that God deliberately made people sinful so that they might suffer:

> Your hands fashioned and made me; and now you turn and destroy me.
> Remember that you fashioned me like clay; and
>   will you turn me to dust again?
> Did you not pour me out like milk and curdle me like cheese?
> You clothed me with skin and flesh, and knit me
>   together with bones and sinews.
> You have granted me life and steadfast love, and
>   your care has preserved my spirit.
> Yet these things you hid in your heart; I know
>   that this was your purpose.
> If I sin, you watch me, and do not acquit me
>   of my iniquity. (Job 10:8–14)

---

[26] <http://www.scripture4all.org/OnlineInterlinear/OTpdf/job3.pdf>, accessed 15 July 2023.

[27] Cox, *Man's Anger and God's Silence*, p. 39.

[28] The Genesis passage continues with the story of Noah: "So the Lord said, 'I will blot out from the earth the human beings I have created—people together with animals and creeping things and birds of the air, for I am sorry that I have made them'" (Genesis 6:7).

According to Cox, the "import of verse 13" is clear and is paraphrased for emphasis: "Yet, after all, you were dissembling, biding your time, I know."[29] The accusation is that humankind was created ("set up") to fail and evokes the response that forms the succinct title that the NRSV has for Job 10: "I loathe my life."

The characters in the book of Job that try to offer comfort to Job would not be accepted in a post-Enlightenment world. One of the friends in the book, named Zophar, argues that God is to be accepted and not "subjected to vigorous logic".[30] Whilst such acceptance might have been imposed in mediaeval times, the Enlightenment sought logic and rationality. Indeed the meaninglessness of tragic events, such as the Lisbon earthquake in 1755 and other such "acts of God" that occurred in Christendom, resulted in a sense of purposelessness. Such purposelessness will for some, as remarked by Cox, be a driver to create authenticity or rationality.[31]

There is a claimed soteriological response within Job (19:25–7). The verses are sufficiently well-known to sometimes be engraved on tombstones and other monuments and form the text of one of the better-known arias in Handel's *Messiah*:

> For I know that my Redeemer lives, and that at the last he will stand upon the earth; and after my skin has been thus destroyed, then in my flesh I shall see God, whom I shall see on my side, and my eyes shall behold, and not another. My heart faints within me!

Comparison of the NRSV translation and the Concordant Hebrew English Sublinear does appear to leave a large gap for the imagination to fill.

- 19:25   and I—I know—one redeeming of me—life—and last—on soil—he shall arise

---

[29] Cox, *Man's Anger and God's Silence*, p. 54.
[30] Cox, *Man's Anger and God's Silence*, pp. 56–7.
[31] Cox, *Man's Anger and God's Silence*, p. 43.

- 19:26 and after—skin of me—they encompass—this—and from flesh of me—I shall perceive—Eloah
- 19:27 which—I—I shall perceive—for me—and eyes of me—they see—and not—alienate. [32]

Although it may be hazardous, and even seem offensive to some, to "read in" the theology of one religion into a text that is sacred to another, if in these translations the "one redeeming of me" גֹּאֲלִי (*gali*) is seen as the second person of the Trinity, and הֱלוֹהַּ (*Eloah*) is likened to the Father, then God the Father could be regarded as our destroyer and God the Son becomes the "one redeeming of me", who defies the Father and thus protects us from the wrath of God. This could lead to an interpretation of the cross and hence a theodicy in which God the Father is not regarded as being benevolent. Whilst according to Cox, "the translation is atrocious because the text is gibberish",[33] there is, nevertheless, a suggestion in this text that the proper and restored relationship between humankind and God that will involve the resolution of the questions of suffering and justice either requires or involves an intermediary, and of course in Christian theology such an intermediary is the person of Jesus Christ.

According to Cox, Job also questions how suffering is distributed, indeed "what kind of God, given man's 'normal lack of righteousness', will mete out suffering and wellbeing arbitrarily?"[34] Contemporary science has demonstrated how suffering from natural causes might be distributed arbitrarily without being deliberately "meted out" to any particular individual, but does not justify suffering *per se*.

Job draws an ancient parallel with the role of the "chaotic" in the cosmos. In Job are the mythic creatures Behemoth and Leviathan, who

---

[32] Cox, *Man's Anger and God's Silence*, p. 68. Trans-literal from <http://www.scripture4all.org/OnlineInterlinear/OTpdf/job19.pdf>, accessed 15 July 2023.

[33] Cox, *Man's Anger and God's Silence*, p. 68. Illustrations of text from <http://www.scripture4all.org/OnlineInterlinear/OTpdf/job19.pdf>, accessed 15 July 2023.

[34] Cox, *Man's Anger and God's Silence*, p. 81.

represent the Chaos from which Yahweh draws order and meaning.[35] Cox describes the natural state of the cosmos thus:

> Chaos is its (i.e. the cosmos's) basic nature, the non-chaotic moral law and chaotic natural law are in disharmony.[36]

Thus the action of Yahweh is to impose the non-chaotic moral law upon the chaos of nature to produce order and meaning. Modern science has described order and meaning in the cosmos, but has confirmed that a chaotic, non-deterministic "quantum" element persists. For Gutiérrez, through suffering Job is enabled to see the cosmos as chaotic;[37] furthermore God is "absent as the one who creates and shapes it into a Universe".[38] For Job, the universe lacks order and meaning, and furthermore Yahweh has not imposed the moral law on nature that would remove the suffering he endures.

According to Cox, one of the justifications for suffering that is proposed in Job is that God is not to be likened to a judge, who gives out rewards and punishment justly, but a poet or artist who creates, for whom suffering is a necessary catalyst.[39] Such a view is supported in Job by the recognition that there is a "mystery and irrationality in Creation"[40] and the "absurdity of Creation" is illustrated by the creation of "magnificent predators".[41] Whilst a (mediaeval) teleological view of Creation may have concurred with the view that the creative process produced the absurd, that found expression in the "dog-heads" and other bizarre creatures that are drawn in mediaeval manuscripts, such

---

[35] The mythology of the Behemoth and Leviathan may have had an origin in the bones of beached whales and other matter whose form originated from living creatures such as fossils. Bauckham, *Bible and Ecology*, pp. 54–5, suggests the mythology may originate from the hippopotamus and crocodile.
[36] Cox, *Man's Anger and God's Silence*, p. 104.
[37] Gutiérrez, *On Job*, p. 62.
[38] Gutiérrez, *On Job*, p. 8.
[39] Cox, *Man's Anger and God's Silence*, p. 126.
[40] Cox, *Man's Anger and God's Silence*, p. 109.
[41] Cox, *Man's Anger and God's Silence*, p. 106.

absurdity and irrationality is counterintuitive to biologists who regard form as an expression of optimized function and that optimized function is necessary for the continued existence of a species. The peacock's spots are there for a reason, "magnificent predators" enable an ecosystem in which the predators paradoxically enable the species on which they predate to survive and benefit other species. The description of god found in Job as a dispassionate poet or artist who permits suffering for the sake of creating the absurd and irrational could be considered to be as morally unacceptable as Laplace's clock-making demon or the gambling "monster" that watches a game of chance being played out. Furthermore, an axiom of science itself is that the cosmos is neither absurd nor irrational, in that order and "Laws" are to be discovered. Whilst even the quantum phenomena of radioactive decay and superposition may appear irrational in their unpredictability and strangeness, they are nevertheless generally consistent in these properties. Radioactive decay has a measurable half-life,[42] and superposition is dependably reproducible.

Cox proposes that Job contains two main arguments to answer the question of why there is suffering. The first is that suffering, combined with unreason and absurdity, adds beauty to Creation. There is no great merit in this argument, as is clearly demonstrable by applying it in a pastoral context: "Surely you do not begrudge a virus with such beautiful symmetry such as the coronavirus from devastating your family?" is unlikely to feature as an appropriate response in a handbook of practical ministry.

The argument can be refined, and the point can be made that if God is able to make creatures as beautiful in their own lethal way as, for example, a tiger, then surely God could have created life in all its fullness without the existence of suffering if it were possible to do so. The Hubble pictures have helped humankind to visualize a cosmos that is much larger than it needs to be to sustain the planet Earth: the current estimate is 10 billion galaxies each with 10 billion stars. On planet Earth is to be found an extraordinary profusion of landscapes, seascapes and icescapes and living creatures in their almost endless variety, many if not most of

---

[42] The half-life is the time taken for half of the remaining atoms in a sample that have not decayed (split into fragments) to decay.

which are not needed to create the ecosystems required to support and sustain human life. There is also evidence of "beyond that which is simply necessary" in the potential for all of the special senses, and some of the other things that humans can sense such as satiety or a deep breath, to imbue a sense of beauty or wellbeing. This suggestion of Creation beyond what is required for human life also points to a creator with the capability to eliminate or at least reduce the existence of suffering if it were possible to do so.

The second argument proposed by Cox that is proposed in Job is that suffering is deserved by both the just and the unjust.[43] Again there is little merit in this: why should the just suffer as much as the unjust, for in effect the unjust go as unpunished as the just; and why should the unjust themselves be punished when presumably they were created with a tendency to be unjust (set up to fail) as in Cox's interpretation of Job 10:13–14? The lack of merit in this argument is also illustrated by another inappropriate pastoral example: "God has deemed that you deserve to suffer like everyone else."[44]

So does God, as Cox claims, argue in Job a case for suffering as "valid as one that is logical", i.e. acceptable to reason?[45] I personally find the two arguments lacking in substance when tested in a pastoral context. Yet the "pastoral" theodicy itself leads to an apologetic dead-end. The sentiment "my thoughts are not your thoughts" (Isaiah 55:8), which suggests a greater and incomprehensible plan that God has that cannot be understood by humankind either now or perhaps ever in mortal life, may be fitting as a response to the question in pastoral care as to where God is to be found in the midst of suffering, but it is a statement that concedes ignorance: "We simply do not know", followed by an appeal to trust God nevertheless. The pastorally gifted Gutiérrez gives a covert warning: "Job's rebellious attitude is due not so much to his suffering as to the arguments that his friends develop in their pompous manner."[46] An

---

[43] Cox, *Man's Anger and God's Silence*, p. 128.
[44] Such Augustinian theodicy is discussed later on in Appendix 1.
[45] Cox, *Man's Anger and God's Silence*, p. 124.
[46] Gutiérrez, *On Job*, p. 56.

unjust or otherwise bad pastoral situation can be worsened by pompous theological justification. The title of Dermot Cox's book, *Man's Anger and God's Silence: The Book of Job*, does lead to the question of whether human anger, or despair, or sorrow, or other generally negative responses to suffering, is in any form of dialogue with God when God seems to be silent? Job asks, "Why me, why am I suffering?" There is no answer, and Job accepts the lack of an answer to be the answer. A more refined description of Job is why is he experiencing meaningless and disproportionate suffering? Job accepts that he is a sinner; his complaint is the level of suffering that he is subjected to.[47] Whilst moral evil is only meaningful in that it is a necessary corollary of human free will, and that natural "evil", or accidents, and the associated finitude mitigate the otherwise devastating effect of death caused by human evil (i.e. murder), they do appear even less meaningful on account of their apparently random distribution. For the time being we see Plato's shadows, the imperfect cast by forms in a cosmos that we almost innately expect to be perfect,[48] and these shadows are seen dimly through mortal eyes, reflected by St Paul's darkened mirror:

> For now we see in a mirror, dimly, but then we will see face to face. Now I know only in part; then I will know fully, even as I have been fully known. (1 Corinthians 13:12).

Gustavo Gutiérrez spent many years working as a priest in the slums of Lima, Peru. In his book, *On Job: God-Talk and the Suffering of the Innocent,* is an expansion of the interpretation of Job that not only includes suffering, but also the question of justice. For Gutiérrez, Job is particularly about social and economic justice, and the way in which the poor are dealt with. In the part of the world from which Gutiérrez is writing, the criminal aspects of social and economic injustice are also overt; they are more covert in other parts of the world but no less harmful, for example such things as the economically significant tax evasion mentioned in the Introduction. Gutiérrez's axiom that "the

---

[47] Gutiérrez, *On Job*, p. 24.
[48] C. Rovelli, *Reality is not what it seems* (London: Allen Lane, 2014), p. 212.

ultimate basis of God's preference for the poor is to be found in God's own goodness"[49] is understandable in the context of his immersion in the plight of the poor. In this, Gutiérrez does have support from Luther, who stated that "God willed that he should be known from suffering",[50] and this is perhaps so in order that God could identify with the less fortunate who would be more receptive to God's love. The poor might be considered to be more receptive to God, because they are less distracted by possessions and the fear of losing them, and the poor also rely on what they might receive through the goodness of God (often expressed through the generosity of others) rather than being self-reliant. Liberation theology, however, speaks of the "evil of misfortune", and, quoting Bishop Desmond Tutu, this "liberation theology stems from trying to make sense of human suffering".[51] It would seem there is another answer required from the questioning of theodicy. It is not that theodicy seeks only to reconcile the loving nature of an omnipotent God and the righteousness of the situation in which such suffering is allowed, but also the injustice of how suffering is distributed.

Perhaps a better summary of the message of Job comes from a philosophical perspective; in Job, there is a dissociation of evil from punishment, and Job looks forward to a world in which a person has a purer motive for seeking God; neither for gain nor the avoidance of punishment.[52]

The Fall
Christian theologians have traditionally taught that the origin of suffering and evil in all of its forms can be traced back to the disobedience of humankind, i.e. the Fall. Bishop Irenaeus of Lyon (c.130—c.202) "presupposes some kind of mystical solidarity, or rather identity, between the father of the (human) race and all his descendants. At the time of

---

[49] Gutiérrez, *On Job*, p. xiii.
[50] Moltmann, *Crucified God*, p. 217.
[51] Gutiérrez, *On Job*, pp. xiv–v.
[52] Peterson et al., *Reason and Religious Belief*, p. 140.

the Fall they somehow already existed in him."⁵³ Origen of Alexandria (*c*.185—*c*.254), however, "transforms the story recorded in Genesis ... into a cosmic myth, and lifts the origination of human sinfulness from the terrestrial to the transcendental plane".⁵⁴ The account of the Fall that appears in Genesis, if it is accepted at all, is now usually accepted as an allegory. For Origen, "the story of Adam and Eve mirrors the experience of every man and woman".⁵⁵ It is not necessary for the purposes of this book to consider whether the Fall might signify a single discrete event that actually happened or whether, as in Bauckham, the early chapters of Genesis describe a "gradual descent into sin".⁵⁶

The theology of Genesis is sophisticated, and since the Fall does not reappear in the Hebrew Bible after Genesis, this suggests that Genesis was written, or at least edited, rather late compared to the other books in the Hebrew Bible. Genesis Chapters 1–11 describe "what has gone wrong in creation", the effects of human sin and wickedness and "people trying to live as though they were God"; the episode in the Garden of Eden with the serpent can be regarded as a pre-presentation of the whole of the section that precedes the Abrahamic Covenant.⁵⁷

Should the notion of the Fall be rejected entirely it is sufficient for the purposes of the hypothesis of this book to acknowledge that, for whatever reason, human beings were created that were imperfect and capable of committing acts of evil, and that is a choice that God makes despite the unwanted consequence of the opportunity for human beings to commit acts of moral evil and the necessary and consequent natural evil required to be present in the cosmos. Such a choice is, or may be, made by God because without the freedom of humanity to do good or evil there can be no possibility of human beings properly loving God: humanity would be akin to angels, animals or robots. In reading further in this book, if the

---

[53] J. N. D. Kelly, *Early Christian Doctrines*, 5th edn (London: Continuum, 1977), p. 172.

[54] Kelly, *Early Christian Doctrines*, p. 180.

[55] Origen, C. Cels 4, 40 in Kelly, *Early Christian Doctrines*, p. 182.

[56] Bauckham, *Bible and Ecology*, p. 23.

[57] D. Atkinson, *Renewing the Face of the Earth: A Theological and Pastoral Response to Climate Change* (Norwich: Canterbury Press, 2008), p. 31.

Fall is not accepted then the creation of deliberate human imperfection will make a substitute adequate for the purposes of this book.

The most direct consequence of humanity's disobedience is the perpetration of moral evil. It is to be emphasized that the Fall, though it may represent an historic transition, is perhaps more significantly also an allegory of a continued state of human rebellion against God in the form of deliberate sin. In the letter to the Romans, the apostle Paul, in attempting to resolve the relationship between human sinfulness and the (Hebraic) Law, recognizes this innate tendency to do what is wrong, even though he was aware of his wrong doing:

> I do not understand my own actions. For I do not do what I want, but I do the very thing I hate. Now if I do what I do not want, I agree that the law is good. But in fact it is no longer I that do it, but sin that dwells within me. For I know that nothing good dwells within me, that is, in my flesh. I can will what is right, but I cannot do it. For I do not do the good I want, but the evil I do not want is what I do. (Romans 7:15–19).

The second consequence of the Fall is that of finitude which may be perpetrated by moral evil (e.g. murder or neglect) or through the natural processes inherent in living in a world with disease and disaster. The natural processes of disease, disaster, degeneration and death are necessary, otherwise the effect of murdering a person who was otherwise immortal would be immense, and so natural evil, by ensuring our mortality, actually mitigates the effect of moral evil. The random element of natural evil, by creating uncertainty of the time when we die, adds meaning to the life we have before death; if we all died in our nineties, those who were in their eighties might control the planet, and matters of faith would wait until we were 89. We would also be likely to ask why we did not live well for ten more decades, and so *ad infinitum*.

Human sinfulness presents moral dilemmas to other humans who wish to live righteously: how to respond when rape is followed by pregnancy, or how to respond when a country is invaded by an aggressive neighbour. Human sinfulness may also present moral dilemmas to God: God has seemingly not chosen to punish the wicked during mortal life but has limited the effects of human sinfulness by ensuring our mortality. But how does God do this? A prejudicial way would result in people being terrified of doing wrong in case they became ill or had a serious accident, to the extent that life may not be worth living. By choosing a random and non-prejudicial way to ensure mortality seems ultimately to be fairer, yet surely God must grieve with us when the wickedness of the whole of humanity results in the suffering of innocents.

The acceptance of the Fall and other tenets of the Nicene Creed have caused problems with writers who have attempted to reconcile modern science and (orthodox) Christian theology.

Peacocke's *Theology for a Scientific Age* found no place for sinfulness or the Fall, regarding disobedience and sinfulness as the expected behaviour of a human being that was not fully evolved and concluding that the Fall is a completely human invention. Similarly, in Peacocke's theology, the Incarnation is no more than a device to secure human evolution in its full and final intention.[58] For Peacocke, salvation is universal, and indeed the uniqueness of Christ is denied, with *any* response to the *logos* in Creation being regarded as salvific, the concept of the *logos* being an expression that the universe is set up to save itself.[59] Peacocke's theology, in denying some of the central tenets of the Nicene Creed, in an apparent act of appeasement to science, ignores the wilful disobedience and rebellion of humankind against God. Even those who do not overtly break "The Ten Commandments" have a propensity to ignore God, as described by St Paul: "they exchanged the truth about God for a lie and worshipped and served the creature [Creation][60] rather than the Creator, who is blessed for ever!" (Romans 1:25).

Such theology also denies the "cosmic" importance of the intense suffering that Jesus underwent to enable a specific salvific path. The

---

[58] Peacocke, *Theology for a Scientific Age*, p. 331.
[59] Peacocke, *Theology for a Scientific Age*, p. 334.
[60] As in <https://www.scripture4all.org/OnlineInterlinear/NTpdf/rom1.pdf>, accessed 15 July 2023. The readership of the King James Version would have understood "creature" to be that which was created; it is surprising that the word was not changed to Creation (as in the NT Greek) in modern translations such as the NRSV.

theology casts some doubt on the love of God towards creatures that are not fully evolved. If sinfulness is a temporary phenomenon produced as a consequence of an incomplete evolution, and if there is no "Fall", then what was the purpose behind God sending a redeemer? If we have only evolved, then can we have any confidence in the reordering of the world to become heavenly? The Fall suggests the possibility of restoration to that which preceded the Fall. For those who accept Peacocke's theology, there can be no sense of forgiveness if human sinfulness is denied, no joy in the incarnation if such an event was deemed inevitable, no hope for miracles since God is valued for being consistent and deemed to be so. Those who believe in this theology presumably are content to take their chance in a Creation that will feel as if they are abandoned by God, even if God works through normal physical means by a "top-down causality", whilst they await transformation to another, albeit heavenly, mode of existence.

Southgate is also dismissive of the need to accept the doctrine of human rebellion. In his book *The Groaning of Creation*, he describes a "spurious appeal to fallenness".[61] It cannot be proven that the "groaning of Creation" is a consequence of humanity's sinfulness, but neither can it be proven that it is not. If, as Peacocke and Southgate suggest, we are purely creatures of evolutionary origin, then what was the purpose of Jesus' salvific ministry?

For St Paul, the groaning of Creation has an expectant quality as it describes a process of change. For St Paul, "the whole Creation has been groaning in labour pains until now", and "we ourselves . . . groan inwardly while we wait for adoption, the redemption of our bodies" (Romans 8:22–3). For St Paul, there was a past event that was responsible and there was (is) hope "that the Creation itself will be set free from its bondage to decay" (v. 21). Southgate points out that St Paul does not mention the Fall in Romans 8.[62] The Fall would have been understood by St Paul's readers, and the word "decay" suggests a former state when the world had not started to decay. Whilst the groaning of Creation in Southgate might

---

[61] C. Southgate, *The Groaning of Creation* (Louisville, KY: Westminster John Knox Press, 2008), p. 47.

[62] Southgate, *Groaning of Creation*, pp. 95–6.

appear to have a perpetual quality, the description of an eternal *status quo*, in Romans 8 there is hope that the cycle will be completed when the groaning of Creation ends as the salvation of humankind will lead to the salvation of all Creation.[63] This has resonance with the Jewish hope of earthly transformation that will come with the Messiah.[64]

Jesus recognized that human sinfulness needed to be dealt with. The cross and resurrection were the cosmic event that achieved this, but Jesus also called people to repent: "the time is fulfilled, and the kingdom of God has come near; repent, and believe in the good news" (Mark 1:15). Jesus' call to repentance occurs early in the other two synoptic Gospels (Matthew 4:17 and Luke 5:32), suggesting that this is an important part of Jesus' message as understood by the Gospel writers. The word for "repent" (μετανοεῖτε (*metanoiete*)) is a present active ("be ye repenting"), and this means a complete change of direction and therefore the call to repentance was about something fundamental rather than an optional extra.

Jesus encouraged the Jews to be outward-looking and inclusive, rather than exhorting the exclusivity necessary to be more in-bred.

Southgate states that animal suffering is a necessary part of an evolved created order and that since animal suffering pre-dates the emergence of humankind and its associated moral evil, i.e. the Fall, animal suffering is therefore not a consequence of a fallen world.[65] In dismissing the Fall, Southgate states that "organisms ... through the power of the Spirit ... explore their landscape ... giving rise to new possibilities of being a self".[66] Southgate implies that Darwinism makes the animal, but the Holy Spirit moulds its behaviour.[67] It is to be noted that an evolutionary sociologist or behaviourist might also claim an evolutionary basis for behaviour. Dividing the Creation between what is of God, i.e. behaviour that is

---

[63] W. Pannenberg, *An Introduction to Systematic Theology* (Grand Rapids, MI: Eerdmans, 1991), p. 61.

[64] Bauckham, *Bible and Ecology*, pp. 95–101.

[65] Southgate, *Groaning of Creation*, p. 18; see also the "*pre-archaios*" proposed in the final Chapter 5.

[66] Southgate, *Groaning of Creation*, p. 61.

[67] Southgate, *Groaning of Creation*, p. 62.

moulded by the Holy Spirit, and that which is not, the body that has been left to "Darwinism", is close to Dualism, except that in Southgate's description the material world is self-created, or at least abandoned by its Creator as in Deism, rather than having been made by another god or demiurge.

One corollary of this description is that if (all) "organisms... explore their landscape through the power of the Holy Spirit", then this does beg the question of how does the Holy Spirit, whilst empowering creatures to explore their landscape, find expression whilst inhabiting either the apparently dispassionate predators or passive grazers with their repetitive lives that constitute much of the animal kingdom? If there is no *expression* in an animal's behaviour of the Holy Spirit, then why should God fill such a creature? Those who have a close bond with a pet animal may feel or at least hope that their pet has a spiritual connection with its Creator, but it is much harder to believe that this would be the case for creatures such as venomous snakes and spiders, and formidable predators such as the massive marine reptile Liopleurodon that is now extinct.[68]

Suffering of human origin: "moral evil"

Before dismissing moral evil as the cause of suffering that is the most easily explained, it is to be recognized that the scale of such suffering has been immense and continues to be so. Much of this inhumanity is inflicted "in the name of god". This must surely question whether humans were indeed created in the image of God. The level of suffering inflicted in the name of faith or religion calls into question whether faith or religion actually benefit humanity. In addition, there is a more profound question: why were human beings created at all?

As a thought experiment, imagine that you live alone on an island that has no macroscopic living creatures. There is no means of contacting the "outside" world, and the island is populated by robotic creatures that you have made and programmed. Perhaps this is how God might have related to God's Creation before the Creation of human beings. From a

---

[68] <http://hansonfamily.org/dino/liopleurodons.html>, accessed 15 July 2023.

Jewish perspective, Abraham Heschel argued that the concern of God for humankind (*pathos*) is such that "God is in need of" human beings.⁶⁹

From a Christian (Trinitarian) perspective, if it is considered that "God is love", then it is plausible that the Triune God of three persons could have spent eternity in a loving relational manner in the sole company of Godself. In this, Barth describes a difference between (Roman) Catholic and Protestant theology. The Catholic view of the Church is one in which human activity is a prime mover and speaks of a created order that was incomplete without a Church. This is contrasted with Protestant theology that does not speak of a God as one who is incomplete without a Church.⁷⁰ If, as in Catholic theology, the creation of human beings was necessary for God, or, as in Protestant theology, the creation of human beings was an option for God, either way that human beings are formed as sentient beings with the capacity to love suggests that God wanted to have a loving relationship with humanity. God may have "created angels that are programmed to simply praise God (in perpetuity), and had created animals to simply live as animals do",⁷¹ but it was only in fulfilling God's desire to create humankind that possessed free will, i.e. human beings that had been given the choice as to whether they might love God or reject God, that God had created "beings fit for fellowship with himself".⁷² With free will, love becomes voluntary and therefore the worship that human beings offer to God becomes authentic. The scientist and bishop David Atkinson answers the question "Why were humans created?" with "That we may be creatures

---

[69] A. J. Heschel, *The Prophets* (New York: Harper Classics, 1962), p. 235, quoted in R. Bauckham, "'Only the suffering God can help': divine passibility in modern theology", *Themelios* 9:3 (1984), pp. 6–12.

[70] K. Barth, *Church Dogmatics* I.1, tr. Geoffrey Bromiley (Edinburgh: T & T Clark, 1975), p. 151.

[71] From a sermon by Rowan Williams given at St John's, Walworth, London, when he was Archbishop of Canterbury.

[72] D. J. Bartholomew, *God of Chance* (London: SCM Press, 1984), p. 138, cited in Peacocke, *Theology for a Scientific Age*, p. 123.

of the seventh (Sabbath) day! To praise God, to reflect God's image, to delight in creation, so that God could enjoy our joy."[73]

It has been proposed that God might have created a world with no evil or suffering in it in which humans were under the illusion that they had moral freedom. The philosopher Antony Flew has proposed that moral evil is not an inevitable consequence of humanity's freedom to choose. Flew suggests that such "free beings" could also always choose to do what is good.[74] According to Peterson, Flew (and Mackie), humanity could have a free choice but would always choose to do "right actions" *that are predetermined*.[75] In this predetermined world, all actions become inevitable, and there are no moral consequences for, or the possibility of blame on, any person including god; a dispassionate clockwork cosmos unwinds. Contemporary science has demonstrated a non-deterministic (physical) world that supports a model in which humans are free to make real choices. Furthermore, whether such "free" beings could always choose to do what is good seems to be an oxymoron; surely always choosing to do good (or evil) suggests that the freedom of choice necessary to be truly "free" is lacking.

The philosopher David Ray Griffin in "A Critique of John H. Hick's Theodicy" (1981) argues that "(Hick's) God could have created us such that we were absolutely convinced that we were free, even though we only did what God willed for us to do".[76] Perhaps angels *are* thus made, and if the freedom of humankind is not an illusion then that is presumably what God has willed for humankind. Whilst it has to be accepted that "free will" *per se* may be an illusion, Griffin's critique seems to have the form of rejecting the idea of god because god has not seemingly behaved in a way that is either expected or wished for. In Christian orthodox

---

[73] Atkinson, *Renewing the Face of the Earth*, p. 79.
[74] A. Flew, "Divine Omnipotence and Human Freedom", in A. Flew and A. MacIntyre (eds), *New Essays in Philosophical Theology* (London: SCM Press, 1955), pp. 144–69, cited in Hick, *Philosophy of Religion*, p. 38 and Peterson et al., *Reason and Religious Belief*, pp. 131–3.
[75] Peterson et al., *Reason and Religious Belief*, p. 133.
[76] D. R. Griffin, "A Critique of John H. Hick's Theodicy", at <http://www.anthonyflood.com/griffincritiquehicktheodicy.htm>, accessed 15 July 2023.

theology, human beings are created by God and may exercise free will and thus accept or reject the good or the bad, and choose to love God or reject God.

It is possible that God, however omniscient, may have had such omniscience overridden by being too pure, holy, loving and good to have been able to foresee just how depraved some human beings would become and the moral evil that would become possible having received this freedom.[77] According to Peacocke, "God took a risk in Creation" and possibly regretted doing so.[78] An action is subject to regret if part of the full implications of the action itself or other consequences of that action are undesirable, and in either case a degree of inability to foresee such consequences is required. It is proposed that God's inability to foresee such consequences is most likely due to God's Holiness. Alternatively, God may have been able to foresee the consequences of humankind's free will but nevertheless placed a higher value on human freedom. The existence of moral evil is an inevitable consequence of the human freedom that God granted, and moral freedom is an essential constituent of being human. Such free acts have no causal explanation, otherwise they would not be free, and to quote Hick, "the origin of moral evil lies forever concealed within the mystery of human freedom".[79] It is outside the scope of this book to try to *prove* whether such freedom is real or an illusion; it is sufficient to be reminded of the common experience of making a free choice rather than a choice that has been imposed: "we can experience free will like we experience bread. I don't need a philosopher to prove that free will is real before I can experience exercising free will."[80]

---

[77] This idea was provoked by the pornographic images that were displayed on my computer when I used the internet to research the innocent word "sunshine". It is difficult to imagine that the creators of such technology had such usage in mind when it was being developed.

[78] Peacocke, *Theology for a Scientific Age*, p. 124.

[79] Hick, *Philosophy of Religion*, pp. 38–9.

[80] My paraphrase similar to an exposition of the "nevertheless" argument by Simone Weil as in Peterson et al., *Reason and Religious Belief*, pp. 107–8.

Philosophy and theodicy

> Hick and I [Griffin] agree that theodicy involves the construction of a metaphysical hypothesis, and that to be successful this hypothesis must be plausible, not just logically possible.[81]

If theodicy "involves the construction of a metaphysical hypothesis", and if metaphysical is to be taken to mean everything, i.e. no less than the cosmos itself, then the metaphysical hypothesis must include a theory of how the cosmos itself came into being that is plausible if the theodicy is to be plausible. Science may be deemed to be the best discipline to use to decide how the cosmos came into being. The proposal that the cosmos somehow created itself is plausible; it is after all one of two mutually exclusive possibilities and "self-creation" seems to have some support from contemporary science even though the narrative is far from complete. The proposal that the cosmos was created by a creator is also plausible; again this is one of two mutually exclusive possibilities and scientific enquiry has also demonstrated an "awesome" cosmos that points to what is a remarkable self-creation for some and for others the work of an imaginative creator God beyond human comprehension. Since the proposals, God-Creation and self-Creation are both plausible, and not just "logically possible", it would appear given the current evidence presented to humankind that a choice can be made between alternatives that are mutually exclusive. It is therefore equally (philosophically) valid to choose to believe in a God-created cosmos rather than a self-created cosmos, and reasonable to suppose that such choices do not rely upon either plausibility or logic, but on human judgement, such judgement being the interpretation of the evidence presented by the cosmos. If it is accepted that the origin of the cosmos is a matter of human judgement, then such judgement forms the basis upon which a theodicy is formulated.

Griffin also states:

> Since Hick thinks that God is limitlessly good, he must try to show that all the apparent evils in the world are necessary for the

---

[81] Griffin, "A Critique of John H. Hick's Theodicy".

greatest possible good. The question is whether Hick has made plausible the conviction that this inherently omnipotent God is perfectly good. I think not.

Whilst Griffin may deny the goodness of an omnipotent God, this is a matter of judgement not derived from any series of cognitive statements. The argument has shifted from the qualitative, that questions the relationship of entities, to the quantitative, i.e. how much suffering would seem to be permissible to maintain belief in God? Griffin seems to be asking Christians to prove that this is the best possible world; this would seem to be impossible and handing opponents a seemingly impossible task is not a way to finally settle an argument.

The philosopher Gottfried Leibniz (1646–1716) suggested that, despite manifest evil and suffering, this is the best of all possible worlds.[82] A Christian may be entitled to believe that God has reduced suffering to the lowest permissible level simply because that is what God would be expected to do on account of the nature of God, even if the necessity of such evil and suffering was hidden. Whilst we are in a quantitative mode of argument, then considering the amount of natural evil that is considered to be required to balance the existence of moral evil, the extent of the natural evil that is required points to how depraved some human beings have been, are and will continue to be whilst the cosmos is configured as it is. If we all behaved well, then there might be a feasible world in which we all passed away quietly in our sleep once we had reached old age.

Peterson states: "If (these) theists can convincingly argue that there is a place for pointless evils within a theistic conception of the world, then they stop the evidential argument (against the existence of god) from going through." According to Peterson, Alvin Plantinga achieved this through the Free Will Defence to "prove that the logical argument does not show theism to be inconsistent". The Free Will Defence (Theodicy) includes the notion that God knowingly created beings capable of evil.[83] In this book, such a defence is modified: if God is wholly omniscient

---

[82] Peterson et al., *Reason and Religious Belief*, p. 140.
[83] Peterson et al., *Reason and Religious Belief*, p. 143.

then God would have known that such beings were capable of evil; if the Holiness of God is such that evil that is or was yet to happen, was, and still is, unimaginable by God, then God may not have foreseen the evil that free beings would create. It is not unreasonable to conclude that God is not capable of doing that which is logically impossible, for example making a round peg to fit a square hole exactly, and similarly God's Holiness may be such that God cannot imagine evil things that are yet to happen. For God, Holiness may be more important than being omniscient.[84]

The Free Will Defence led to the emergence of an evidential approach in the 1980s which attempted to disprove the existence of God.[85] The philosopher Michael Tooley (2015), for example, used mathematics derived from Bayes' theorem to conclude via calculation that it is most likely that God does not exist. The evidential problem of evil is not that belief in God and evil are inconsistent, but that they are implausible.[86] Statistically based implausibility was proposed by Wesley Salmon, and rejected by Plantinga on the grounds that "there is a lack of clear criterion for judging the probability of one statement on the basis of another" as well as "the tendency of critics to let their own presuppositions affect their assignment of prior probabilities".[87] Another major flaw in this approach is that such calculations are dependent upon judgement to estimate input values. For example, how does one compare quantitatively the human affliction of malaria, that has been calculated during prehistory to have killed more than half of the human population, and is still a major cause of mortality on this planet, with sickle cell disease, that is a severe and potentially fatal illness, the only apparent benefit of which is that being

---

[84] The importance of God's Holiness was inspired by part of a prayer of consecration: "Lord, you are holy indeed, the source of all holiness; grant that by the power of your Holy Spirit, and according to your holy will..." The Archbishops Council, *Common Worship* (London: Church House Publishing, 2000), p. 189.

[85] Peterson et al., *Reason and Religious Belief*, p. 137.

[86] Peterson et al., *Reason and Religious Belief*, p. 133.

[87] A. Plantinga, "The Probabilistic Argument from Evil", *Philosophical Studies* 35, pp. 1–53, cited in Peterson et al., *Reason and Religious Belief*, p. 134.

a sickle cell trait carrier affords some natural resistance to malaria? The third major flaw in this approach is that we can factor in past events, and include data from the present, but the proof or otherwise of the existence of God should surely include the future as well; without a complete set of data such proof has little validity. Fourthly, to use a mathematical tool to disprove the existence of God as a benevolent deity is surely as flawed as the argument that the improbability of a cosmos complete with living forms that are self-aware provides "proof" of a creator.

The *prima facie* evidence of the implausibility of the existence of God is natural evil, for which there seems to be no good explanation. A lot of types of natural evil are described in the book, and "good explanations" from contemporary science for why they might exist are given, and not just "for a greater good" but because, as contemporary science can demonstrate, natural "evils" are inevitable components of a physically and biologically complex cosmos. An essential element of this book is to demonstrate, by referring to contemporary science, that the created world includes natural "evil" as an unavoidable necessity.

Tooley states that "many of the very undesirable states of affairs that the world contains are such as could be eliminated, or prevented, by a being who was only moderately powerful",[88] and furthermore that

> the argument from evil focuses upon the fact that the world appears to contain states of affairs that are bad, or undesirable, or that should have been prevented by any being that could have done so, and it asks how the existence of such states of affairs is to be squared with the existence of God.[89]

The objection from theodicy is a source of the Jain religion in denying that a Creator made the world: "If he created the World out of love

---

[88] M. Tooley, "Theodicy and the Problem of Evil", <http://plato.stanford.edu/entries/evil>, accessed 11 July 2023, 1.1.

[89] Tooley, "Theodicy and the Problem of Evil", 1.2.

for living things and need for them, why did he not make the World completely happy and free of misfortune?"[90]

To eliminate or otherwise prevent "states of affairs that are either bad or undesirable" would require much, including, for examples, genetic coding that could only combine to produce beneficial outcomes, a planet (such as Earth) that is rich in the resources needed to sustain life but without posing any risk to its inhabitants, and the ability to prevent all accidents and crimes whilst preserving human freedom to act. Tooley starts to attempt such a reimagining of Earth by proposing that "the world could perfectly well have contained only human persons, or only human persons plus herbivores".[91] If such herbivores were mortal, then without predation most would die of disease, rotten teeth or starvation and so a swift end by a carnivore might be a desirable alternative. Without animals, from what would Tooley's humans have evolved? Such an idealized existence might exist but be inhabited by robotic creatures. Such a logic-driven robotic existence may appeal to some; for others it may not even be considered to be life at all. Even if we were to live in some form of "heavenly perfection", some would doubt the existence of an all-powerful, all-loving God even if, for example, only one person per million died suddenly and inexplicably each year. If we lived in "heavenly perfection", some would doubt the existence of an all-powerful, all-loving God if no such deaths ever happened. For some, to ever believe in God they will probably need to meet God. The incarnate-revealed God of the Hebraic–Christian tradition is such a person who has been experienced by some people already, albeit in the imperfect "darkened mirror"[92] of mortal existence. The statements of Griffin and Tooley contained in this section seem to allow opinion or matters of judgement to be clouded by deeper longings, and ultimately read more as expressions of desire for a world that is better, or at least more understandable.

It is possible to believe that God limits natural suffering, i.e. suffering of non-human origin, to the lowest possible level, and this belief is not

---

[90] F. Pirani and C. Roche, *The Universe for Beginners* (Cambridge: Icon Books, 1993), p. 27.
[91] Tooley, "Theodicy and the Problem of Evil", 7.1.
[92] 1 Corinthians 13:12.

possible because of the findings of any comprehensive and detailed calculation, and not only as a simple matter of faith and trust, but through reasoning that (a good) God would not be expected to have allowed the level of natural suffering to be higher than that necessary for God's purposes. Jesus did speak of God's care for the creation:

> Are not two sparrows sold for a penny? Yet not one of them will fall to the ground apart from your Father. (Matthew 10:29)

In his book *The Crucified God*, Jürgen Moltmann refers to the theologian Erik Peterson, who makes the point that in the "final age" the world will be Godless and abandoned by God prior to the second coming. If this happens, then at such a time the effect of God in reducing suffering will be apparent.[93] Continuing with Griffin:

> Hick's free will defence is of a hybrid nature. That is, he says that freedom is a contingent aspect of the actual world, given to it by God's voluntary choice. This means that God could suspend or interrupt this freedom at any time ... Accordingly, Hick must defend God's decision to allow every instance of moral evil that has occurred.

As previously discussed, the interventions that Griffin would like to see universally applied would nullify human freedom of choice and would render human existence illusory.

The theologian Bishop David Jenkins stated that for God to intervene to prevent disasters would make God a "meddling demi-God".[94] Whilst such a view would be a poor response in a pastoral context, we do not know to what extent God *does* intervene in the world. History, from the personal level to international levels, is certainly full of significant "near-misses" that would have seemed unpredictable. If we believe that God exists, then a better question might be "Why does God not intervene to prevent disasters more often?"

---

[93] Moltmann, *Crucified God*, p. 54.
[94] Peacocke, *Theology for a Scientific Age*, p. 143.

From Griffin:

> While one may be able to make a somewhat plausible case for God's goodness when discussing moral and natural evil in the abstract, when we are confronted with concrete, horrendous instances of evil, this abstract justification loses its convincing power.

Such "instances" of evil are the exception, and that is why they are regarded as "instances" rather than examples of what is normative. Most people spend their lives without wishing serious harm upon anyone else, and whilst we are all mortal, in any particular year most people will not endure substantial suffering as a direct consequence of "accidents" or "natural evil". It could be argued that many of the "concrete, horrendous instances" of moral evil of the last century of human history have occurred as a consequence of non-belief in God's eternal judgement. The consequences of the behaviour of non-believers are no reason to suggest those who do believe in God, and God's eternal judgement, are wrong.

Griffin questions why God:

> who creates us so that moral evil is necessary—moral evil that can produce "Hiroshimas" and "Auschwitzes"—is a deity who would do all this, solely for the sake of knowing that some of its creatures came to love their creator freely, "limitlessly good?" Again, Hick has not made this plausible.

However dreadful, whilst Hiroshima may have saved human life overall by swiftly ending a war, the death camps such as Auschwitz have no redeeming factors whatsoever. Auschwitz and such atrocities have effectively buried the metaphysical god who is all-loving, all-knowing and all-powerful, in which the future is a script written by God that humans enact as God's puppets. It might be claimed, however, that the Incarnate and Revealed God of the Hebraic–Christian tradition can be believed to be both creative and loving, as such a Holy and loving God may not have been able to foresee and thus prevent the dreadful things that human beings would do with the freedom that they were given. It might also be believed that such a God truly and with integrity grieves as God journeys through such events with God's people.

Griffin continues:

> Furthermore, such a deity, given a reasonable amount of circumspection, would surely know that it was not worthy of love.

The inability of God to foresee the human capacity for evil is a sufficient answer to how humankind came into being as it is, and perhaps God, as well as humankind, has felt the chasm between the good, just and beautiful in the world and the dreadful things which exist. God may also have wondered whether human beings should continue to be part of Creation.[95] This "groaning of Creation" has already been discussed. Later in this chapter, there is a discussion of human response to suffering and what might be God's response.

Griffin continues:

> God wants true faith, which is in things unseen. But this raises the distinction between faith and foolish credulity.

Faith does not require wisdom; it is as available to the wise as the unwise. Faith requires the humility that Griffin, in this critique, appears to lack, and this lack of humility is a potential difficulty for many people. Griffin, for example, suggests several times that God could have designed a better world in which we could live and reveals some bias by describing a deity whose motivation is to "put one over on them (humankind)". Those who have faith can distinguish faith from "foolish credulity" and indeed willingly enter discussions such as this one. Foolish credulity would be manifest in a belief that Harry Potter, Mickey Mouse or Obi-Wan Kenobi will take us to Paradise after we die. The Christian faith is neither rooted in pure fantasy or a work of literature however inspired; it is rooted in the historical person of Jesus Christ, the Church's one foundation, plus the record and experiences of his witnesses and followers that continues

---

[95] As in Genesis 6:7: "So the Lord said, 'I will blot out from the earth the human beings I have created . . . for I am sorry that I have made them."

to this day. As for "credulity", it is surely better in all aspects, even in the exercise of the imagination, to attempt to understand the world in which we actually live rather than to believe that the world could, or should, have been created differently. "He has scattered the proud in the thoughts of their hearts" (Luke 1:51) might also apply to those who are proud on account of their intellectual prowess.

Regarding the evidential problem of evil, Peterson states "[William] Rowe has provided a formulation of this argument which is now a standard in philosophical discussions":

> 1. There exist instances of intense suffering which an omnipotent, omniscient being could have prevented without thereby losing some greater good or permitting some evil equally bad or worse. (Factual premise)
> 2. An omnipotent, wholly good being would prevent the occurrence of any intense suffering it could, unless it could not do so without losing some greater good or permitting some evil equally bad or worse. (Theological premise)
> 3. There does not exist an omnipotent, omniscient, wholly good being. (Conclusion)[96]

The justification for the acceptance of human free will has already been made in this book, there being little point in a God whose nature is to be relational[97] having the entire cosmos filled with that which is predictable to God. Human free will is of benefit to both the Creator and the Creator's creatures. This is the greater good of both the factual premise and theological premise in Rowe's syllogism that would be lost were the intense suffering caused by moral evil to be eliminated.

---

[96] W. Rowe, "The Problem of Evil and some Varieties of Atheism", *American Philosophical Quarterly* 16 (1979), p. 336, quoted in Peterson et al., *Reason and Religious Belief*, p. 135.

[97] The relational nature of God with belief in the Holy Trinity of Father, Son and Holy Spirit, and thus an implied relationship between each person of the Trinity, is one of the defining characteristics of the Christian understanding of God amongst the "Abrahamic" faiths.

It is self-evident that human beings, when exercising free will, can act to produce intense suffering. Were such acts of "moral evil" to be committed in a cosmos in which there was no natural evil, then the effects of such moral evil would be greater; for example, murder would be the cessation of an otherwise immortal life rather than its premature ending. Natural evil is required to exist within the cosmos in a proportionate manner; it would be no match for the comprehensive slaughter of innocents by evil people if the natural evil that existed could result in no more than minor discomfort or else the illness and death that occurred only in the very elderly. Natural evil leads to death and this creates space, resources and opportunities for subsequent generations; natural evil, i.e. suffering of natural origin, is a necessary part of a cosmos in which human beings are allowed to express free will.

Suffering of natural origin

Christian theology has had a Dualistic tendency. In this Dualism, the spiritual is part of the good world created by God. The material world, however, from which suffering of natural origin arises, is either the Creation of a malevolent demi-god or else is considered to have fallen under satanic control or else been abandoned by God. The material world is also the source of "fleshly desires" that are at the root of moral evil.

Whilst theologians as early as Augustine of Hippo "reject the ancient prejudice that matter is evil", nevertheless whilst the Nicene Creed itself proclaims "the Father, the Almighty, maker of heaven and earth" and that "through him (Jesus Christ) all things *were* made", there is no mention in this creed of the current *status quo*. There is no affirmation of the goodness of Creation. Mainstream Christian theology now teaches the Lordship of God over all Creation, and the part of humankind in the proper stewardship of God's Creation.[98] St Augustine also stated that

---

[98] One of the "Five Marks of Mission" that is a benchmark in the Church of England includes "To strive to safeguard the integrity of creation and sustain and renew the life of the earth"; cf. <https://www.anglicancommunion.org/mission/marks-of-mission.aspx>, accessed 15 July 2023.

"evil is a perversion in a fundamentally good Creation",[99] and this accords more with an Eastern Orthodox view of a fundamentally good world, rather than the more North European mediaeval view of a world that was seemingly cursed and inhabited by people whose natural state was evil who thus only deserved God's wrath and from which the only escape was through death, provided salvation had been provided for. Such theology that regards human beings as fundamentally evil who deserve God's wrath and damnation now seems alien, yet this quote is from Article 9 of the 39 Articles in the Book of Common Prayer:[100]

> Whereby man is very far gone from original righteousness, and is of his own nature inclined to evil, so that the flesh lusteth always contrary to the spirit; and therefore in every person born into this world, it deserveth God's wrath and damnation.[101]

Such theology has its roots in Scripture, particularly St Paul's writings, e.g. "Instead, put on the Lord Jesus Christ, and make no provision for the flesh, to gratify its desires" (Romans 13:14). St Paul and later Christian writers may have had an ascetic predisposition that saw their physical appetites to be something which they should resist. Since the New Testament was written, there is now another, arguably deeper understanding of the Incarnation in which God became flesh (Latin *carnis* = "of the flesh") and thus sanctified all of Creation: "the Incarnation, when God declared all things holy".[102]

---

[99] In Hick, *Philosophy of Religion*, p. 37.

[100] The Book of Common Prayer is held in high regard and has some well thought-out and inspiring services but is perhaps rarely read in its entirety.

[101] One possible cause of the revulsion against "the flesh that lusteth always contrary to the spirit" by religious people in both ancient and mediaeval times is the occurrence of erotic "wet" dreams, particularly in those who are both young and celibate. Contemporary psychoanalytic theory has demonstrated the innocence of such phenomena by explaining how that which is to be rejected by the mind whilst awake can be the focus of attention, with a different response, whilst asleep or whilst hypnotized.

[102] J. A. T. Robinson, *Honest to God* (London: SCM Press, 1963), p. 87.

If it is accepted that the natural world is as much of God as the spiritual realm, then the question of the necessity of natural evil needs to be addressed. "Natural" suffering may be permitted by God, or even purposefully created by God, although in theistic terms these are the same thing since God is omnipotent. Natural sufferings such as disease, degeneration and disaster all result eventually in finitude, and this diminishes the impact of deadly moral evil since through such natural processes all humans are rendered mortal and will die eventually whether or not they are the victims of the perpetrators of moral evil. Sadly, one tragic consequence of this is that whilst death may not be considered to be "evil" if it occurs at the end of a fulfilled life, natural causes often prevent lives from being fulfilled.

There may in addition be a reason why this "natural evil" "seems to be built into the very structure of our world", and that is because a permanent hedonistic paradise could not forward the Hebraic-Christian Divine purpose, and also because it is required such that humans can grow in a world that has the capacity for them to do good, that would be lacking in a world devoid of all forms of evil.[103]

A contemporary "scientific" response to the question of God's righteousness in the face of suffering is to be found in Peacocke, who described "natural evil" as an inevitable consequence of "chance" acting within an ordered framework "law". Peacocke recognized such evil to be a major stumbling block to belief in an omnipotent and loving God, yet afforded just one page to the problem of theodicy in his chapter titled "Divine becoming".[104] Does the acceptance of chance *alone* really mitigate the problem of evil? This explanation ignores the supposed omnipotence of God who created a cosmos with a chance element within it, and questions the kind of God who would observe but never act.

Animal suffering

In the account of the Gadarene swine, Jesus was apparently content to have a "large herd of swine" drown (Matthew 8:28-33). Although the two demoniacs were rid of their demons, it is not certain that Jesus had to agree

---

[103] Hick, *Philosophy of Religion*, pp. 40-1.
[104] Peacocke, *Theology for a Scientific Age*, p. 125.

the demons' request to enter the swine, and therefore he could have dealt with the demons in a way that did not involve the suffering of animals. The swineherds and owners did not benefit directly from this episode either. Jesus also extends this destructive behaviour to plant life: "And seeing a fig tree by the side of the road, he went to it and found nothing at all on it but leaves. Then he said to it, 'May no fruit ever come from you again!' And the fig tree withered at once" (Matthew 21:19). These two episodes do not form a blueprint for Christian attitudes towards the natural world, and there is much in the Hebrew Bible about care for the natural world. Much of Jesus' teaching is about stewardship and the appropriate use of resources, and this implies a need for the proper care of the world. The fallenness of humankind is not only manifest in interpersonal behaviour but is also expressed in how humankind has treated creatures and the environment with contempt.

Darwinism proclaims that it is the one and only possible means of creation of living things, and therefore morally neutral.[105] If Darwinism is correct, then God does not have to receive creatures into eternity since creatures live and die in the "only way" that is possible. Southgate, however, suggests that although animals are innocent, and lack "moral content",[106] because they suffer then it would seem correct that animal suffering will be answered by some form of redemption in a new soteriology.[107] Most visions of a new Creation include animals, and the solution to the problem of predation, the hunter and the hunted living well together, is almost an icon of this new Creation. Such a vision is in Isaiah, who also foresaw what the "new" lion would eat:

> The wolf shall live with the lamb, the leopard shall lie down with the kid, the calf and the lion and the fatling together, and a little child shall lead them. The cow and the bear shall graze, their young shall lie down together; and the lion shall eat straw like the ox. (Isaiah 11:6–7)

---

[105] Southgate, *Groaning of Creation*, p. 65.
[106] Southgate, *Groaning of Creation*, p. 4.
[107] Southgate, *Groaning of Creation*, p. 10.

In John's Gospel, Jesus states that *all Creation* (πάντα, *panta*) will be restored through his cross and resurrection (John 12:32). Apart from the scriptural texts and the requirement to compensate an animal for a poor earthly life, a "suffering innocent", the other reason why animals might be expected to have the possibility of eternal life is because if they are required for human life to be the best possible in this life on Earth, so why not in Heaven too?

Even if it is accepted that (adult) humans may sometimes "deserve" to suffer, animals, which are widely regarded as morally incapable throughout their lives and are therefore deemed to be innocent by default, undergo suffering less explicably.[108] Although animal pain is observable, with its accompanying physiological reflexes and pain-induced behaviour such as limb withdrawal and vocalization (cries), it is not known by humans how animal pain is *experienced* by the animal concerned, particularly when the animal is considered to be lacking the existential, psychological and spiritual factors that affect the perception of pain. There is thus the problem of knowing if a creature is self-aware as humans are, and if so, whether emotions can be experienced.[109]

Those who have had pain inflicted upon themselves for the purposes of experiment know that it has a very different quality that is difficult to

---

[108] Consideration of animal suffering also calls into question the precise definition of whether a creature is an animal or a human being. The increase in the cultural and social awareness of humans and their evolutionary ancestors that occurred circa 30,000 years ago predates the tragic extinction 12,000 years ago of Homo Floresiensis, a dwarf hominid from the Indonesian island of Flores (Southgate, *Groaning of Creation*, p. 15). For any lover of animals, this is a sad event, and these hominids may have been cultured, sensitive and kind, but it is only conjecture to suggest that they were fully human with a spirituality that reflected God's image.

[109] J. Al-Khalili and J. McFadden, *Life on the Edge: A Coming of Age of Quantum Biology* (London: Black Swan, 2014), p. 315, questions whether a fossilized dinosaur felt fear as it drowned in the mud that preserved its skeleton; there is also the question of what emotions were experienced by its prey as they were being predated.

describe.[110] In describing animal behaviour, including the response to suffering, anthropomorphic language is used, since we have "no other way of accessing the experience of animals. Renouncing anthropomorphism altogether is bound to be reductionist, resulting in the explanation of animal behaviour in wholly mechanistic terms".[111] But could animal behaviour be mechanistic? It is not reasonable to assume that an animal necessarily experiences pleasure or pain as we do simply because they (a) appear to do so and (b) it suits the language that we use to "access" their experience.

If animals do not have the language to express their reactions, then they are in this regard what would be a vegetative state for a (sentient) human being. Without the language to express the existential, psychological and spiritual factors that affect the perception of pain in human beings, pain may have a very different subjective quality. Pain itself is a necessary sensation and humans (and presumably animals too) that do not have the ability to experience pain inadvertently cause themselves serious and debilitating harm. Having said that, this book does accept that animal pain is noxious and confirms the view that animal suffering should always be alleviated where practical.

It is recognized that animal suffering, if claimed to be a consequence of moral evil, through the necessity of natural evil that human moral evil creates, predates the origin of human beings on this planet. If it is considered that the Fall was an event within Earth time this creates a significant paradox, or contra-diction. Although a natural paradise that existed on Earth would have left no archaeological footprint, for the Fall to have occurred in Earth time on a planet that had already been prepared to accept the emergence of "fallen" human beings, then the consequences of the Fall would have had to have been preknown by God. The construction of a planet that was prearranged for such human

---

[110] Whilst I was a medical student, one method used was by placing a sphygmomanometer cuff (such are used when taking blood pressure) around a limb and leaving it inflated for prolonged periods of time. Although my arm "hurt", it did not bother me; I knew the pain could be stopped at any time without any lasting consequences.

[111] Bauckham, *Bible and Ecology*, p. 53.

failure is not compatible with the hypothesis that a Holy God was unable to foresee the consequences of human freedom. It is to be noted that a Holy God may have been able to foresee the consequences of human freedom but nevertheless valued human freedom too highly not to grant human beings free will.

It is proposed that the Fall did *not* occur within the current geographical and historical framework (i.e. the cosmos as we know it) but in some eternal mode of existence, the "*pre-archaios*". It is proposed that the *pre-archaios* predates the existence of any sentient creatures on Earth. Such a *pre-archaios* would seem a more probable setting for a rebellion amongst God's creatures than a specific time and location on planet Earth. If the allegorical "Adam and Eve" had been expelled from such a heavenly realm, there is no reason why the translocation to Earth would have needed to have been instant. For humanity, the transition from the *pre-archaios* in which a Paradise once existed may have been a move from Heaven "time" to Earth "time" rather than a spatial transition across the face of the Earth. That "Adam and Eve" would have had to wait in Paradise's "departure lounge" from the emergence of cellular life 1,850mya[112] to the emergence of humanoids 0.25mya (Earth time) as God created a fallen world for them, points to the enormous disparity between temporal (Earth) time and eternal (heavenly) time. Whilst nearly two billion years may seem an excessive length of time in which animal suffering occurred prior to the emergence of prehumans, it is not likely that even the most sentient creatures would have been aware of, or complained about, the longevity.

Human fallenness could be the reason that human beings were sent to live in a world in which natural evil pre-existed; (mortal) human beings therefore evolved in a world that had natural evil to counter the moral evil of humanity. It is somewhat tragic that such natural evil affects animal life. My own preference is to hope that animal pain is experienced (subjectively) neither in the manner nor in the extent to which human pain can be experienced. Others have suggested that such animal suffering means that animals both deserve and are granted an eternal

---

[112] mya is an abbreviation for "million years ago".

existence.¹¹³ Even though such suffering may provide a means to eternal life for an animal, we should surely have compassion on animals that suffer. In a new creation the "lion will lie down with the lamb"; however, for the time being such innocent creatures suffer as a consequence of our moral failings. There is surely a duty to reduce animal suffering and thus a justification for compassionate farming, and cruel "sports" such as fox hunting should only be regarded as a form of depravity.

Dinosaurs existed for $c.160$ million years before the emergence of mammalian species from which human beings evolved. It may be questioned as to why such a period of animal suffering was so prolonged. Perhaps the creatures of previous archaeological ages did not suffer? If during this long passage of time animals did not actually suffer in this prehuman era, then God may have taken great pleasure from allowing and even assisting the evolution of the enormous beasts and monsters whose skeletons now only adorn our museums. Only mammals seem to be able to bond closely with human beings; birds, reptiles, insects and arachnids when kept as pets are often psychologically "cold" and unengaged.

Alternatively this delay of the emergence of the origin of human beings is similar to the other seemingly unanswerable question, why is the *Parousia*¹¹⁴ delayed? A philosophical answer is the rejoinder that however long such periods of suffering existed, or will exist, it could always be hoped that they would be shorter. A Christian response is to have faith that God is to be trusted to know the best timing for such events. This book is specific; it is an answer to the question of theodicy from a Christian understanding. There are matters for which faith is required, such as belief that the risen Jesus Christ offers his followers hope of eternal life and that God can create an eternal heavenly existence in which human beings can live life in all its fullness whilst retaining their free will. In John 10:10, Jesus states, "I came that they may have life, and

---

[113] Southgate, *Groaning of Creation*, p. 43. According to Richard W. Kropf, animal suffering leads to a resurrected existence. Cf. R. W. Kropf, *Evil and Evolution: A Theodicy* (Eugene, OR: Wipf & Stock, 1984), pp. 118–27.

[114] The Parousia is the Christian expectation of the return of Jesus Christ and the judgement and redemption of the cosmos.

have it abundantly." Perhaps such a description is that of a fully lived life that will only occur in a heavenly existence in which the joys of this life such as the beauty of nature, art and music, spiritual experience and other joys unlimited are even more intense. The mystery of how our earthly life might relate to our heavenly life is discussed in the final chapter.

Natural accidents

In 2007, the Revd Tom Honey, a parish priest, delivered an essay at a TED conference that was written as a theological response to the 2004 earthquake and tsunami in the Indian Ocean that resulted in the loss of an estimated 250,000 human lives.[115] An article in the *Sunday Telegraph* (2 January 2005) by the then Archbishop of Canterbury, Rowan Williams, had stimulated the essay. According to Honey:

> the essence of his (Williams') words was this: the people most affected by the devastation and loss of life do not want intellectual theories, about how God can let this happen. "If some religious genius did come up with an explanation of exactly why all these deaths *made sense*,[116] would we feel happier, or safer or more confident in God?"

The justification for describing this theodicy to be broadly philosophical in approach derives from the specific appeal for the deaths to make "sense". What sort of "sense" would this be? Would this "sense" include the ability to demonstrate an overall plan in which the deaths were a necessary step? This would assume that the cosmos proceeds in a predetermined manner. The use of the word "genius" seems almost pejorative, as if an explanation would not be an improvement upon leaving the question of theodicy as a mystery. My recollection is that at about that time Bishop John Sentamu, who was about to be consecrated as the Archbishop of York, also expressed a view that people in distress did not want others to expound theories, they wanted people to offer practical help. That

---

[115] T. Honey, "How could God have allowed the tsunami" (2007), at <https://www.youtube.com/watch?v=2wdkxdiOFJA>, accessed 16 July 2023.

[116] My italics added for emphasis.

the two senior appointees in the Church of England did not apparently wish to provide any explanation as to why these events had happened must have rung a little hollow with the churched and unchurched alike. It is fully accepted that in the acute event a theory of theodicy would not be at all helpful. Honey illustrates this with the image of a father holding the hand of his dead child. At a later time, however, if the understanding of God as "a policeman in the sky who orders everything and causes events to happen" is rejected, and a more contemporary scientific understanding of how the cosmos works is applied, it can be seen that such tragedies are not necessary *steps* in the unfolding of a predetermined cosmos, that move inexorably from one time frame to the next as in the relativistic description, but that such tragedies are necessary *consequences* of human life occurring in a cosmos in which there is a random element that renders the cosmos non-deterministic.

In the acute event, no theory would make us "feel happier, or safer or more confident in God", but such theories might provide for a more robust apologetic. Surely wishing to understand God, rather than proclaiming holy mysteries, is the driver for all theology and many would feel comforted to know why and how they can nevertheless feel loved by God despite such events. Such understanding might also lead to a greater future hope as well as a less unjust planet as people are more minded of their Creator to whom they are answerable.

Honey questions whether God interacts in the cosmos, quoting the words of a harvest hymn, "the wind and waves obey him", concluding "Do they? I don't think we can sing those words again." Rather than the binary question of whether God does control every single event, or does not, the causal nexus model of the cosmos provides a hybrid economy that indicates that God creates the laws that enable the (necessary) existence of the wind, ocean waves and even earthquakes, and also, crucially, suggests a loose control of such phenomena. Had Honey been more minded of Scripture, then Jesus' response to the tragedy of the tower of Siloam might have been recalled and found to be helpful. However ghastly the loss of life and destruction of the Boxing Day tsunami, it is possible, although not provable (either way), that God has limited the total amount of suffering of natural origin in the cosmos to the lowest possible level. It is possible that no other cosmos, in which we are placed as we are, can exist. A Christian, or other person of faith in a loving God, would find it difficult to accept that God would allow more suffering than necessary. If we believe that God made everything, then God made the Boxing Day tsunami. The cynics of the time concluded that God was too busy after His Son's birthday celebrations to intervene (the tsunami having occurred on Boxing Day), but they did not describe what sort of life humans could ever enjoy were they to live in such a protected illusion. As an example, I could question whether I would have been a loving parent if I had never allowed my children to be exposed to the slightest risk. To do this would have meant home education, no travel and, for example, no hill walking in Eryri (aka "Snowdonia"). Since they attended an inner-city comprehensive school, travelled by bus, rail, car and air, and had the experience of climbing a few of the peaks in Eryri, does this mean that I did not love them properly?

Honey's response is forged in the binary question and deterministic view that God is either "in control" or not, leading to the conclusion that "maybe God doesn't do things at all" and the question "what if God is in things?" Honey describes a "compassionate presence" but does not explain why such a god of everything should have this quality. This is particularly noticeable in a view of god that has been proposed to answer the question of why natural accidents occur.

The faith proposed by Honey is similar to faith in nature: "faith in this God would be more like trusting an essential goodness and benevolence in the universe". It can only be assumed that this belief in an "essential goodness" is derived from the observation that many human lives are lived without becoming victims of a natural accident, and as such is close to the assertion that God has reduced the level of suffering through natural accident to the lowest possible level.

The "god in everything" panentheism that Honey describes is characterized by a loss of Christian identity and a pluralist outlook and can become the basis of a type of spirituality. It is reminiscent of the "Temples to Nature" created in post-revolution France. With Honey, however, vestiges of Christian belief are still to be found, for example in the "awareness of my own infinite value" that requires some external reference since who or what has deemed a person to have infinite value? It would seem that Rowan Williams and John Sentamu had responded to the tsunami by saying that we do not have a complete theodicy (and even if we did it would not be helpful). Tom Honey is saying that we know nothing, so let us try and find god in everything. Further examination of the cosmos to provide an answer to the question of the necessity or otherwise of suffering of natural origin reveals that the cosmos has a predictable foundation based upon physical laws, but within this there are random processes that produce beneficial effects, for example the diversity of evolution that occurs at the boundary of the predictable and non-predictable. Such a boundary also produces creative opportunities that will be described and discussed later in this book. These random processes, however, that are an intrinsic part of what may be the only possible cosmos may also be responsible for disease and other natural disasters. Volcanoes exist at the fault lines between tectonic plates, and it is in these places that humans have mined minerals and metals from the Earth's crust, so they have sadly also been the places where human beings have tended to live and thus increased the number of deaths when the volcanoes have erupted. Scientific study, for example, in describing the complexity of biological systems, may support the assertion that disease is an inescapable part of the natural world. The pathogens of communicable diseases are similar to those that form a beneficial element of the biosphere: fungi recycle carbon, viruses enable bacterial evolution via plasmid transference; bacteria are needed to recycle biological "material", and in human therapeutics bacterial metabolism is required for the combined oral contraceptive pill to work. Variability within the natural world, however, leads to harmful or lethal variants. There may be no completely "bad" genes but numerous harmful combinations of good ones that lead to a predisposition to disease, analogous to the machine code errors in computing where "good" information and instructions are read as a "bad" instruction. If such bad combinations of "good" genes are the source of much illness, it would explain why very few diseases appear to have specific genetic markers. The fact that bad genes, and bad combinations of good genes, persist suggests that either "removing" such bad genes completely or the prevention of harmful combinations is not possible, either for God or via an evolutionary process.

This does, however, beg the unpleasant question, "did God create cancer?" The question is unpleasant, because the answer has to be "yes", since God created everything. This is unsettling and counter-intuitive for those who believe in a loving God, and unsettling for those who publicly deny the existence of god yet inwardly cling to a hope that they might be wrong. Cancer could not have arisen by an evolutionary process in the way that infectious diseases (bacterial, viral, fungal and parasitic) may have arisen since cancers do not replicate from host to host; they arise in the tissue of the person with the disease. There are approximately 200 cancers that affect human beings, and most have a fairly consistent biology.[117] There are, of course, many other illnesses apart from cancer, such as motor neurone disease and rheumatoid arthritis, that appear in the sufferer without being transmitted by a biological agent. I believe that God wept when God first knew that such bad combinations, or "machine errors", would produce cancers that particularly affect the newly born. The genetics that are responsible for the propensity to lethal cancer in the newborn and children do not have the ability to be passed to the next generation. That they have a consistent biology suggests they are not the product of a random, e.g. radiation-induced, process. My conclusion is that the propensity to such cancers is the consequence of a combination of otherwise innocuous genes.

How we respond to the consequences of such faults or accidents in human biology is a matter of attitude and interpretation, notwithstanding how being personally affected by such illnesses might profoundly affect such responses. It could be said that 200 types of human cancer are evidence that God is incompetent. Those who trust in God, and/or have an appreciation of the intricacies and complexities of cellular and molecular biology, will more easily accept that the number of human cancers of "only" 200 is astonishingly low.

---

[117] Biological phenomena that occur with each type include susceptibility (or otherwise) to radiotherapy and specific chemotherapeutic agents, propensity to develop in response to carcinogenic agents such as tobacco smoke, mode of spread, non-metastatic phenomena and histological (microscopic) cellular characteristics.

Tooley describes theodicies, that is "attempts to explain why God permits evil", to be "tepid, shallow and ultimately frivolous".[118] The underlying reasons for this appear to be a naïve interpretation of omnipotence, i.e. expecting God to do the impossible, together with an understanding that evil is permitted by God only for the sake of some greater good. Tooley sets out a "direct inductive" argument from evil to deny the existence of an omnipotent and loving god. The examples cited are "animals dying an agonizing death in a forest fire and a child's undergoing lingering suffering and eventual death due to cancer".[119] It is to be noted that both examples concern the suffering of innocents and thus any argument from the freedom to do evil, and then "reap the just rewards", is inapplicable. Both examples are those of suffering from natural accidents; wild animals have freedom to move, experiencing pain helps animals to limit injury, sunshine enables growth but also dries out forests and makes them susceptible to lightning that forms an essential part of the natural nitrogen cycle that is in turn essential for the plant life on Earth on which all living things depend. In the case of the child example that Tooley gives, as I have suggested, there are some dreadful gene combinations. Such tragedies are not accepted without protest by those who do profess faith in a benevolent God.

Tooley also lists four other sources of theodicy:

First, to the value of acquiring desirable traits of character in the face of suffering
Tooley may be referring to Hick's thesis that evil and suffering enable our souls to mature.[120] Hick's theory of the cosmos being a place where souls mature does not fit with those who die young or even unborn; perhaps there is a "mixed economy" in Heaven, and there will be some relationship between how our earthly lives are led and how Heaven

---

[118] Tooley, "Theodicy and the Problem of Evil", 7.
[119] Tooley, "Theodicy and the Problem of Evil", 3.5.
[120] J. Hick, "An Irenaean Theodicy" and "Response to Critiques", in S. T. Davis (ed.), *Encountering Evil: Live Options in Theodicy*, 1st edn (Edinburgh: T & T Clark, 1981), pp. 39–52 and 63–8; see also Peterson et al., *Reason and Religious Belief*, p. 139.

will be experienced, for without such a relationship the pre-*Parousia* cosmos seems to be without value. In defence of this first source, we cannot ourselves evaluate how living in the world we live in affects our development since no corresponding control environment exists from which to make comparison. It is difficult to imagine how traits such as bravery and heroism can arise without "bad" people to be our foes, nor indeed can we easily imagine a world in which neither heroic people nor their adversaries existed.

Secondly, to the value of libertarian free will
There is some irony that Tooley places little value on libertarian free will. Although, as Tooley states, there is "no satisfactory account of the concept of libertarian free will",[121] i.e. a proof founded on cognitive statements, it is common human experience that free will exists, and that it is valuable. When freedom is no longer available, for example during imprisonment or as the consequence of illness, the lack of physical freedom is distressing and the world *feels* a very different place. If free will is restricted and thus an illusion, it is difficult to imagine the mechanism through which human free will may be restricted in a cosmos that has a random and non-determined element. If human free will was restricted by an omnipotent god who had willed that humans should live according to a predetermined plan, what would be the purpose of allowing human beings to believe that they possessed free will? It would take extraordinary faith to believe that such a god existed.

Thirdly, to the value of the freedom to inflict horrendous evils upon others
Tooley's third point is a gratuitous embellishment of Point 2; again Tooley wishes to reimagine the world: "individuals could, for example, have libertarian free will, but not have the power to torture and murder others".[122] This does beg the question as to exactly how a person might be able to scythe wheat in order to harvest the grain, but not be able to turn the sharpened blade on their perceived adversary. To have this

---

[121] Tooley, "Theodicy and the Problem of Evil", 7.2.
[122] Tooley, "Theodicy and the Problem of Evil", 7.2.

free will repeatedly available and then withdrawn would render human experience chaotic.

Fourthly, to the value of a world that is governed by natural laws[123]
A world that is governed by natural laws seems to require both order *and* chaos; the chaos within the cosmos also creates that which is tragic. Prior to this Tooley had offered a challenge:

> One possibility is the offering of a complete theodicy. As I shall use that term, this involves the thesis that, for every actual evil found in the world, one can describe some state of affairs that it is reasonable to believe exists, and which is such that, if it exists, will provide an omnipotent and omniscient being with a morally sufficient reason for allowing the evil in question.[124]

This is surely a matter of judgement rather than the application of pure logic. It can be argued that in the causal nexus, it is true that the predetermined and the random elements are both completely essential for human life to be lived in its fullness, and that there are also unfortunate consequences of this through which natural accidents (or "evil") occur, such consequences being unavoidable even for God, who, though omnipotent and omniscient, cannot do what is impossible. If this is accepted, then the question of "morally sufficient reason" becomes that of whether God should have created humankind and the cosmos in which we live at all; to doubt that God exists because simply we are discontent with what God has made is not logically defensible.

Tooley's entry in the *Stanford Encyclopaedia of Philosophy*—"Theodicy and the Problem of Evil"—has a third attempt to reimagine the created world, by denying any necessity for divine intervention. Tooley suggests that the

> very close relations between human and chimpanzee DNA, and the fact that known mechanisms of chromosome rearrangement

---

[123] Tooley, "Theodicy and the Problem of Evil", 7.
[124] Tooley, "Theodicy and the Problem of Evil", 4.

render the transition from some non-human species to Homo sapiens not at all improbable, the postulation of divine intervention at that particular point does not seem plausible.[125]

Such a statement underlines how important the interpretation of the natural world is. Tooley is (presumably) reassured that the human and chimpanzee have 98.5 per cent of their DNA in common; detailed comparisons of the chromosomal structure reveal differences that place a chasm between the two. Chromosomal rearrangement, in human medicine, normally produces severe disease or debility. Whilst evolutionary processes, over time, could have made such "quantum leaps" in chromosomal structure, to disagree with Tooley and nevertheless suggest that divine intervention is required to bridge this chasm is a somewhat pyrrhic victory, as it begs the question as to why humans are more closely related to chimpanzees, with their common pattern of aggression, rather than the generally more placid orangutan. In creating a body for fallen humankind there is no reason why God would have needed to do this *de novo*, and starting with the common ancestor of the great apes would have been sufficient for the purpose.

Although the world that we and the animals inhabit is not Paradise, there may be "good" reasons why some "bad" phenomena exist at all. Griffin questions belief in "a creator who has the power to create a completely different type of world and yet who deliberately builds earthquakes, tornadoes, and cancer into the structure of the world". As stated previously, earthquakes are found at the junction of tectonic plates, and as this is also where the metallic deposits are that have benefitted human beings with the metals used to make agricultural and carpentry tools, such junctions or "fault" lines are thus unfortunately places with high levels of human habitation as the metallic deposits are mined and put to use. Tornadoes are extreme examples of one of the "natural" distributions of phenomena that constitute the weather system that brings water from the sea to the earth, thus rendering life on land possible. Lightning strike is the natural process through which nitrogen returns from the air to the land and sea that enables plant life, and thus

---

[125] Tooley, "Theodicy and the Problem of Evil", 7.5.

all forms of life, to exist. Cancer and other diseases seem to have no benefit apart from sparing many of us from death by slow degeneration. Griffin's point is acceptable but only if such a world that he hopes for can be shown to be physically possible. The eradication of what has been termed "natural evil" from the cosmos may be impossible even for God. Although the term "evil" signals an intention, those on the receiving end of such "accidents" frequently feel less generously towards the ultimate source of their affliction.

Consciousness and the innate

That we question why suffering exists might suggest a primaeval memory of a better time and place. As humankind strives for Utopia, an ideal world in which every problem in medicine, politics, economics and safety has been solved, such that we could live forever on this planet, would that be like living in the heavenly realm that many feel, by instinct, to be our destiny? Human consciousness has been demonstrated to possess innate qualities such as an understanding of the concepts of grammar that underpin the use of language (Chomsky). There is a proposed innate sense of morality, i.e. what is self-evidently right and what is self-evidently wrong, the "natural philosophy" described by the mediaeval historian and Christian writer C. S. Lewis (1952) in *Mere Christianity*. This innate sense of morality was thought to be such an inherent part of human nature it had been referred to as the "Law of Nature";[126] furthermore it is an essential part of Christian doctrine. If our moral compass is simply formed by external factors such as nature (genetics) and nurture (our environment), how could we possibly be condemned (more positively why would we need salvation) on account of where we were placed as we were being formed? If we are not condemned, we do not need the salvific ministry of Jesus Christ. There is a critique of faith that claims that it is no more than a "psychological crutch".[127] Perhaps this reflects how we are made by God with an innate sense of needing to connect with our creator. As Augustine wrote, "You have made us for yourself and our heart

---

[126] C. S. Lewis, *Mere Christianity* (Glasgow: Collins Fontana Religious, 1952), p. 16.

[127] Hick, *Philosophy of Religion*, p. 36.

is restless until it rests in you."[128] If it is accepted that the human mind, or soul, has such innate capacities, then an innate sense of another mode of existence that predates the Fall is not unimaginable.

There would also appear to be an innate desire for people to "achieve harmony within themselves and within their environment".[129] It is perhaps an innate sense within us that God should be good that leads to such distress when the unacceptable aspects of God's Creation are considered. The actor and comedian Stephen Fry has posted a video on YouTube in which he describes how he is angry with God because of what the (Christian) God has created, for example malignant bone disease in children. Fry states how he would not have a problem meeting a "classical" god.[130] Assuming that Fry has no actual expectation of meeting a "classical" God, this is similar to "Protest" atheism, such as that of the Dostoyevsky character Ivan Karamazov, who can accept the existence of God but not that God made the world, with its inherent suffering and injustice.[131] It is a variant of atheism that "does not doubt the existence of God but doubts whether the world of experience is grounded in a divine being and is guided by this divine being".[132] Such a form of atheism deals with the philosophical problem of not being able to prove that something (e.g. god) does not exist.

But how might such innate senses be transmitted from generation to generation? One possibility is that innate senses are transmitted through consciousness that has no material form, yet it inhabits and finds expression through the biochemical and electrical activity of the brain.

"The origin of consciousness is as great a mystery as the origin of the universe and the origin of life."[133] Defining consciousness is challenging; the eminent scientists Jim Al-Khalili and Joe McFadden state: "but what is consciousness ... we will take the cowards' way out by not attempting

---

[128] St Augustine, *Confessions* I i 1.
[129] Hick, *Philosophy of Religion*, p. 78.
[130] <http://www.youtube.com/watch?v=-suvkwNYSQo>, accessed 16 July 2023.
[131] Moltmann, *Crucified God*, p. 227.
[132] Moltmann, *Crucified God*, p. 226.
[133] Al-Khalili and McFadden, *Life on the Edge*, p. 360.

any rigid definition".[134] "The mind-body problem or the hard problem of consciousness is surely the deepest mystery of our entire existence."[135] How does the consciousness, that has no material presence, effect an electrochemical change in our brains that, for example, will make us decide to play a violin? A rather empty explanation of consciousness is provided by the "sheer complexity of the human brain".[136] Does this mean that a rock has a miniscule "quantum" of consciousness too? Does this mean that the worldwide web is conscious that it exists?[137]

Whether a creature (or object) may be conscious might be defined by the following: "our starting point is an insistence that those of our ancestors who painted the ideas of bears, bison or wild horses on ancient cave walls were definitely conscious".[138] It is difficult to accept that a bacterium is conscious, and therefore during the evolutionary process consciousness developed after bacteria and before modern human beings: "a bizarre property appeared in the living matter of which organisms are composed".[139]

Peacocke has proposed that consciousness is "derived" from complex organization, e.g. from highly organized neural networks such as brains.[140] How this "derivation" occurs and what level of organization is required in a neural network to become self-aware is pure speculation. The molecular neurobiologist Axel has used the word "percept" to describe what higher brain centres *generate* in response to the scent of "lilac, coffee or a skunk";[141] however, there is no notion of what such generation is, whether a physical or electrical entity. When describing olfaction (or

---

[134] Al-Khalili and McFadden, *Life on the Edge*, p. 314.
[135] Al-Khalili and McFadden, *Life on the Edge*, p. 323.
[136] Al-Khalili and McFadden, *Life on the Edge*, p. 323.
[137] A similar question is posed in Al-Khalili and McFadden, *Life on the Edge*, p. 332, in which silicon-based computers are deemed to be zombies whereas flesh-based "computers" are conscious.
[138] Al-Khalili and McFadden, *Life on the Edge*, p. 316.
[139] Al-Khalili and McFadden, *Life on the Edge*, p. 316.
[140] Peacocke, *Theology for a Scientific Age*, p. 67.
[141] Al-Khalili and McFadden, *Life on the Edge*, p. 200. Al-Khalili has used the term "blips" that, for example, create the perception of an object.

sense of smell) Al-Khalili stated: "the key event in this whole process is *of course* the capturing of the odour molecule by the olfactory neuron".[142] This may be the key event in terms of the function of the sensor but for human beings the important thing is not that electrical signals are sent to the brain, but that the brain can, in this example, "experience" the smell of the odour molecule. If the process of experience is no more than electrical activity within the brain, then we must also conclude that a simple measuring device such as an ammeter[143] is conscious in some manner. There are further questions that seem to be outside of the envelope of what science can explain, such as why would a person wish to repeat some olfactory experiences?

The development of artificial intelligence may produce insight into what constitutes consciousness. One example might be if a computer were to be made that was sufficiently complex such that the machine exhibited phenomena associated with "consciousness". One test of consciousness might be the ability of such machines to speak unprompted. Whilst it is claimed that science is not able to explain "subjectivity"[144] on a practical level, neurosurgeons, in eradicating disease, strive to preserve brain function during surgical procedures with neurophysiological monitoring and other techniques that include "awake craniotomies"; the main driver is to preserve speech function. It is sadly difficult to imagine the self-awareness or consciousness that a person retains if they lose the ability to speak even to themselves.

There is of course no evidence from standard biochemical and electrical testing that the soul exists, although this is to be expected since such testing of neural tissue is restricted to equipment that can (only) detect biochemical and electrical phenomena. That "the concept of a soul, [is] no longer part of modern *science*"[145] is certainly true and is perhaps a good thing, since *science alone* does not have the language or method to describe the soul or investigate further.

---

[142] Al-Khalili and McFadden, *Life on the Edge*, p. 198.

[143] An ammeter (ampmeter) is a device to measure the strength of electrical current using either an electromagnetic mechanism or digital electronics.

[144] Peacocke, *Theology for a Scientific Age*, p. 110.

[145] Al-Khalili and McFadden, *Life on the Edge*, p. 48.

It has been proposed that if consciousness can "inhabit" the electrochemical apparatus of the brain, then might not a "soul" also inhabit a person, or inhabit more than the higher centres of the brain:

> The soul "is an individual essence that makes the body a human body and that diffuses, informs, animates, develops, unifies and grounds the biological functions of the body. The various chemical processes and parts (e.g. DNA) involved in morphogenesis are tools, means or instrumental causes employed by the soul as it teleologically unfolds its capacities toward the formation of a mature human body that functions as it ought to function by nature."[146]

If non-physical consciousness ("the soul") is accepted, this provides an explanation as to how God might be able to "speak" to humankind without altering matter or energy. Such communication from God to humankind may help form our conscience and other manifestations of the innate.

God and suffering

As the creator of the cosmos, God is ultimately responsible for everything, including the tragedies that result from all forms of suffering and evil. There is a question of justice: what has God done in response to the suffering and evil in the cosmos?

Christian theology teaches that despite evil being contrary to God's nature, God nevertheless intervened in a fallen Creation, with the Incarnation of Jesus and the ultimate triumph of the cross and resurrection. The theology of the Incarnation and the cross provides an answer to the question of the justice of what God has done in response to the suffering and evil in the cosmos.

---

[146] J. P. Moreland and S. B. Rae, *Body and Soul: Human Nature and the Crisis in Ethics* (Downers Grove, IL: InterVarsity Press, 2000), p. 202, cited in Peterson et al., *Reason and Religious Belief*, p. 201.

Michael Ramsey, whilst Archbishop of Canterbury, gave his response to the question and problem of suffering. His response was to remind people of the right of God Almighty to judge people[147] and, by implication, to remind people that God would ensure that the consequences of such judgements were enacted. This understanding is shocking, inasmuch as it was stated in a book written as recently as 1972, and moreover in a book intended as a guide for pastoral ministry. It would appear that the understanding of God within mainstream Christianity (or at least the Church of England) has changed much in the last 50 years, and that God is no longer so seemingly remote, uncaring and willing to punish.

In Job, there is an uncompromising message: God created the world; the world belongs to God, and God can do as God wishes. Job's protest is turned to repentance as God describes the chasm between God's power and creative abilities and those of Job (42:1-6). This is, in fairness, the essence of the response given in the above paragraph by Michael Ramsey, except that in Job God is claiming creative rather than moral superiority, and it is also similar to the response to suffering that those who adhere to other world faiths might give. It is also the response that might be given by a Christian whose principal metaphor for the understanding of God is God as a judge.[148] If, however, Christians believe in a God who loves the creatures that God has made, and is by nature a loving God who longs for and deserves our worship but does not impose God's will upon us, then belief in such a God as judge who deliberately has "reserved a right" to inflict suffering is not possible. One major problem with the "God can do just as God wishes" belief, particularly when combined with the belief that the cosmos unfolds according to a detailed plan that God has determined, is that these two beliefs create a fatalistic sense of hopelessness in that any response that we might have to God is either illusory or without effect. These two beliefs also undermine hope for an experience of eternal life in which there is a continuation of freedom that is seemingly precious to us.

---

[147] M. Ramsey, *The Christian Priest Today* (London: SPCK, 1972), p. 22.

[148] This and other metaphors are discussed in S. McFague, *Metaphorical Theology: Models of God in Religious Language* (Philadelphia, PA: Fortress Press, 1982).

Apatheia: The impassibility of God

The Platonic and then Stoic concept of the soul described a lower part with emotion and a higher part with thought and reason, and hence god [lower case g used for non-Jewish-Christian God] was imagined to have the latter without the former.[149] The early Christian Fathers had been influenced by the Jewish theologian Philo, who had made "*apatheia* a prominent feature of his understanding of the God of Israel".[150] *Apatheia* is essentially a description of inertia, the inability to be passive or to suffer, or the inability to sense emotions both welcome and unwelcome and the inability to "be affected by something else". Thus emotions such as anger or empathy are not possible since these may be induced by others. This doctrine of *apatheia* is a consequence of God being believed to be "absolutely self-sufficient, self-determining and independent".[151] A God with such *apatheia* seems completely devoid of the essential characteristics of a person, and this presents a terrifying prospect if it is true.

Perfection

Another argument for God's inability to change is because perfection, should it change, can only become imperfect. For Thomas Aquinas, who broadly attempted to reintegrate classical philosophy and Catholic theology, God is *actus purus*; and passion, that implies change, would not be compatible with God's true Being.[152] Heschel states that in the biblical understanding of God, God is not described as "perfect", since this suggests a standard against which God is judged.[153] Kant is quoted in Moltmann stating that "the Holy One of the gospel (Jesus) must first be compared with our ideal of moral perfection".[154] In writing a book called *Religion within the Limits of Reason Alone*, Kant made the error of writing a theology *for* a particular purpose rather than *from* a particular

---

[149] Heschel, *Prophets*, p. 322.
[150] Bauckham, "'Only the Suffering God Can help'", p. 7.
[151] Bauckham, "'Only the Suffering God Can help'", p. 7.
[152] Heschel, *Prophets*, p. 337.
[153] Heschel, *Prophets*, p. 352.
[154] Moltmann, *Crucified God*, p. 93.

aspect. For surely God is God, and so theology is trying to understand who God *is* rather than developing ideas about God in order to fit a particular purpose. If it is believed that God created humankind, then God also enabled humankind to develop an ideal of moral perfection. Christians can read about a small fraction of the earthly life that Jesus lived and regard it as an attempt to describe a life lived as an example of moral perfection:

> Then he (Jesus) said to them, 'is it lawful to do good or to do harm on the sabbath, to save life or to kill?' But they were silent. He looked around at them with anger; he was grieved at their hardness of heart. (Mark 3:4–5a)

If Jesus' life was moral perfection, then moral perfection appears to include a wide range of responses, including righteous indignation or "plain" anger. Strong's (NT) Greek, however, defines "anger" (ὀργή, *orge*) as a controlled and considered reaction, and not an emotional outburst.[155]

A perfect being could, however, have more than one form or mode of operation. As a visual analogy, a vista of ocean waves crashing on a rocky shore may appear perfect, but in this vista the changeability is an important element of the perfection. There is an analogy in music: the interval of the perfect fifth (3:2) has a beauty on account of it being an interval between natural harmonics, yet there is also the equal tempered fifth (1.4983:1) that transformed the tuning of keyboard instruments and led to complete freedom of modulation between keys. In Trinitarian theology, God is a perfect unity, but God is also Father, Son and Spirit, three different and separate "perfections".

Pathos: The passibility of God

Theodicy has developed with the acceptance of the *passibility* of God, and the theodicy proposed in this book accepts the passibility of God. Bauckham credited R. H. Relton for first proposing, in 1917,

---

[155] <http://biblehub.com/str/greek/3709.htm>, accessed 16 July 2023.

the understanding of a God who suffers,[156] and this theology has been subsequently developed by others. In his book *The Crucified God*, the theologian Jürgen Moltmann argues the case for Divine passibility and commences by challenging the assumptions made by the early Church Fathers who envisaged God as the deity invented and described by classical metaphysics and Greek philosophy. The analogical (Platonic) principle of knowledge was adopted by early Christian theology (i.e. like can only know like), and this precluded revelatory theology.[157]

In his book (1962) *The Prophets*, the Jewish theologian Abraham Heschel comments on the notion of *pathos*. Although *pathos* is etymologically related to *apatheia*, Heschel used *apatheia* to describe an understanding of God derived from that of the divine *apatheia* of the Greeks; *pathos* is used to "describe God's concern for and involvement in the world".[158] Heschel states that when the Hebrew Bible speaks of the *pathos* of God, it is a quality that "evokes pity or sadness"; *pathos* is etymologically related to *paskhein* meaning to suffer and *penthos* meaning grief. According to Heschel, the *pathos* of God is described more frequently in the Hebrew Bible than the normative "goodness, justice, wisdom and unity".[159] Examples of God's *pathos* include: "The ox knows its owner, and the donkey its master's crib; but Israel does not know, my people do not understand" (Isaiah 1:3) and "Thus says the Lord: what wrong did your ancestors find in me, that they went far from me, and went after worthless things, and became worthless themselves?" (Jeremiah 2:5). In Genesis 6:5–6, God laments the creation of humankind with its wickedness.

There is thus a stark contrast between the God of Israel and the classical philosophical God thought to be *anankē*, i.e. unknown and indifferent.[160]

---

[156] H. M. Relton, *Studies in Christian Doctrine* (London: Macmillan, 1960), p. 79, in Bauckham, "'Only the Suffering God Can help'", p. 6. The rediscovery of a Franciscan understanding of the suffering God may be more.

[157] Moltmann, *Crucified God*, p. 21.

[158] Bauckham, "'Only the Suffering God Can help'", p. 9.

[159] Heschel, *Prophets*, p. 286.

[160] Heschel, *Prophets*, p. 289.

For Heschel, *pathos* is not an unreasoned emotion, and the expression of the *pathos* of God is firmly within God's control.[161] Self-limitation would appear to have been rooted within contemporary New Testament culture and found expression in the Aramaic *makikhe*, "the lowly ones", as in the *Magnificat* (Luke 1:52), or voluntary self-humbling where an inner strength is controlled or repressed,[162] and later in the concept of *kenosis* or voluntary self-limitation as in the self-emptying of Jesus: "Jesus . . . emptied himself, taking the form of a slave" (Philippians 2:5–7).

Justice

For Heschel, "divine pathos may explain why justice is not meted out in the world".[163] For Gutiérrez, human freedom to choose is reflected in, or similar to, God's freedom to be unconfined to a system of reward and punishment.[164] For Cox, who like Gutiérrez is commenting on Job, "the key is not so much the 'justice of man, injustice of God'; it is the erosion of the intellectual basis for 'faith'".[165] Cox also states that the wicked and the unrighteous are part of the cosmic whole; they represent the liberty that God has inserted into Creation,[166] and God will decide where, when and how moral inequity is dealt with.[167]

These threads portray God as one who is able, through the suffering and grieving connotations of *pathos*, to tolerate injustice by the "internalization" of God's grief. Whilst a contemporary psychologist might describe the process as an internalization, Heschel points out that the "divine pathos" is a "unique theological category", and not a "common psychological concept",[168] and if this is true, then any such

---

[161] Heschel, *Prophets*, p. 290.

[162] The meaning of the Aramaic *makikhe* is from N. Douglas-Klotz, *Prayers of the Cosmos: Meditation on the Aramaic Words of Jesus* (San Francisco, CA: Harper, 1990), p. 54.

[163] Heschel, *Prophets*, p. 305.

[164] Gutiérrez, *On Job*, p. 80.

[165] Cox, *Man's Anger and God's Silence*, p. 83.

[166] Cox, *Man's Anger and God's Silence*, p. 107.

[167] Cox, *Man's Anger and God's Silence*, p. 99.

[168] Heschel, *Prophets*, pp. 347–8.

psychological analysis should be seen as an analogy or model and not an explanation. God does not seek immediate revenge or other form of retribution, but is able to compensate by existing in a state of sorrow. To determine whether such tolerance by God should erode the "intellectual basis for faith" would need consideration of what sort of cosmos would it be in which righteousness, and its converse, were fully dealt with in this mortal life? Would such a world be possible? And what sort of God would even attempt to do such a thing in this fallen world? If all good behaviour were rewarded promptly in this mortal life, we would become like Pavlov's dogs who salivated when a stimulus associated with the imminent provision of food was made. We would nearly always behave well, and the reward received would not even be appreciated; since we would live as all others did, the rewards would only become apparent when absent. Those who did not consistently behave well would not be regarded as bad or evil, but regarded as being either mentally or psychologically deficient in some way, and thus human existence would no longer have the moral dimension that would appear to be important to God. It is self-evident that human beings can, for the time being, enjoy the liberty that God has placed in Creation. How, and whether, God will deal with moral inequity is ultimately a matter of faith.

Bauckham describes the prevailing Jewish and philosophical view of the time, adopted by the early Church Fathers, to be that "suffering and emotion are both incompatible with the nature of a God who never becomes, but is".[169] Had they not been minded of the description of the LORD in Exodus 3:14, אֶהְיֶה (aeie), that is not to be translated as "I AM" but as "I shall become, I am becoming"?[170] Bauckham states that to the ancient Greek mind stability was attractive; yet the Hebrew Scriptures contain accounts of three covenants that God made with the ancient Hebrew people, the Noahide, the Abrahamic and the Mosaic. It seems remarkable that such a history that defined the identity of the Jewish people could be apparently so easily abandoned in favour of Greek philosophical ideas. As Heschel states, "to the biblical mind the

---

[169] Bauckham, "'Only the Suffering God Can help'", p. 8.
[170] <https://www.scripture4all.org/OnlineInterlinear/OTpdf/exo3.pdf>, accessed 16 July 2023.

conception of God as detached and unemotional is totally alien".[171] If God is not detached, then it must be recognized that God interacts with God's Creation.

The crucified and resurrected God

Bauckham notes how the Fathers understood the love of God in the "benevolent attitude and activity"[172] of God, although this seemed to ignore the hardship and suffering that constituted much of human life at a time of Christian martyrdom. There was a difficulty in reconciling the benevolence of God in Creation with the "real sufferings of Christ".[173] Moltmann pointed out that the error the early Church Fathers made was to recognize "only two alternatives: either essential incapacity for suffering or a fateful subjection to suffering". For Anselm, God's perfection implies impassibility, for God cannot suffer;[174] for later theologians, perfection also means perfect love that does run the risk of being hurt. Moltmann, however, recognized a third form of suffering, "the voluntary laying oneself open to another and allowing oneself to be intimately affected by him (another); that is to say, the suffering of passionate love".[175] The self-limitation of such voluntary action accords with the concept of *kenosis*.

Moltmann, however, looks for continuity in the understanding of God as a person with mystery who revealed Godself to the ancient Hebrews and their successors.[176] In Mark 15:34 (and Matthew 27:46) is a proclamation by the crucified Jesus: "At three o'clock Jesus cried out with a loud voice, '*Eloi, Eloi, lema sabachthani*' which means, 'My God, my God, why have you forsaken me?'" The use of Aramaic in the Gospel texts ("*Eloi, Eloi, lema sabachthani*") suggests a verbatim record of Jesus' words. For Moltmann, the essence of his book is the interpretation of

---

[171] Heschel, *Prophets*, p. 330.
[172] Bauckham, "'Only the Suffering God Can help'", p. 8.
[173] Bauckham, "'Only the Suffering God Can help'", p. 8.
[174] Peterson et al., *Reason and Religious Belief*, p. 61.
[175] J. Moltmann, *The Trinity and the Kingdom of God: The Doctrine of God*, tr. Margaret Kohl (London: SCM Press, 1981), cited in Bauckham, "'Only the Suffering God Can help'", p. 8.
[176] Moltmann, *Crucified God*, p. xi.

this phrase;[177] for in this "dying cry of godforsakenness" Jesus takes up the protest against suffering.[178]

When first heard, the phrase "the crucified God" is shocking and causes distress amongst those who place their trust in God to protect them and to bring them to life eternal whatever obstacles might be placed in their way. The "crucified God" is, however, shorthand in Moltmann's writing for whom "the crucified God" is also the risen Christ. It is also to be understood that the suffering and crucifixion of God did not occur because God was helpless but because God chose to identify with those who were suffering, and deal with a fallen world and broken humankind on behalf of humankind. Moltmann presents the crucifixion of Jesus as an axiom of Christian faith: "Christian identity can be understood only as an act of identification with the crucified Christ."[179]

Whilst Christian identity may be bound with the crucified Christ, the experience of suffering is in the present. Although the crucified Christ rose from the dead, followers of the "Easter faith", as Moltmann describes them, believe that there is a sense that the crucifixion of Jesus and the suffering God continues into the present. "The curtain of the temple is torn forever."[180] This short statement illustrates well the notion of the death of Jesus, and thus the breaking of the barrier between God's heavenly Kingdom and God's earthly Kingdom, as an ongoing event, and not something that is to be only interpreted as a completed action that happened once. Jesus died once and once only, but the repercussions and consequences continue into the present. Moltmann also quotes Bultmann: "the cross is an eschatological event 'in and beyond time'".[181]

Bauckham used a quote from Bonhoeffer's *Letters and Papers from Prison* to title his critique of Moltmann "only the suffering God can help".[182]

---

[177] Moltmann, *Crucified God*, p. x.
[178] Moltmann, *Crucified God*, p. xii.
[179] Moltmann, *Crucified God*, p. 13.
[180] J. B. Metz, *Theology of the World*, tr. William Glen-Doepel (New York: Seabury, 1969), p. 113, in Moltmann, *Crucified God*, p. 39.
[181] Moltmann, *Crucified God*, p. 57.
[182] D. Bonhoeffer, *Letters and Papers from Prison*, the Enlarged Edition (London: SCM Press, 1971), p. 360, in Moltmann, *Crucified God*, p. 43.

Although published in 1971, the texts were written when Bonhoeffer was a prisoner during the Second World War. Bauckham recognized a pattern in this: *The Impassibility of God: A Survey of Christian Thought* was written by Mozley in 1926 in the aftermath of the First World War; Kitamori's *Theology of the Pain of God* was published in 1946 in Japan soon after Hiroshima; and Moltmann's theology was influenced by his time as a prisoner during the Second World War and is an attempt to do theology "after Auschwitz".[183] Such theology came from the perspective of those whose lives are dominated by the suffering of themselves and others. That Christ brings help as someone who did suffer and continues to do so, brings comfort and consolation to those who have faith in him but also suffer. Key to understanding this consolation as more than a warming empathy is how the emotional situations of not being loved and of being abandoned, and the powerlessness of unbelief, are the same as those that the crucified Jesus experienced with his suffering, wounds and pain; and thus if or as we suffer with Jesus, we are with him and so might also share in his resurrection.[184] As well as resurrection hope, when we pray to Jesus we pray to a God who is on, or who certainly knew, the one side of the cross where we are placed. All the other gods, those of riches, power and domination, are on the other side.[185]

This theology, which is in essence pastoral, may help to bring comfort to the afflicted, but does not progress an understanding of theodicy itself, i.e. how might it be just that there is so much suffering in this world when it is apparently something that God could stop?

Key to the understanding of how the crucified God might contribute to the question of theodicy is the recognition that the God proclaimed by Christians is not faith in a god that might be derived from a philosophical approach or metaphysical exercise: "Christian faith basically lives only as a profession of faith in Jesus."[186] The question of theodicy from a Christian perspective, therefore, is such that criticisms directed against particular properties and attributes of the metaphysical and philosophical

---

[183] Bauckham, "'Only the Suffering God Can help'", p. 9.
[184] Moltmann, *Crucified God*, p. 42.
[185] Moltmann, *Crucified God*, pp. 200–1.
[186] Moltmann, *Crucified God*, p. 80.

understanding of who or what god might be do not require an answer. The Jesus of history does not correlate well with a metaphysical understanding of god that is intransitory, immortal and impassible.[187] There is also a mysterious aspect of the nature of Jesus that accords with the Hebraic understanding of God,[188] and indeed some of the words of Jesus himself are far from being those of one who is impassible.

According to Moltmann, the "task of theological reflection is ... to seek the truth of Jesus himself".[189] Scholars such as Albert Schweitzer and Paul Tillich, in discovering the historical Jesus through Christological revisionism, not only criticized doctrine but also the testimonies of the primitive faith gathered in Scripture, almost making faith an arbitrary choice.[190] Friedrich Schleiermacher (1768–1834), however, had argued that important knowledge in matters of faith comes via emotions and feelings, and that a more valid Christology arose from a personal relationship with Jesus.[191] Schleiermacher stated: "Religious experience is not an intellectual or cognitive experience, but a feeling of absolute or total dependence upon a source or power that is distinct from the world"; the deeper aspects of belief cannot be known by reason, they are known by feeling.[192] In 1916, Karl Barth, in a context that was not only the ongoing war being fought in Western Europe and beyond, but also his reaction to the "undertaker–scholars", who had tried to bury Scripture during the two previous generations, defined the kind of writing in the Bible to be "revelatory and intimate rather than informational and impersonal".[193] This discovery, or "new awakening", was developed by Barth over the next 50 years. William James (1958) described feelings

---

[187] Moltmann, *Crucified God*, p. 86.

[188] Moltmann, *Crucified God*, p. 90.

[189] Moltmann, *Crucified God*, p. 116.

[190] Moltmann, *Crucified God*, p. 118.

[191] Moltmann, *Crucified God*, p. 93.

[192] Peterson et al., *Reason and Religious Belief*, p. 19, quoting F. Schleiermacher, *The Christian Faith* (Edinburgh: T & T Clark, 1928), p. 17.

[193] K. Barth (1978), *The Word of God and the Word of Man*, tr. Douglas Houghton (London: Hodder & Stoughton, 1928), cited in E. Peterson, *Eat this Book: The Art of Spiritual Reading* (London: Hodder & Stoughton, 2006), p. 6.

as a "deeper source of religion",[194] and therefore religious experience is foundational and reflection, both theological and philosophical, is derived from such experiences. Therefore such reflections cannot refute the truth of religious experience. Cognitive processes, however, *are* required to translate religious experience into truth-claims.[195]

It is to be noted that religious feelings have their limitations and are not the exclusive basis of Christian faith. Peterson states:

> In short, those who describe religious experience as mere feeling encounter a dilemma. If the religious experience is ineffable, then it cannot be used to ground religious beliefs, for it provides no content for grounding. If, however, the experience has conceptual content, then it cannot be independent of conceptual expression and immune from criticism. Those who make religious experience into mere feeling cannot have it both ineffable and the foundation for a religious conceptual system.[196]

Whilst feelings may modulate Christian experience, *the* foundation of Christian faith is Jesus Himself. This has been handed down via the three pillars of Hooker: Scripture, reason and tradition; however, the foundational nature of Jesus is to be recognized.[197] We are thus returned to Moltmann's assertion that the "task of theological reflection is ... to seek the truth of Jesus himself".[198]

For an authentic Christian faith, we must try to discern the teaching of Jesus in the "common ground" of teaching found in all four of the canonical Gospels, and not allow our theology to be dominated by others such as John the Baptist and St Paul who interpreted his teaching. For example, John the Baptist was preaching repentance and judgement,

---

[194] W. James, *The Varieties of Religious Experience* (New York: New American Library, 1958), p. 329, cited in Peterson et al., *Reason and Religious Belief*, p. 20.

[195] Peterson et al., *Reason and Religious Belief*, p. 20.

[196] Peterson et al., *Reason and Religious Belief*, p. 26.

[197] As is discussed in Brooks, "The Church's One Foundation".

[198] Moltmann, *Crucified God*, p. 116.

whilst Jesus preached repentance and forgiveness.[199] John continued to baptize disciples after Jesus' followers started to baptize people:

> After this Jesus and his disciples went into the Judean countryside, and he spent some time there with them and baptized. John also was baptizing at Aenon near Salim because water was abundant there; and people kept coming and were being baptized. (John 3:22-3)

Whereas the apostle Paul preaches the righteousness of God, Jesus preached about the kingdom of God, and it is noted how Jesus' teaching is "irrelevant for St Paul";[200] the teaching of Jesus is quoted just once in all of Paul's writings. Whilst the difference in the teaching of Jesus and St Paul is that one precedes the cross-resurrection and the other succeeds it, this is only in an historical sense for, as Bultmann pointed out, there is an emphasis on eschatology in Jesus' preaching.[201] Jesus did not teach his followers the "early chapters" that would need completion by another. Since Jesus' preaching has a unique character in that it relates to him alone and to no other, in consequence this preaching "could not be handed on unaltered"; Jesus speaks about himself; we speak of Jesus.[202]

In understanding the meaning of "the crucified God", we can place this in the context of Jesus who was also a teacher, and therefore not the diminished version that St Paul presents, a total innocent who became the sacrificial offering made to satisfy the righteousness of God and thus the redemption of humanity and the world. It is very likely that Jesus would have been forgotten except for his resurrection, but there was a further significance of the resurrection: it vindicated and provided proof of the validity of his teaching.[203] That Jesus' teaching has survived is not the only evidence of his resurrection. Moltmann asks: "Why must

---

[199] Moltmann, *Crucified God*, p. 131. Pannenberg, *Introduction to Systematic Theology*, p. 60, also makes this distinction.
[200] Moltmann, *Crucified God*, p. 121.
[201] Moltmann, *Crucified God*, pp. 122-3.
[202] Moltmann, *Crucified God*, p. 125.
[203] Moltmann, *Crucified God*, p. 166.

the absolute claim of Jesus be accepted?"[204] In answer to this question, there is non-Scriptural contemporary literary evidence from Josephus that Jesus existed. There is also the historical record of the times in which Jesus lived, as the community of those who believed in the risen Jesus grew in number, developed their understanding of Jesus and impacted upon world history. Today there is evidence from the manner in which Christian theology engages constructively with other academic inquiry together with the experience of Christians for whom knowing Jesus is "revelatory and intimate".[205] The "body" of teaching that Jesus gave, plus the "body" of the risen Christ that is alive in the minds and souls of believers and is celebrated to this day, gives authenticity and authority to an answer to the problem of theodicy in which the revelation of God is understood and accepted by those who adhere to the Christian faith. Whilst a theodicy that has its basis in Christian theology (rather than classical metaphysical descriptions of god) may not be fully acceptable to those who are not Christian believers, for those who are Christian believers a sound reasoning that explains theodicy in their Christian terms will hopefully be an asset to apologetics even if limited in its ability to provide comfort and reassurance in moments of acute grief.

That God was crucified is not an answer as to why there is suffering. However, the cross-resurrection, amongst other consequences, does provide a response to suffering and also proclaims the need for the redemption of (fallen) humanity and the created world. In Judaism, theodicy, the "justice of God", is achieved by the raising from the dead and God's final judgement such that the innocent go to eternal life and others eternal damnation.[206] Indeed the belief in the resurrection of the dead seems to be derived in Judaism from the expectation of God's justice which cannot occur except by recompense or even retribution in a post-death existence.[207] For, "if the death boundary is understood as a judgement of Yahweh, then his power also extends beyond death."[208]

---

[204] Moltmann, *Crucified God*, p. 96.
[205] Peterson, *Eat this Book*, p. 6.
[206] Moltmann, *Crucified God*, pp. 178–9.
[207] Moltmann, *Crucified God*, p. 181.
[208] Moltmann, *Crucified God*, p. 119.

Furthermore, in *Theology of Hope* (1967), Moltmann states that in the Old Testament there is an understanding of the interpretation of history that not only demonstrated what God had done but also spoke of promises for the future,[209] and this also fits with the Jewish belief that some form of eternal life *has* to exist because only through this can injustices be reconciled. Such recompense or even retribution in a post-death existence may provide an answer to how God will deal, or deals, with moral evil, but not natural evil.

This reasoning that the cosmos requires completion is similar to the unpublished syllogism (quoted in Chapter 1) that I wrote in 1975 that had a salvific emphasis:

- *There is sense in Creation.* There is evidence of design and innovation that could not have happened by accident.
- *With no Saviour there is no sense in Creation.* The injustice in the world suggests that there is a means of ultimate justice and restoration.
- *Therefore there has to be a Saviour.* If there is a Creator, then there is presumably also a Saviour.

In Christian theology, the new "righteousness" comes from a rejected and crucified God. God manifests his true righteousness "in this crucified figure". Thus in the cross of Christ the sin of the world is dealt with such that "the resurrection hope of Christian faith is unequivocally a joyful hope and not threatened by an uncertain final judgement".[210]

The cross-resurrection leads to salvation and was the recompense for the sins of the world and other evils for which God holds ultimate responsibility. There is the question of individual human responsibility for sin. If—as it is believed—God created everything, then God must have created the potential for human sin. It is not, however, inevitable that humankind would exercise this freedom to do evil, and our laws

---

[209] J. Moltmann, *Theology of Hope: On the Ground and the Implications of a Christian Eschatology*, tr. James W. Leitch (London: SCM Press, 1967), p. 103.

[210] Moltmann, *Crucified God*, p. 180.

and other societal governance are founded on the basis that choosing to commit acts of evil, where freedom to choose exists, is undertaken voluntarily such that the perpetrator may be blamed or otherwise held to account.

The notion of the cross-resurrection in providing an eschatological panacea[211] begs the question of why this type or mode of Creation is not here today, and why this "interim" world is required at all. If, for example, as Moltmann suggested, the victims of an act of murder and their murderers are treated in the same way,[212] then is this justice? Moltmann seems to be promoting Universal Salvation. Jesus preached a message of God's forgiveness, but Jesus did also call people to repent and not to "sin again". For example, "the woman caught in adultery":

> Jesus straightened up and said to her, "Woman, where are they? Has no one condemned you"? She said, "No one, sir". And Jesus said, "Neither do I condemn you. Go your way, and from now on do not sin again. (John 8:10–11)

If victims and their murderers are treated the same way, why did Jesus teach, or be known to humankind at all?

The teaching and ministry of Jesus may be regarded as further evidence of God's love for the cosmos. Jesus' ministry was not only about the creation of a pathway from Earth to Heaven, but also that "Thy Kingdom come, on Earth as it is in Heaven". The cosmos is precious to God, and God wanted humanity to live well whilst living their mortal lives, and hence the moral teaching of Jesus. If the quality of mortal human life was of no importance to God, and yet the cross-resurrection was necessary for salvation, then God could presumably have succeeded in such purposes by arranging a private crucifixion known only to God.

If, however, there is no relationship between this earthly life and Heaven, then this earthly life, which is unpleasant for many, is apparently

---

[211] Moltmann, *Crucified God*, pp. 181–2.
[212] Moltmann, *Crucified God*, p. 183.

without purpose. Was Moltmann in a state of post-*Shoah*[213] emotional and moral exhaustion that sought a totally benign future; so exhausted by human inhumanity even to the extent that the wicked should go unpunished? The resurrection appearances of Jesus looked forward to the coming glory of the Kingdom of God and also back to the past with the marks of crucifixion,[214] and this suggests that something of mortal existence will continue in, affect, or relate to, heavenly existence.

If there is some relationship between our earthly lives and heavenly existence this contradicts the proposal that the record of our earthly lives is of no account once Heaven is entered. One resolution is the notion of purgatory, a place where justice is meted out prior to the experience of eternal life, noting that an eternity that follows such a period of purgatorial time is no lesser an eternity.[215] Whether or not "purgatory" is accepted, I am not concerned that this book presents an unanswered question for *how* eternal existence will be experienced, and *how* God will deal with people, "saints and sinners alike", justly; it is sufficient for me to have attempted to explain the how and why of mortal existence.

The cross-resurrection did not lead to the immediate Creation of a new Heaven and a new Earth, and it is for this reason that Jesus is not recognized within Judaism as the Messiah. Yet "Christ could only be resurrected *for* us by being resurrected *before* us".[216] In this interim time, this "delay of the *Parousia*", for Christians there is a need to affirm the risen Christ as Lord and Saviour. Whilst during this delay there is earthly life with all of its wonders and joy, and the freedom to voluntarily seek God, there is, however, considerable suffering and injustice, and this pleads for an answer to the question of theodicy that arises. Christ indeed could only be resurrected for us by being resurrected before us, but the passage of time since AD 33 seems unbearably long already. Heschel states

---

[213] Shoah is used as a preferred term to Holocaust, as the latter has the connotation that God approved of such a sacrifice.

[214] Moltmann, *Crucified God*, p. 172.

[215] Infinity may be defined mathematically as a "number" that when a finite number is subtracted from it is not diminished and is still equal to that "number".

[216] Moltmann, *Crucified God*, p. 189.

that God's compassion enables the temporary situation of the triumph of evil deeds over the just,[217] and in this delay such "compassion" seems to unjustly favour those who commit evil.

The suffering God

What of the suffering of "the crucified God", and how might this help to understand suffering?

The penal-substitution theory of the cross would have appealed to St Paul. For St Paul, whose former religion involved sacrifices made in the Temple, the suffering Christ was a special sacrificial offering made to appease God. Jewish scholasticism of the Middle Ages describes an apathic God apparently immune to unfairness or suffering. The wrath of God was deemed to be a consequence of God's love, the opposite of love being indifference.[218] The penal-substitution theory of the cross, which has been termed "cosmic child abuse", is not tenable in a faith that understands God as love. In order to convince a person that a god was justified in having god's own son crucified, then such a god would have to primarily be regarded as a god of vengeance and judgement.[219] As God loves as a person loves, then such love, which is the acceptance of the wellbeing of another without regard to one's own wellbeing, contains the possibility of suffering.[220] This possibility of suffering will be present if it is accepted that God is by nature loving and cannot exist in any other way. This possibility of suffering will also be present if the exercise of true love involves the possibility of it being withdrawn.

For Cyril and Athanasius, Christ's desolation and suffering was an intellectual challenge since God, as in the dual nature, could not be "defeated".[221] This challenge persisted as the classical metaphysical

---

[217] Moltmann, *Crucified God*, p. 368.//
[218] Moltmann, *Crucified God*, pp. 280–1.
[219] As in Sallie McFague's *Metaphorical Theology*. I sometimes wonder how mediaeval Christian missionaries first convinced "heathen" Vikings that theirs was a God of love, who had had his own Son crucified. Were the Vikings impressed or disgusted?
[220] Moltmann, *Crucified God*, p. 237.
[221] Moltmann, *Crucified God*, p. 236.

concept of god expounded by those early Church Fathers remained dominant. Bauckham states that it was in the mid-thirteenth century that depictions of Christ on the cross illustrate a shift from the apparently unperturbed crucified Christ more preoccupied by the glory to come, to an introspective Christ with the marks of suffering, although such depictions did not indicate a shift in the theology of the divine nature.[222]

Although sculptures and paintings of the suffering Christ had appeared before the beginning of the twelfth century,[223] the adoption of such images in central Italy has been linked to the influence of Franciscans and Dominicans.[224] Did Franciscan spirituality, with its affinity for and its inclusion of and love and respect for the natural world, together with a desire to "live the Gospel", lead St Francis and his followers to see in Jesus a fully human person, capable of human emotion, and able to suffer as humans do? Of possible significance is the occurrence in 1257 of the catastrophic volcanic eruption of Samalas in Lombok, Indonesia[225] that led to crop failure in both hemispheres of the Earth. There is evidence of mass starvation in London in the aftermath of this eruption,[226] and similar food shortages would be expected to have occurred in central Italy (Tuscany and Umbria). It might be expected that those living through such devastation might have looked to their Saviour and seen Jesus as a

---

[222] Bauckham, "'Only the Suffering God Can help'", p. 8.
[223] For example, the Gero Crucifix c.965–70, Cologne Cathedral, see <http://www.medievalists.net/2015/04/the-crucifixion-of-jesus-in-medieval-art/>, accessed 16 July 2023.
[224] See e.g. Miri Rubin at <http://histflorence.blogspot.co.uk/2013/01/a-stylistic-analysis-of-two-crosses-by.html>, accessed 16 July 2023.
[225] C. Vidal, N. Métrich, J-C. Komorowski et al., "The 1257 Samalas eruption (Lombok, Indonesia): the single greatest stratospheric gas release of the Common Era", *Scientific Reports* 6 (2016), 34868 at <https://doi.org/10.1038/srep34868>, accessed 16 July 2023.
[226] Dalya Alberge, "Mass grave in London reveals how volcano caused global catastrophe", *Observer*, 5 August 2012, <https://www.theguardian.com/uk/2012/aug/05/medieval-volcano-disaster-london-graves>, accessed 16 July 2023.

person who, like them, was one for whom the sky darkened as He suffered and for whom only the image of a properly suffering Christ would suffice.

Martin Luther later understood that as Jesus dies on the cross so does God die, for God does not provide a creature to solve the problem of human sinfulness and a corrupt Creation, but became, and continues to be, the solution. Luther, however, avoids commenting on what happened to the relationship between Son and Father, and Son and Spirit, as Jesus died.[227]

The suffering of Jesus on the cross—"My God, my God, why have you forsaken me?"—whose apparent abandonment by God stimulated the one recorded complaint that Jesus had about his suffering, is "something which separates the Son from the Father and is something that takes place within God himself",[228] but "What dichotomy does this presuppose of God? Jesus dies as God the Father whilst God the Father witnesses the (his) death?"[229]

The cross is where "only a fully divine God who suffers can help us".[230] But how does the suffering and death of God help humankind and the created world? Moltmann phrased the question: "How can deliverance and liberation for godforsaken man lie in the figure of the godforsaken, crucified Christ?" According to Moltmann, the cross leads to the separation of the three parts of the Trinity[231] more than any other event;[232] the Son is forsaken by the Father and suffers abandonment, and the Father grieves as his Son dies. The separation between the Father and

---

[227] Moltmann, *Crucified God*, p. 241.
[228] Moltmann, *Crucified God*, p. 154.
[229] Moltmann, *Crucified God*, p. 208.
[230] Moltmann, *Crucified God*, p. 212.
[231] An understanding of the Trinity may be found in quantum logic. In binary logic, the states of 0 and 1 are mutually exclusive. In quantum logic, both states can be considered to be present simultaneously in a manner analogous to superposition. Therefore the "anomaly" of the Trinity has a solution: "God is Father; God is Son, and God is Spirit; Father is not Son; Son is not Spirit; Spirit is not Father" becomes acceptable; in quantum logic same and not same can coexist.
[232] Moltmann, *Crucified God*, p. 213.

the Son is filled with love: "the Holy Spirit is the powerful love which proceeds from this event to reach godforsaken human beings".[233] In such "staurocentric (cross-centred) theology", the cross becomes the basis for belief in the Trinitarian nature of God.[234]

It is supposed that "somehow", within the internal economy of God, the cross-resurrection event has led to the opportunity of the redemption of all that God has created, including all of those people God has created. The theologian Kitamori has produced this explanation:

> In the face of sin, God's immediate love turns to anger, but since he continues to love those who should not be loved, he suffers the conflict of love and wrath within him. In the victory of his love over his wrath God's pain mediates his love to sinners.[235]

Such a "somehow" proposition is unacceptable to those whose understanding of god is that of classical philosophy or metaphysics, but for those who have the Hebraic–Christian understanding of God, whose nature is mysterious, then no complete explanation, even if such were possible, is necessary. Christian theology is not, or should not be, however, the end of metaphysics.[236] It would be arrogant to assume that all theology could be imagined or otherwise contained within the human mind. A Christian is, however, also commanded to love God by trying to comprehend God: "You shall love the Lord your God with all your heart, and with all your soul, and with all your *mind*, and with all your strength" (Mark 12:30; cf. Deuteronomy 6:4–5; author's emphasis). Such comprehension, to quote the "Hooker" triad,[237] is required to be able

---

[233] Moltmann, *Crucified God*, pp. 240–9, and *The Trinity and the Kingdom of God*, pp. 75–83, in Bauckham, "'Only the Suffering God Can help'", p. 11.

[234] Moltmann, *Crucified God*, p. 249.

[235] K. Kitamori, *Theology of the Pain of God* (London: SCM Press, 1966), especially Chapter 10 in Bauckham, "'Only the Suffering God Can help'", pp. 10–11.

[236] Moltmann, *Crucified God*, p. 225.

[237] For Hooker, the triad of Scripture, reason and tradition are the foundations of Christian faith.

to reason theologically and also use reason to interpret tradition and Scripture. Such an intellectual component ensures that the "Hooker" foundations of Christian faith are not solely reliant on the unthinking acceptance of what others have written or how Scripture has been interpreted (or ignored) in the past as tradition developed.

Jesus is quoted, somewhat enigmatically, in John 12:32, in referring to the cross-resurrection that "I, when I am lifted up from the Earth, will draw all people to myself"; except that πάντα (*panta*), translated in this NRSV text as "people", is more commonly translated in the NT as "all", or "all things", implying that the whole of Creation is to be redeemed.[238] There was a Pauline understanding of the redemption of the whole of Creation as in 1 Corinthians 15:28: "When all things are subjected to him, then the Son himself will also be subjected to the one who put *all things* in subjection under him, so that God may be all in all", and also Colossians 1:20: "and through him God was pleased to reconcile to himself *all things*, whether on earth or in heaven, by making peace through the blood of his cross" (author's emphasis in both texts).

The crucified God is thus the response of God to the suffering of humankind *and* the whole of Creation. As God is omnipotent, then God has ultimate responsibility for human sin and the consequences thereof, for God created humankind with this capacity, and God in some way in the cross-resurrection also makes recompense for the "natural evil" in what God has created, even if such "natural evil" might be necessary toitigate the effects of otherwise unlimited moral evil. It might also be that through the cross, God, who would otherwise be limited by God's Holiness, is able to commune with sinful human beings.

I referred earlier to the apparent injustice of a victim and murderer being dealt with by God in the same way. It *might* follow from this that if God regards Godself as the ultimate source of both natural evil and moral evil, then the murderer is not to be blamed for being the result of his nature and nurture. This would suggest a bi-directionality of the atonement as God makes an extreme "penitent" gesture for the suffering

---

[238] <http://www.scripture4all.org/OnlineInterlinear/NTpdf/joh12.pdf> and <https://www.biblestudytools.com/search/?s=references&q=panta>, accessed 16 July 2016.

of the world and thus God offers us the means of forgiveness and offers Godself as an act of wishing to be forgiven, and provides a means through which Creation will ultimately be redeemed from the effects of both moral and natural evil. I do not hold this view of the cross-resurrection, since it denies the existence of deliberate acts of human evil. For me, the cross provides a means of restoration and forgiveness for those who are penitent; God alone will judge and deal with unrepentant murderers. Is there not, however, *some* element of bi-directionality of the atonement: God making amends for those who have suffered as a result of natural evil and moral evil by dealing with this on our behalf and offering us blissful immortality, and in so doing *also* performs an act of penitence?

An experience of abandonment by God, as Jesus experienced, is a common human reaction when evil and suffering are experienced within an otherwise "good", even beautiful Creation. Were Creation generally other than a source of joy and beauty then belief in a benevolent Creator would surely be impossible. Job relented (42:1-6) and was crushed, humiliated and defeated in the face of a powerful God. God is otherwise silent and humiliates Job by pointing out who the Creator is.[239] Bauckham summarizes the situation: "God puts Job in his place".[240] Yet could this humiliation *really* have led to the "deep spiritual joy" that Gutiérrez interprets in this text?[241] Atkinson describes how the experience of Job—"a seemingly harsh and unfeeling perspective—can lead us to worship".[242] Bauckham also looks for the "good" in the "bad":

> For Job to realize his true position in the scheme of things is painful, but the pain is the sort of pain that can be necessary for effective healing.[243]

These somewhat paradoxical responses are reminiscent of the Stockholm syndrome, a psychopathology in which a captive finds a coping strategy

---

[239] Atkinson, *Renewing the Face of the Earth*, p. 56.
[240] Bauckham, *Bible and Ecology*, p. 39.
[241] Gutiérrez, *On Job*, p. 12.
[242] Atkinson, *Renewing the Face of the Earth*, p. 57.
[243] Bauckham, *Bible and Ecology*, p. 45.

for dealing with imprisonment by forming an emotional bond with their captors. It may be that for some there is "faith that God can bring a greater good even out of the most devastating pain",[244] but for many such a "pastoral" answer to suffering rings hollow in the aftermath of a tsunami, lethal viral epidemics, or other manifestations of natural evil.

There is a notion that suffering should be accepted because there is an apparent acceptance of suffering that has roots in the Old Testament, the belief that "God's ways are higher than our ways". Such "higher" ways could represent a "lower" morality than our own. Peterson asks: "How can we love such a God and how was our more compassionate moral sense created?"[245] It could be said that this is a repugnant[246] argument that places God's morality lower than our own. It is also flawed since it defies logic, for how was our seemingly more compassionate moral sense created? The passage sometimes quoted from Isaiah to "support" this view does no such thing:

> Let the wicked forsake their way, and the unrighteous their thoughts; let them return to the Lord, that he may have mercy on them, and to our God, for he will abundantly pardon. For my thoughts are not your thoughts, nor are your ways my ways, says the Lord. For as the heavens are higher than the earth, so are my ways higher than your ways and my thoughts than your thoughts. (Isaiah 55:7-9)

Isaiah is claiming that God's ability to pardon the wicked exceeds human imagination; Isaiah is not claiming that there is a mysterious "higher" morality that provides an adequate explanation for suffering and evil.

The "goodness" of suffering has roots in the New Testament:

> And not only that, but we also boast in our sufferings, knowing that suffering produces endurance, and endurance produces

---

[244] Atkinson, *Renewing the Face of the Earth*, p. 57.
[245] Peterson et al., *Reason and Religious Belief*, p. 141.
[246] I feel righteously indignant when it is suggested that the God whom I worship has a lower moral standard than that which human beings can achieve.

character, and character produces hope, and hope does not disappoint us, because God's love has been poured into our hearts through the Holy Spirit that has been given to us. (Romans 5:3–5)

Paul presumably felt he deserved to be punished on account of his persecution of Christians prior to his conversion, and also wished to be "identified" with the sufferings of Christ. Whilst suffering may have helped a remarkable person like Paul in his journey of faith as his past beliefs were discarded as he placed his trust in the New Covenant, they are hardly applicable in most cases of suffering and bereavement.

The notion that a benevolent and loving God deliberately inflicts suffering for the purposes of a greater good is rejected; it is the antithesis of what is proposed. Evil and suffering exist but not because they were deliberately created by God, but because they are a necessary consequence of the sinfulness that resulted from human free will.

In 1972, Archbishop Michael Ramsey told people to accept the judgement of Almighty God who inflicted punishment upon sinful people. In 1974, Jürgen Moltmann called us to abandon our protest and look into the face of the crucified and risen God who suffered and died for us. Jesus' death was no cosmic act of sympathy to make humankind feel better about what it had been given by God in this mortal life, but a precursor, a *sine qua non*, for an opportunity for eternal life that transcends death itself. In 1991, Wolfhart Pannenberg was able to write of the "old problem of theodicy" that was apparently resolved by stating that something more is required, namely the redemption and final salvation of creatures.[247]

Whilst it is surely true, however, that hope in a better life after death must help to alleviate those who are suffering or grieving now, if the "old problem of theodicy" has its resolution in an eternal life then does it not follow that it is only proper that we reserve drawing any conclusions about suffering and justice until either we, or those that do, arrive in Heaven?

---

[247] Pannenberg, *Introduction to Systematic Theology*, p. 12.

When discussing the question of "Why do bad things happen?", I was told by a bishop that he pointed people in the direction of the wounds of the risen Christ. In my role as a minister, this is a concept that I use because this may offer comfort to believers who can know that God understands what it feels like to suffer because God has experienced suffering, and that their suffering does not mean that they are abandoned by God. An atheist philosopher might ask: "How do we accept that God allows a person to be afflicted on the basis that God also afflicted God's own Son?" This is not a matter that two "wrongs" make a perverted "right" in the Divine economy, but that if we identify with and share Christ's suffering we might also share in an eternal resurrected life.

Summary

The logical problem of evil arises when attempting to reconcile (1) that an omnipotent, omniscient, perfectly good God exists with (2) the evil that exists in the world. The problem arises if certain definitions of "omnipotent, omniscient and perfectly good" are chosen, and they *can* be chosen (with prejudice) to ensure inconsistency. The main supposition is that humans are entitled to live eternally in a perfect world. "The theistic defender must show that both claims (1) & (2) can be true, though he need not show that they are in fact true."[248] There is a "requisite statement" needed to link (1) and (2): "God is omnipotent, and it was not within his power to create a world containing moral good but no moral evil."[249] I have provided such a requisite statement: that God's Holiness, whilst granting authentic free will to human beings, prevented God from being able to foresee the extent or even the occurrence of human evil: thus God's Holiness limited God's omniscience. It has been stated that some things are impossible even for God to achieve, for example making a planet that is both cuboidal and spherical, and there may be circumstances in which God cannot be all-powerful, all-knowing and all-loving, particularly if

---

[248] Peterson et al., *Reason and Religious Belief*, p. 130, quotation in this text from Alvin Plantinga.

[249] Peterson et al., *Reason and Religious Belief*, p. 131.

being all-loving requires that humanity possesses its freedom to love, and in so doing exercises a potential to cause pain to humanity's Creator, the God who loves and therefore suffers. "The Free Will Defender insists that God cannot determine the actions of free persons."[250] Is this not the ordinary experience that constitutes a properly basic belief? Paul (in Romans 7:19) wrote candidly and concisely about his knowing the right and the wrong and sometimes deliberately choosing to do wrong: "For I do not do the good I want, but the evil I do not want is what I do." The non-deterministic physics within the cosmos disables God from being able to consistently and precisely determine the actions of free persons.

I have described a cosmos in which random occurrences are necessary parts of the created order. I have described how the malign consequences of human free will may not have been foreseeable by a Holy God. I propose that I have demonstrated adequate reasons why moral and natural evil exist.

---

[250] Peterson et al., *Reason and Religious Belief*, p. 132.

4

How might God act in the cosmos?

> For as the rain and the snow come down from heaven, and do not return there until they have watered the earth, making it bring forth and sprout, giving seed to the sower and bread to the eater, so shall my word be that goes out from my mouth; it shall not return to me empty, but it shall accomplish that which I purpose, and succeed in the thing for which I sent it. (Isaiah 55:10–11)

The predictable deterministic (Newtonian) physics gives order and structure to the cosmos, and God ensures our mortality in a non-prejudicial manner by ordering the cosmos with a "deeper" physics: the non-predictable, non-deterministic (quantum) physics that produce random effects in the cosmos. Such a random quality means that misfortune can be distributed in a non-prejudicial manner. Chaos theory and statistical clustering explain how random events, whilst being distributed in a sporadic manner, can produce extreme events. Deterministic order and non-deterministic factors facilitate creative processes.

Physics: Theological reflections

Newtonian physics (specifically Newton's mechanics) had led to a description of a cosmos in which the course or outcome of events was fully predictable, and such a cosmos in which events could also be considered to have been predetermined by a Creator who had set up such a cosmos fitted well with theologies such as the predestination of "Calvinism". I have placed Calvinism in inverted commas to denote a predeterministic understanding of God that is in common usage, although it does not accurately portray the theology of John Calvin himself.[1]

When quantum theory and quantum mechanics first entered into public debate, they were adopted by Eastern mysticism such as Daoism and similar theosophical belief collections because the new physics described a cosmos that was uncertain, in which "nothing is real". It was partly as a reaction to this assimilation of quantum theory by Eastern mysticism that Gribbin wrote *In Search of Schrödinger's Cat*.[2]

The adoption of quantum theory by Eastern mysticism may be the reason that Christian theologians were relatively late to examine the interface between their understanding of God and the new physics. In 2007, the physicist and theologian John Polkinghorne published *Quantum Physics and Theology: An Unexpected Kinship*. In Chapter 2, "Comparative Heuristics", Polkinghorne noted the similarity between the "subtle and creative interaction between experience and conceptual analysis"[3] in both physics and theology particularly as the new understanding of physics came to rely upon theoretical ideas and thought experiments rather than a sole reliance upon the interpretation

---

[1] "Pre-destination is not a common phrase in Calvin's Institutes (there are a few references in the index, but not nearly as many as 'love' or 'grace'). It does not, I believe, really mean determinism in the philosophical sense. I think in Calvin it is not so much a word about God's (unfair) decrees, as a word about Christian experience. Calvin wanted Christians to be assured, confident and joyous in their faith, and God's decree was a doctrine of comfort and assurance. I do not have to try to save myself: everything is from God's call, God's grace and God's spirit. I think it is a doctrine to liberate believers from insecurity. I find it regrettable that the term 'Calvinist' is used very often these days to describe a view of God as inscrutable, cruel, detached, deterministic—which may have been the view of some of Calvin's followers—whereas I don't at all think that is Calvin's view of God." Personal communication from Bishop David Atkinson.

[2] J. Gribbin, *In Search of Schrödinger's Cat* (London: Transworld Publishers, 1984), pp. 8 and 16.

[3] J. Polkinghorne, *Quantum Physics and Theology: An Unexpected Kinship* (London: SPCK, 2007), p. 25.

of data obtained in a laboratory, although such data is essential for the verification of theoretical ideas in the physical sciences. A parallel in theology was claimed, for example, in the study of Christology, in which there is interplay between the "objectivity" in the search for the historical Jesus and the "subjectivity" of the "experience of the very early Church".[4]

In order to reflect theologically from a Christian understanding on the impact of quantum theory on theological understanding of the universe, and in particular the question of theodicy, an historical perspective may be helpful.

Laplace's "demon"

In 1814, almost a century before the emergence of quantum theory and the description of quantum phenomena, the French mathematician and physicist Pierre-Simon Laplace proposed a "demon" in which if there were sufficient computational power, then measurement of how things are placed at one point in time could be used to calculate both the exact sequence of events leading to that point in time, and also predict the sequence and outcome of all future events. This "demon" was described at a time when all physics was classical: "classical physics is deterministic and leaves no place for human free will or chance".[5] Thus there would be no opportunity for human intervention to affect outcomes. The "infinite accuracy needed for the total predictability that *Laplace* assured us was possible"[6] may have been considered to be a possibility in Laplace's era. However, as in Berry's calculations, if an electron placed at the edge of the cosmos may affect the course of a game of billiards, then so most certainly would such a computational machine affect the outcomes that it was attempting to predict. Thus, acquiring the "infinite accuracy" seems unattainable, even if Laplace himself was certain that his "demon" would function accurately. The Heisenberg Uncertainty Principle that states "it is impossible to measure precisely certain pairs of properties,

---

[4] Polkinghorne, *Quantum Physics and Theology*, p. 27; see also Barth versus the "undertaker-scholars" on p. 159.
[5] Gribbin, *In Search of Schrödinger's Cat*, p. 27.
[6] Peacocke, *Theology for a Scientific Age*, p. 48.

including position/momentum, simultaneously"[7] might also render this computation an impossibility, even if God were to attempt to use such a machine. Hawking, in *A Brief History of Time*, stated: "the uncertainty principle signalled an end to Laplace's dream of a theory of science, a model of the cosmos that would be completely deterministic".[8] As well as signalling an end to a completely deterministic cosmos, that included a deterministic approach to human behaviour,[9] the uncertainty principle also removed the basis of Marxist scientific determinism.[10]

Peacocke dismissed Laplace's demon, but on uncertain grounds: Laplace specified that sufficient computational power was required, and Peacocke thought such computational power was improbable.[11] However, the improbable is not the same as impossible for an omnipotent Creator. Nevertheless, as "Quantum Theory cuts free from the determinacy of classical ideas", Laplace's demon, even if operated by God, assuming God would wish to, would seem an impossibility, since "we cannot know the position and momentum of even one particle precisely".[12]

Even if such a "computational machine" was not part of the cosmos in which we exist, the "supply of information", through whatever means, would have to interact in an unimaginable way with our cosmos, and therefore Heisenberg Uncertainty, which may be likened to an extreme form of observer effect[13], would be manifest. The gravitational effects of such interactions would also affect what was being measured.

The demonic quality of the mechanical nature of the cosmos that it describes arises from the assumption that it has within it no place for human free will; the cosmos becomes an object of "clockwork", and the Creator becomes a passive observer as the mechanism unwinds. Even if it is accepted that the cosmos unfolds according to the path set by its

---

[7] Gribbin, *In Search of Schrödinger's Cat*, p. 161.
[8] S. Hawking, *A Brief History of Time* (London: Bantam Books, 1988), p. 63.
[9] Hawking, *A Brief History of Time*, p. 61.
[10] Hawking, *A Brief History of Time*, p. 59.
[11] Peacocke, *Theology for a Scientific Age*, p. 48.
[12] Gribbin, *In Search of Schrödinger's Cat*, p. 207.
[13] Observer effect occurs when the activity of observation alters that which is being observed.

creator, there would be something "demonic" in the nature of such a creator that had created beings such that their perception of free will was an illusion.

In the twentieth century, the theories of Einstein, that were a development of classical physics inasmuch as that they did not incorporate quantum theory in any form, were adopted by moral philosophers to produce a relativistic morality. The term relativistic is derived from relativisticism and not from relativism.[14] Relativistic morality proposed a cosmos of entire predictability as people and other objects moved through space but also from one time frame to another, leading to the notion of "over then". In this relativistic mode of thinking, time was likened to one of the three spatial dimensions (height, width and depth) with which we are more familiar; relativistic morality depends upon the acceptance that time is one of the four dimensions in the space–time continuum. The past was considered to be as real as the present or the future; just as places that are separated by space are equally "real", then so are spaces that are separated by time. The dead were not to be mourned inasmuch as "their" past was as real as "our" present. Since there is neither moral responsibility nor *moral* consequences of people thus described who move through time on an inevitable path, as such relativistic *amorality* may be a better term. The humans who populate such a cosmos were thought to be no more than puppets that follow a predetermined "script". It is noteworthy that there is an expected contrast between relativistic morality that is driven by inevitable causality and quantum theory that is characterized by a lack of causality.

If the cosmos, conversely, is purely that of "quantum" unpredictability, then within this cosmos is a "monster": a creator who watches the cosmos unravel in a random manner whilst observing dispassionately, if at all. To regard such a "monster" to be a loving creator is almost as impossible as regarding the creator of a cosmos fitted with Laplace's demon to be a loving creator. If the cosmos does exist as a sequence of relativistic timeframes, the "over then" as described, then it is theologically possible

---

[14] Relativism is defined as "the doctrine that knowledge, truth, and morality exist in relation to culture, society, or historical context, and are not absolute" (OED).

that God creates and sustains each timeframe that has passed as God transcends past time, with a perfect memory. God would, however, nevertheless have to wait for the future to happen just as we do on account of the random element inherent in the modus operandi of the cosmos, and the consequences of human free will. The unknowingness of God does mean that if God travels through our time with us and experiences things as they happen, then God can truly grieve when tragic events happen. As a pastoral example, could God honestly share the joy of an event such as a marriage whilst knowing that the two persons who were being married were soon to meet an untimely end? This does not deny the idea that God prescribes the ultimate destiny of the cosmos. For some, the unfolding of a "script" that God has planned in every detail may offer comfort; others will find comfort in believing in a "greater" God who can achieve God's purposes through a myriad of possibilities.

If the gravitational effect of an electron placed at the edge of the cosmos can affect a game of billiards, and if the behaviour of sub-atomic particles has a random function such as the "quantum leaps" as an electron moves from one shell to another, or at the atomic level the massive effect of random nuclear decay, then the non-random, purely deterministic cosmos as described by pure classical physics, even when refined by Einstein, cannot exist since it is affected by the random behaviour of its constituent particles.

The quantum mechanical description of the cosmos, that seems to have an inherent random quality, also has a deterministic, even "superdeterministic", interpretation. For example, rather than being a random event, the exact time in which each atomic nucleus in a sample of radioactive matter decays may simply reflect the age of formation of that particular atom or some other as yet unidentified or measurable property. The table of Standard Model of Elementary Particles may one day be simplified, or even made more complex, such that the particles no longer behave in an unpredictable manner. If it is postulated that the Creator monitors and controls the entire cosmos such that only one predetermined script is followed, it has to be asked why then would a Creator pursue such an objective when it would seem that the creation of free will in human beings, that produced the possibility of authentic love, was the primary reason for the creation of human beings. Quantum indeterminacy would render the future unknowable, perhaps even for God. Similarly, what is now in the past would have been unknowable at the time, since it would be the future when "looked forward to" at an even earlier point in time.

A mixed model: laws and chaos

A model of the physical cosmos which has the characteristics of both the determined and the non-determined is now to be assumed. It is possible that such a mixture of the determined and the non-determined may be the only cosmos suitable for human inhabitation. The former classical "Laws of Nature" give structure and predictability in what would otherwise be utter chaos. The unpredictable non-deterministic element within the cosmos provides part of the answer to the problem of why there may be harmful things present that are not directly intended by the Creator, although it is to be noted that the notion of allowing harm to exist non-intentionally is no defence for an omnipotent and omniscient Creator. The inclusion of the unpredictable may form part of the answer as to how suffering comes into being and also may explain the reason for the apparently random distribution of harmful natural phenomena, such as disease, "untimely" or "premature" death, degeneration and disaster. It is assumed that death that occurs with minimal suffering at the end of normal life expectancy is acceptable, for without such death occurring new life would not be possible on a planet with limited resources.

If it is accepted that God has seemingly allowed both the determined and the non-determined to play their part in the Creation of the cosmos, then this also implies that both are part of the means by which humans are created and therefore all people, irrespective of their gender, orientation, sexual identity, ethnicity, predisposition to disease, inherited illnesses, abilities and neurotypicality or otherwise, are of equal worth to God. It is no longer possible to claim that God loves any "type" of person less than others since such variation is produced by non-predetermined processes. That God has created a cosmos that enables the existence of human beings with such a wide spectrum of variability of features suggests that

God has not intended a particular perfect form.[15] If it were to be decided that God holds an ideal of such perfection, and merely tolerates the "less-than-perfect", then this would imply that all others are of lesser value, and that God was prejudiced against such "variants". Jesus Christ, whose example and teaching is surely the basis of proper Christian faith, was as welcoming to all people as was possible within the constraints of the danger-laden society in which he lived and did not appear to place a lesser value on any of the people he encountered. For example, Jesus' encounter when he healed the daughter of a Syrophoenician woman, who was noted in Mark 7:26 to be "a Gentile", would have been seen to be controversial at the time, but nevertheless Jesus "took the risk".

The random element that is part of the physical "fabric" of the cosmos leads to the conclusion that, if created by God, then God abides with the outcomes of random and chaotic processes. Accepting that it is necessary for God to do this enables humankind to proclaim that the love of God does exist in a Creation in which there is human freedom, joy, creativity and beauty but also suffering and animal and human mortality. It is possible to believe that God can also truly love humankind because humankind exists in what *could* be the best possible world given the two necessities of moral evil that is a by-product of human freedom and the natural evil that is necessary to ensure mortality and to mitigate the effects of moral evil. Whether the cosmos is founded upon probabilities or certainties, for God to continually override the structure of the cosmos would render the cosmos illusory for any sentient beings living within it, and effectively deny humankind the ability to exercise free will. To quote the theologian Martin Buber, God "deals with us in ways that respect our personal freedom and responsibility".[16] For Luther and Pascal, the hidden God, *deus absconditus*, preserves human freedom.[17] Another theologian, Austin Farrer, went further: if universally applied "divine intervention

---

[15] For clarity, I am contrasting the perfect with the imperfect, rather than the perfect versus Plato's shadows cast by the perfect forms.

[16] J. H. Hick, *Philosophy of Religion*, 2nd edn (Hoboken, NJ: Prentice-Hall, 1973), p. 10.

[17] Hick, *Philosophy of Religion*, p. 63.

to alleviate suffering would lead to a world deprived of physicality",[18] and therefore such interventions would be a bar to the very existence of the physical cosmos as we know it. This supports the statement that humankind, in its current form, exists in what could be the best possible world.

A cosmos free of all suffering where "death will be no more; mourning and crying and pain will be no more, for the first things have passed away" (Revelation 21:4), and the relationship between this new Creation and the cosmos as it is now, is discussed in the final chapter.

Those who pray to God do so in the belief that God can, and does, intervene in the cosmos that God has created by the exercise of *occasional* intervention within the causal nexus, even if such interventions are open to non-Theistic interpretation. I have used the term intervention in this context to denote a surprising, unexpected or otherwise remarkable occurrence, usually of a beneficial nature. It is to be emphasized that my understanding of such "interventions" is that they occur within a cosmos in which God is present always and everywhere: God is not "only" the Creator but also the Sustainer of the cosmos. That is the full meaning of the Incarnation. For those who pray it can be helpful to imagine God *not* as a person who is distanced physically—"up in Heaven"—but, as Tillich described, God is more than this and is the "infinite and inexhaustible depth and ground of all being",[19] and this image fits better with God acting through a causal nexus rather than God being imagined as an aloof manipulator or cosmic puppeteer.

Since humankind has seemingly prayed to gods and God since the emergence of cultured "pre-humans", it is not possible to determine scientifically if prayer works. To determine if prayer works then another "half" of the controlled experiment, in which the sentient beings on a planet such as Earth have never prayed, would need to be discovered to provide the control conditions against which a valid scientific comparison could be made. If God were to be made the subject of a

---

[18] C. Southgate, *The Groaning of Creation* (Louisville, KY: Westminster John Knox Press, 2008), p. 75.

[19] P. Tillich, *The Shaking of the Foundations* (London: SCM Press, 1949), p. 57, in Pannenberg, *Introduction to Systematic Theology*, p. 25.

selective prayer experiment, then any data that was obtained might not be reliable since God might not allow Godself to be thus tested. It is a matter of pure conjecture to consider what would happen to the causal nexus of the cosmos, with its physical laws and the chaotic elements within it, together with the mysterious forces that move matter and distort time and space, if no single person had ever prayed to the God who created it, but fascinating nevertheless.

On an individual level, whilst there are some who believe that through prayer God was responsible for a miraculous cure or escape from danger, there are sadly many for whom there was no such beneficial outcome to their prayer. I am minded of the impact of the *Shoah* upon human belief in a powerful and benevolent God. Surely many of those who were murdered had prayed for deliverance. Even those who only saw the acts of God in the broad sweep of history rather than at a personal level would have had any understanding of God with power without limit swept away. I am proposing that the ultimate quality of God that limits God's power in this mortal life is God's Holiness: as such God would have wept with those who suffered and died.

If the cosmos was completely random, then it would not be possible for God to act in such a cosmos in a meaningful manner because the result of such interventions would be unknowable, possibly even for God. If the cosmos was completely predictable, then it would not be possible for God to act in such a cosmos without all such interventions being clearly identifiable to any present observers, and observing such interventions would deny such observers the free choice between either accepting God or else rejecting God. It would seem that a mixed model of the cosmos is an essential requirement for a suitable world in which creatures can live with freedom to chose or reject God, and also provides the conditions for God to act within the cosmos.

Theology of nature

Miracles
A Christian theological description of the cosmos would be incomplete without some reference to the Incarnation and Resurrection of Jesus, the

basis of the "Easter" faith. Such events are special cases of miracles. Hick stated: "if a miracle is defined as a breach of natural law, one can declare a priori that there are no miracles".[20] This is another way of stating that natural laws cannot be breached or broken. We have no explanation of how the four forces (strong and weak nuclear, electromagnetic and gravitational) arise, and if it is believed that a creator God not only made the cosmos but also sustains the cosmos by ensuring that laws and natural forces are consistently applied, then a believer only has to believe that such consistent applications are occasionally withheld to be able to believe that miracles can occur. For if such laws should owe their existence to a Creator, could not the Creator also suspend the law? For a Christian to believe in the Resurrection of Jesus is to believe that a miracle occurred, and there would seem to be no reason why God should restrict Godself to one miracle only.

Peacocke objected to miracles on the grounds that God is required to be consistent,[21] but who (or what) has the authority to require that God should be consistent? The God of the Hebraic–Christian tradition is full of surprises and innovation. The history of the Hebrew people recorded in their Bible lists three covenants: the Noahide, Abrahamic and Mosaic. A "consistent" god would surely have made just the one covenant. Peacocke defined a miracle as an event "not fully explicable by naturalistic means",[22] and if so, then we are immersed in miracles because much of science is a description rather than an explanation for which I have already given examples. The "force" of gravity, when it causes objects to fall, is commonplace and almost passes unnoticed, but when the force is seen to move objects sideways, for example as mercury droplets coalesce on a flat level surface, for some observers it acquires a mysterious quality that verges on the miraculous.

If I was standing on the North Pole of the moon and I had an exceptionally good camera, then I could take a picture of an Arctic explorer standing on the North Pole of the Earth. I could then point

---

[20] Hick, *Philosophy of Religion*, p. 46.

[21] A. Peacocke, *Theology for a Scientific Age: Being and Becoming—Natural, Divine, and Human* (Minneapolis, MN: Fortress Press, 1993), p. 269.

[22] Peacocke, *Theology for a Scientific Age*, p. 270.

my camera a little lower and take a very similar picture of an Antarctic explorer standing on the South Pole of the Earth, except that the explorer would appear completely "upside down". I could then point my camera at the edge of the Earth at the equator and take a picture of a giraffe, except that the giraffe, the horizon and all other objects would appear rotated through a right angle and appear "sideways". The giraffe photograph would be technically more difficult since whilst in the case of all three photographs the Earth, as it orbits the sun, would be moving at 66,600mph (fortunately the moon also orbits the sun at this average speed and always, rather curiously, "points" the one side towards the Earth), in the polar pictures the subjects would complete one rotation every 24 hours, yet the equatorially placed giraffe would be moving either towards me or away from me at 1,040mph.

Al-Khalili's book *Life on the Edge* describes "spooky" quantum effects such as tunnelling, superposition and the Einstein-Podolsky-Rosen effect or "spooky action at a distance".[23] These are not easily observable yet how would the effects of magnetism or static electricity be regarded if they were viewed for the first time? I recall my childhood fascination after I had been introduced to magnets and later to the electrostatic phenomena produced by a Van de Graaff generator such as floating hair and miniature lightning.[24]

Magnets that can be made to "float" in the air and the phenomena of super-conductivity and super-fluidity have similar "unnatural" qualities when observed. Nor has science explained the profound effects of art, music and transcendental experience: for some they might be perceived to be miraculous too. It might be concluded that the Creator can intervene in what the Creator has created, and that we are so immersed in the miraculous that when phenomena occur as a consequence of natural forces, their appearance has lost the element of surprise.

---

[23] J. Al-Khalili and J. McFadden, *Life on the Edge: A Coming of Age of Quantum Biology* (London: Black Swan, 2014), p. 46.

[24] For example, see <https://en.wikipedia.org/wiki/Van_de_Graaff_generator> (accessed 17 July 2023) for a photograph of a woman touching a Van de Graaff generator at the American Museum of Science and Energy. The charged strands of hair repel each other and stand out from her head.

I am not claiming that miracles exist and therefore so does God. I am, however, pointing to the miraculous nature of the cosmos. It is for each individual to decide if the cosmos points to a creator, or if it is easier to accept that the cosmos somehow created itself. From a philosophical perspective, there is no definitive answer. Whilst "[Theists] want to expand the definition [of a miracle] to cover any event in relation to which God can be viewed as having directly manipulated the natural order, regardless of anyone's ability to construct plausible alternate causal scenarios"[25] and also "might maintain that unless it can be shown that a given occurrence is not a direct act of God, they are justified in claiming that it is",[26] atheists (naturally) might wish to challenge these statements. The philosophical argument is barren, however, since "few philosophers today maintain that the existence of a supernatural being, or the ability of such a being (if it exists) to intervene, can be demonstrated to be impossible".[27]

It cannot be proven that other "plausible alternate causal scenarios" will never be constructed to *explain* the four forces, and other features of the cosmos. Even if this were to be achieved, then the definition given of a miracle will still be valid, and proving that a miracle could never happen might arguably be even more challenging. The improbability of the cosmos existing at all, and its alone having living things within it, is so unlikely that it could be regarded to be as providential and miraculous as the most unlikely scenario that the human imagination can create.

Given the tendency of materials to become distributed randomly, it is remarkable that in one part of the cosmos there exists a place where the diversity necessary for life to be sustained should exist at all. The place is the Earth: "a place in our solar system where the basic ingredients that make up rocks and stones have been brought together in such a variety of forms, functions and chemistry that just one gram of the resulting

---

[25] M. Peterson et al., *Reason and Religious Belief*, 3rd edn (Oxford: Oxford University Press, 2003), p. 175.
[26] Peterson et al., *Reason and Religious Belief*, p. 184.
[27] Peterson et al., *Reason and Religious Belief*, p. 176. This is discussed further in Peterson, Chapter 5: "Theistic Arguments: Is there a case for God's existence?"

material exceeds in diversity all the matter found elsewhere in the known universe".[28]

Theology and science

Whilst Polkinghorne (2007) had discussed the interface between quantum physics and theology, earlier books, such as Arthur Peacocke's *Theology for a Scientific Age* (1993), had commented upon the interface between theology and science. There are numerous definitions for theology. Translation from the Greek origins of the word reveals the study (λόγος, *logos*) of God (θεός, *theos*). Theology, in the Hebraic–Christian tradition, is not to be constructed; it is to be discovered through the contemplation of and response to God's self-revelation and Incarnation. Whilst theology might be inspired by or derived from e.g. Black, feminist or liberation perspectives, these are attempts to understand God in a way that can be more easily understood from the particular experiences of particular groups of people. Whilst it is self-evidently right that theology can be written *for* a particular group of people in the sense that they can easily identify with the language and concepts that are used, there is a danger that the theology makes the Procrustean error of appeasing the audience. Having the "aim of constructing a theology believable in a scientific age",[29] Peacocke goes beyond making a theology that contains concepts with which a scientific readership might be familiar, and abandons orthodox theology in order that, presumably, such a reduced version is easier for scientists to believe.

Peacocke implies in his title that there is (or once was) a "scientific age", and whilst such an age may have occurred in the imagination of some people, to write a theology for a scientific age is no more reasonable or acceptable than those written to appeal to, for example, legalistic or materially driven ages. Rather than understanding God from a scientific perspective, Peacocke seems to be using science to create a new theology the essence of which is that God created the world, that humans evolved by the purely natural processes of "chance" operating within "law", and that through the "Christ-event", namely the resurrection of Jesus, humankind

---

[28] Al-Khalili and McFadden, *Life on the Edge*, p. 43.
[29] Peacocke, *Theology for a Scientific Age*, p. 271.

will be able to attain its final destiny by becoming fully evolved into persons who are in full communion with God. Peacocke seems to have discarded much of the "traditional" Christian understanding of the nature of humankind and the relationship that God has with God's people.

Monoliths and paradigms

Dictionaries contain numerous definitions for monolith, and in this book a monolith can be likened to a massive tablet of stone engraved with a series of statements. To use the word monolith to describe God suggests an intransigent and impersonal nature that has no internal contradictions. It is not likely that God could be written about in this way by a human being with human limitations, since to understand God in God's fullness would require such a being to be the intellectual equal of God and would also require the language to express such a monolith. There is, in contrast, no one description of God within Scripture. The Hebrew Bible and New Testament have a spectrum of views, and there are apparent inconsistencies. For example, in Luke is a parable of Jesus in which God, likened to the "Good Shepherd", actively *seeks* the "lost" who are likened to lost sheep (15:3–7). Four verses later is another parable (15:11–32) that is known traditionally as the parable of the "Prodigal Son", in which God, who in this parable is likened to the "Forgiving Father", *waits* for his lost son to return to the family's home. Whilst some may believe that the Bible is perfect, and that it is the intrinsically sinful nature of humanity that leads readers to conclude that there are contradictions and inconsistencies, a response is that to claim that a work of human authorship attains such perfection is idolatrous, even if the writing is wholly inspired by God. Those who are Christians are called to obey Jesus' command to worship God with our minds, and this will mean deciding how best to use the rich inheritance of the Scriptures, and also to understand God as a person too complex for a simple description. The command in Mark 12:30 is "you shall love the Lord your God with all your heart, and with all your soul, and with all your *mind*, and with all your strength" (author's emphasis).

Theology will therefore, of necessity, include ideas that are in tension, and thus may be unpalatable to the scientist or pure philosopher seeking a unified "truth". Humankind meets the Hebraic–Christian God on an intellectual level as a paradigm and not as a monolith. Whilst dictionaries contain numerous definitions for paradigm, a paradigm is understood in this book to be a collection of statements that form a description that may contain internal inconsistencies. Examples already given are four tensions within evolutionary theory, the incompatibilities of gravitational theory and quantum theory[30] and the parables of Jesus. A paradigmatic description of God may hold such inconsistencies that are unresolvable by the human mind but may be resolvable by the divine intellect since God is not limited by the human imagination or intellect. Accepting the description of God as a paradigm rather than a monolith is more consonant with the belief that God is a person rather than a machine.

The modus operandi of God
It might be argued that St Paul knew and accepted the resurrection of Jesus and used this to transform his religious understandings that were dominated by the belief that God demanded sacrifice to atone for human failings. For Peacocke, the risen Jesus is the "Christ-event" that transforms a world view that is dominated by science by (only) completing a path that enables naturally evolved humankind to come into the presence of God. Peacocke makes an Ebionitist[31] assertion with an attempt to characterize the dual nature of Jesus as the human "mechanism" of Jesus that had been perfectly informed by God.[32] This assertion also denies the principle of *kenosis* that would have limited such perfection.

If, for Peacocke, faith is centred in the "Christ-event", then this faith is, by definition, recognizably Christian. That Peacocke suggests that the

---

[30] "In physics it may be necessary to use different formulations in different situations, but two different formulations would agree in situations where they both can be applied. The whole collection of different formulations could be regarded as a complete unified theory, though one that could not be expressed in terms of a single set of postulates." Hawking, *A Brief History of Time*, pp. 200–1.

[31] Ebionitism: "An early Christological heresy, which treated Jesus as a purely human figure". A. E. McGrath, *The Christian Theology Reader*, 2nd edn (Oxford: Blackwell, 2001), p. 582.

[32] Peacocke, *Theology for a Scientific Age*, pp. 298–9.

theology of this faith can be rewritten for the Scientific Age is derived from an approach to theology that is overly reliant upon human reason. Peacocke states that the "search for meaning characterizes religion".[33] But do most people search for such meaning? Perhaps academics in many disciplines do; it is more common experience in Christian ministry to find that most seek *relationships* with each other and their Creator. To state that "belief bears only a distant genetic relation to what was believed a millennium ago"[34] denies the historical roots of two sources of the Christian religion, namely Scripture and tradition. Whilst Peacocke describes a fluid theology, his attitude seems to be that scientific "truth" is everlasting such that "new perceptions are *irreversibly* established".[35] This is an error that some scientists have made, for example Einstein, who believed his theories to be unsurpassable and thus found it difficult to accept quantum theory. Newton, however, was aware of his place in the progression of science as he likened his contribution to one who stood on the "shoulders of giants"[36] and presumably anticipated that he would provide the beginning of another theory that would surpass his own. If scientific truths are surpassable, then, since we do not know what may be surpassed, we cannot say for certainty if a claim made through science is a scientific "truth". For the purposes of discussion, it will, however, be assumed that there are scientific truths even though they may be surpassed.

For Pannenberg (1991), "the story of Jesus has to be history, not in all its details, but in its core, if the Christian faith is to continue".[37] If the Christian faith is ultimately rooted in the person of Jesus Christ and if it is assumed that the record of events surrounding Jesus' ministry, teaching, example, life, death and resurrection are historically accurate, then if

---

[33] Peacocke, *Theology for a Scientific Age*, p. 5.
[34] Peacocke, *Theology for a Scientific Age*, p. viii.
[35] Peacocke, *Theology for a Scientific Age*, pp. viii–ix.
[36] I. Newton, *Letter from Sir Isaac Newton to Robert Hooke, in the Historical Society of Pennsylvania*, at <https://digitallibrary.hsp.org/index.php/Detail/objects/9792>, accessed 17 July 2023.
[37] W. Pannenberg, *An Introduction to Systematic Theology* (Grand Rapids, MI: Eerdmans, 1991), p. 5.

Christian faith is authentic it is to be expected that the new discoveries of science should fit in with this religious truth. This may be expressed another way: according to Bauckham, "these biblical beginnings and endings (of the meta-narrative) need not compete with our developing scientific knowledge of the universe".[38] Scientific knowledge may give some support to understandings that have biblical origin: "how might science inform theology" is an important part of this book.

For Moltmann, "Christian theology ... speaks about all reality and therefore must engage in critical dialogue with other interpretations of the world and human experience",[39] and for Pannenberg "coherence provides the final criterion of truth"[40] and proper coherence is interdisciplinary. Scientists, theologians and artists discover and then create theories to explain what has been revealed to them, and as such they may offer to God what they have created or discovered as an act of worship if they so choose.

Although *creatio ex nihilo*[41] is humanly unimaginable, other modes of God's action may be knowable, but only to an extent since trying to examine the world to determine *exactly* how God interacts in the world would involve "proving" the existence of God. Perhaps to the great annoyance of antagonists, it is frequently suggested that God has chosen to be able to be dismissed in order to preserve human free will, and that this free will is presumed to be a feature of humankind that is very important to God, as it is to humankind. Peacocke attempts to describe the one way in which God interacts with Creation.[42] Science may rejoice

---

[38] R. Bauckham, *Bible and Ecology: Rediscovering the Community of Creation* (London: Darton, Longman & Todd, 2010), p. 143.

[39] J. Moltmann, *Theology of Hope: On the Ground and the Implications of a Christian Eschatology*, tr. James W. Leitch (London: SCM Press, 1967), p. xvii that describes the function of Chapter 4.

[40] Pannenberg, *An Introduction to Systematic Theology*, p. 6.

[41] The doctrine of creation is based upon *creatio ex nihilo*. However, many creation mythologies speak of the creative process being the ordering of chaos; the mixed-mode model of the physical world suggests that order and chaos were created simultaneously.

[42] Peacocke, *Theology for a Scientific Age*, pp. 149–51.

in unifying theories, but could God ever be so reducible to be contained in the human imagination, however gifted some philosophers, scientists and theologians might be? Whilst it might be conceivable that a full understanding of God as a machine could be held within the human imagination, as seems to have been close to the metaphysical, philosophical understanding of the impassible god, the incarnate-revealed God of the Hebraic–Christian faith is believed to be a person with all the added complexities of having a "personality". This "God as person" nature of God suggests there might be more than one *modus operandi* in which God might interact with God's Creation, for even human mortals have the capacity to act in more than one way. Furthermore, the revealed God of the Hebraic–Christian tradition is not "monolithic" in form, but has been likened to a "faithful husband" (Hosea), the "good shepherd" (the Psalmist), the notion of "Sophia" being God's agent and expression within Creation (Wisdom) and, in the Christian tradition, the Incarnation of God in the person of Jesus Christ.[43] The incarnate-revealed God of the Christian faith is Triune: God is the Creator, immanent in the world, knowable through the cosmos that God has created and sustains. God "begets" the Son, becoming incarnate in the world, and in so doing fuses Heaven and Earth into one, the temporal and the eternal coexist. The Son spoke, and continues to speak to those who would listen, for example Jesus' exhortation in Matthew 13:9 "Let anyone with ears listen!" God is the Holy Spirit, present yet also transcendent in and from the world. God interacts with the human souls that inhabit those living on Earth in ways that are unknowable. Since Christian faith is rooted in God who is believed to be immanent, incarnate and transcendent, then it is surely possible for Christians to believe that God may act in the cosmos in more than one way.

God's activity in the world

The theologian and philosopher Owen Thomas, in his book (1983) *God's Activity in the World,* provides a classification of "how" in the question:

---

[43] Peacocke, *Theology for a Scientific Age*, p. 167.

"how does God act in the world?"[44] I have used Thomas' questions to critique Peacocke.

"By what means?"

Peacocke argues the case that there is a "top-down" causality in which processes that are seemingly dependent upon other processes are nevertheless able to influence such "lower" processes:

> Might we not properly regard the world-as-a-whole as a total system so that its general state can be a "top-down" causative factor in, or constraint upon, what goes on at the myriad levels that comprise it? I suggest that these new perceptions in the way that causality actually operates in our hierarchically complex world provide a new resource for thinking about how God could interact with that world.[45]

This theory of top-down causality, if applied to the relationship between God and the cosmos, hands the final say in how things are to God, despite, for example, the purely natural random processes that are cited in Peacocke to produce human beings, that according to orthodox Christian theology have in some way been created by God *to be* in God's image.

Peacocke asserts that God acts by being the source of an "input" of information,[46] yet has to concede that this has to be in the form of matter or energy because the cosmos is made of matter and energy.[47]

Yet there is a further problem with top-down causality based upon the philosophical concepts of cause and effect. As an analogy, how could it be possible that the higher levels of organic function, for example behaviour (or even consciousness itself), that are so dependent on the biochemical

---

[44] O. Thomas, *God's Activity in the World: The Contemporary Problem*, AAR Studies in Religion 31 (Chicago, IL: Scholars Press, 1983), pp. 234–5, cited in Peacocke, *Theology for a Scientific Age*, pp. 163–4. Italicized questions are from this text.
[45] Peacocke, *Theology for a Scientific Age*, p. 158.
[46] Peacocke, *Theology for a Scientific Age*, p. 161.
[47] Peacocke, *Theology for a Scientific Age*, p. 164.

components of that organism, can cause change in the constituents from which it is made? For a simple example, consider a man attempting to "will" himself sober after drinking an excess of alcohol. This illustrates well the conceptual problem with defining the "top". When sober, the man could decide to pour himself a succession of alcoholic drinks and having done this he would imbibe alcohol via the use of neural networks initiating limb movement and the swallowing reflex. Once in the brain the alcohol molecules would eventually have the upper hand as they render the man incapable of rational thought or coordinated movement by the effect of alcohol that inhibits most known cellular processes. The study of physiological reflexes (rather than chemical pathology) also demonstrates an interdependence rather than a top-down hierarchy, for example the reflexes that govern the level of thyroid hormone (thyroxine) in the blood. The hypothalamus, situated in the brain, senses the level of thyroxine and alters the level of thyroxine by producing different amounts of thyroid-stimulating hormone as in a negative-feedback loop. Yet is the hypothalamus controlling the thyroid, or is the thyroid using the hypothalamus as a functionary to achieve the purposes of the thyroid, namely to govern energy production and growth in the formative years of an animal? It is recognized that the hypothalamus has a primary role in the initiation of change, for example the onset of puberty. Biological systems seem to be of the form of interdependent components, for example the heart pumps blood to the thyroid gland and allows the thyroid tissue to function; the hormones the thyroid produces in turn affect heart (cardiac) function. Thus interdependence is a more fitting description of biological systems, and by analogy interdependence may be a better description of the relationship between the cosmos, that includes human beings, and the Creator.

There is the further question of by what means might God interact with human consciousness? This is difficult to answer if a person's consciousness and self-awareness is only and no more than a function of electrical and biochemical brain activity. In this scenario God would need to alter the biochemical and electrical make-up of the brain in order to interact with human consciousness. It is perhaps less problematic to accept that God communes with our souls in non-physical and supernatural ways through or with a non-physical consciousness in which consciousness and self-awareness are immanent within, "inhabiting" and using the electrical and biochemical function of the brain as a mechanism of expression. Accepting that the human soul is immanent in the human brain is conceptually similar to accepting that God is immanent in the cosmos. There is supportive evidence for this non-physical immanence in the beneficial experience of simply *being* with another person in an empathetic, but almost silent manner. This is well recognized in pastoral ministry, as is also the sense of peace or wellbeing that can enfold someone who is being prayed for.

Whilst Peacocke may have likened non-physical consciousness to a "dualistic mind and body belief"[48] that is to be rejected as a "ghost that haunts theological thinking",[49] it could be argued that this rejection is unwarranted since it is not currently explained how consciousness arises, and non-physical consciousness is not unproven. It is conceptually difficult to imagine how the ultimate in the subjective, i.e. consciousness, could be described scientifically when science is concerned with observing and drawing conclusions from the "objective". St Paul wrote: "Do you not know that you are God's temple and that God's Spirit dwells in you?" (1 Corinthians 3:16) If this is true, then it is difficult to accept Peacocke's assertion that "Christian anthropology has no vested interest in any form of vitalism",[50] unless the Holy Spirit is composed of physical matter.

Both quantum mechanics and the detailed examination and consideration of the cosmos as the deterministic entity that classical physics described, with the associated enormity of measurement and control in the latter for the cosmos to be fully predetermined, point to there being a substantial random element within the "fabric" of the cosmos. As such it would be possible for God to intervene in the cosmos with the insertion of energy or matter (being minded that God can create *ex nihilo*) in a manner that such interventions were either

---

[48] Dualistic is to be contrasted with dualism, in which one demi-God creates and sustains the good spirit world and the other demi-God creates the evil physical world.
[49] Peacocke, *Theology for a Scientific Age*, p. 139.
[50] Peacocke, *Theology for a Scientific Age*, p. 245.

markedly perceptible, for example the resurrection of Jesus, or else more "normally" imperceptible. If the "interventions" that God makes are infrequent they might be discrete and separable; it is possible that there is a continuous flow of such interactions that occur imperceptibly. Peterson has described "a universe that can be honestly and sensitively characterized by 'mystery' or 'divine hiddenness' or perhaps even 'divine absence'",[51] and this creates "room" for God to be immanently present at all times throughout the cosmos. Thus God may be considered to be not only the Creator but also the Sustainer of the cosmos. This accords with an early understanding of God being in the present as well as the future, and by deduction the past as well as the present; הָיָא (*aeie*) is not to be translated as "I AM" but as "I shall become; I am becoming" (Exodus 3:14).[52]

"In what way or manner?"

Peacocke suggests that a top-down agency might continuously interact without "rupturing previously observed regular relationships".[53] Whilst God might generally continuously interact in an imperceptible manner, as described in the paragraph above, yet one undeniable characteristic of the incarnate and revealed God of the Hebraic–Christian tradition is that God does reveal Godself, and an essential element of such revelations is the rupture of such "previously observed regular relationships". In Exodus 3, Moses observed a bush that burned, and the volatile oils produced by some bushes sometimes do spontaneously ignite in the desert heat, but the bush that Moses observed was not in a "regular relationship" with the fire as it was not consumed by the fire.

We may receive the accounts of the "miracles of Jesus" as in the Gospels and those recorded in Acts, such as Pentecost, with some liberty, yet the *sine qua non* of Christian faith is the miracle of the resurrection of Jesus. Whilst there may have been some subtlety in this, for example Jesus was not immediately recognizable, the preceding death of Jesus for those who were present was not easy to ignore. Matthew's Gospel

---

[51] Peterson et al., *Reason and Religious Belief*, p. 12.

[52] <http://www.scripture4all.org/OnlineInterlinear/OTpdf/exo3.pdf>, p. 2.

[53] Peacocke, *Theology for a Scientific Age*, p. 164.

records that during the death of Jesus the fabric of the curtain of the Temple was not merely ruptured, it was torn in two as rocks were also split: "At that moment the curtain of the temple was torn in two, from top to bottom. The earth shook, and the rocks were split" (Matthew 27:51). It is characteristic of the most deeply longed for answers to prayer that "previously observed regular relationships" will be suspended, either permanently or at least for a little longer.

"To what effect?" "With what meaning or for what reason or purpose?" "To what extent or degree?"
It can only be supposed, with due reverence, that God created and now sustains the cosmos to satisfy God's purposes. Those who do not believe in God will see no reason to ask if the cosmos has meaning.

"On analogy with what?"
To complete Thomas' classification of "how", Peacocke uses his model of top-down causality to liken the action of God on the cosmos to that of the human mind controlling the body. In this, there may be an analogy if it is assumed that God acts primarily by the transfer of "information".[54] The human brain may be considered to act *internally* by the transfer of information when cerebral function such as consciousness and self-awareness that includes the use of the imagination (not only visual imagination but any of the special senses, e.g. auditory or olfactory, and other senses such as pain, satiety and hunger) and the spectrum of thinking, meditation and prayer occurs. This may be analogous to God working within the human mind to provide emotional and spiritual change. The brain effects *external* change by only two methods. In both, "information" is transferred via neural impulses to either initiate muscular contractions (hence speech and movement) or else stimulate the secretion of substances by glands, for examples the production of saliva by the salivary glands when prompted by hunger or the production of adrenaline by the adrenal glands when anxious. This may be analogous to God acting in the cosmos, either directly by effecting change in the time, energy, matter and space that constitutes the cosmos in which

---

[54] Peacocke, *Theology for a Scientific Age*, p. 164.

we exist, or else via human effort by communicating directly into our thoughts.

The notion of God acting in the cosmos has been taken to an extreme view in the form of process theology:

> Process theism typically refers to a family of theological ideas originating in, inspired by, or in agreement with the metaphysical orientation of Alfred North Whitehead and Charles Hartshorne. For both Whitehead and Hartshorne, it is an essential attribute of God to be fully involved in and affected by temporal processes.[55]

In process theology, there is a description of the transfer of "information" between the persons of the Trinity, although I prefer a description that is less concrete or digital to describe thoughts, prayers, emotions and aspirations. In this, I am minded of St Paul's exhortation, "the Spirit helps us in our weakness; for we do not know how to pray as we ought, but that very Spirit intercedes [for us] with sighs too deep for words" (Romans 8:26). Despite what I have stated about the essential nature of a speech centre, there is in Paul's writing a description that will be familiar to some that our deepest thoughts are transcendental and cannot be expressed in words, i.e. verbal *information*. It is comforting to those persons of faith that the "very Spirit" may also intercede for us if we become incapable of doing so ourselves, for example because of dementia or other brain dysfunction.

When process theology is unpacked, it reveals that the cosmos *is* god's body, that god [god used to denote a non-Christian understanding of God] transcends the world, the world transcends god, the world created god and vice versa.[56] Such theology is essentially the worship of nature, preferring to worship what God has created rather than worshipping

---

[55] Alfred North Whitehead (1861–1947), an English philosopher-mathematician, and Charles Hartshorne (1897–2000), an American philosopher–ornithologist, in D. Viney, *Stanford Encyclopaedia of Philosophy*: Process Theism abstract. First published 2004; revised 2014, at <https://plato.stanford.edu/entries/process-theism/>, accessed 17 July 2023.

[56] Peterson et al., *Reason and Religious Belief*, pp. 66–7.

God the Creator. Since the world might transcend god, then this theology denies both the act of Creation and the need for salvation and seems to be a less honest form of atheism. Process theology may also lead to a view of god that is impersonal. Peterson is forthright in linking any activity that God might have in the world with the personal nature of God: "divine action only becomes a serious possibility if God is conceived as *personal*... an impersonal deity may be the power behind *everything* but cannot be the doer of *particular* actions."[57] The personal nature of God is required such that God is both aware and interested in those matters in which God intervenes.

If God is believed to be a person who acts in the world, then such "acts of God" will affect human beings, and therefore some consideration of human free will is required since human actions may be affected by such "acts of God".

A philosophical definition of *truly* free will has been produced by Basinger: "a person has it in their power to perform A or not to perform A. Both A and not A could actually occur; which will occur has not yet been determined."[58]

This definition is in contrast with the compatibilist conception of free will, in which the agent has a desire and produces the action without *feeling* compelled to do so and the agent *feels* that they could have acted differently. The action produced, however, is not a free choice but that which has been predetermined by God.[59]

Such compatibilism will fit with "Calvinist" theology, that of the theological determinism that regards human beings to be "puppets being manipulated by a puppet master". Therefore the compatibilist notion of free will is merely an illusion: the agent *feels* free to choose, does so without *feeling* coerced and then *feels* they could have acted differently. Human "free will" thus produces results that are compatible with the unfolding of the divine script, not because free will has been exercised

---

[57] Peterson et al., *Reason and Religious Belief*, p. 154.
[58] D. Basinger, "Middle Knowledge and Classical Christian Thought", *Religious Studies* 22 (1986), p. 416, cited in Peterson et al., *Reason and Religious Belief*, p. 158.
[59] Peterson et al., *Reason and Religious Belief*, p. 132.

but only that it is felt to have been exercised. As Peterson asks: "How can God place any value on the love that human beings express towards him, when that love is simply the inescapable result of God's decree that those humans shall love him?"[60] Furthermore, what would be the point in God creating a cosmic puppet show, and in what sense would any of the puppets be guilty and in need of salvation? The rejection of "Calvinist" predeterminism does not imply that God is incapable of acting through persons since, as in the Basinger definition, a person may have a free choice to either perform or not perform an action, but that God may influence their decision. Put simply some may answer the call of God positively, and others simply ignore the call of God. A "Calvinist" description would have to conclude that God induced the decision in a manner that was inescapable, however "free" the choice felt at the time.

"Calvinism" may produce a description of God who is lacking in compassion, as those who are predetermined to suffer do so. The "Calvinist" defence is that "the anger of God [is] against sin".[61] If, however, God has predetermined the course of the cosmos, then God has directly created sin and the consequences thereof, so why should God create something to be angry about? It is more plausible that God's anger (if it exists) might be revulsion against the humans who commit acts of evil, and God's anger may also be as a consequence of God's indignation (and sadness) that God has become required to create necessary natural evil in the cosmos to mitigate human moral evil. If God is, as some "Calvinists" decree, to have created a script, how could God in any sense enjoy the celebration of, for example, an infant baptism with any integrity if God were to foreknow that some terrible affliction or premature death was in the inescapable near future of the infant?

If the "cosmic script" is not predetermined, then the outcomes of events are unknown, and in such open theism, the future is unknown to God who becomes more personal, nurturing and relational, having granted a degree of freedom to creation.[62] Such freedom not only includes the freedom of human beings to make "Basinger" quality choices, but also

---

[60] Peterson et al., *Reason and Religious Belief*, p. 159.
[61] Peterson et al., *Reason and Religious Belief*, p. 159.
[62] Peterson et al., *Reason and Religious Belief*, p. 167.

the freedom inherent in the physical creation through the indeterminacy of quantum mechanics. The freedom of open theism releases humans to truly love, worship and pray to God with the hope that God will effect change.

"Calvinists" reject open theism on the grounds that God has a "lack of absolute control".[63] But why is this lack a problem? A god with absolute control is more like a machine than a person and furthermore, as already described, a God who achieves God's purposes through a myriad of possibilities, in which "truly" human free will exists, is more worthy of praise.

Molinists reject open theism on the grounds that it is "morally intolerable if God could not be guaranteed the precise outcome of his creative ability" and also that "God has taken a risk in creating free persons".[64] There is a question of the moral intolerability of God not knowing precise outcomes, but this is surely less than the moral intolerability of God creating beings that *believe* they are able to make free choices that are actually mere illusions. It is accepted that God took a risk in creating free persons: this points to God being more personable than machine-like. What enjoyment would God have of the cosmos and human "company" if those humans were programmed machines themselves?

"Another criticism is that open theism cannot account for *predictive prophecy*."[65] It is to be noted, however, that biblical prophecy is imprecise in time, manner or place. Such predictive prophecy is often seen to be valid in retrospect. Open theism does not deny the ability of God to achieve God's purposes, but the detail may be left open until it happens. As an example (already given) it is possible to believe that Jesus would have been crucified "one way or another" given the antagonism his teaching and claims he made about himself would have created in a religiously intolerant and brutal society. It is also possible to believe that it was not essential that Jesus was betrayed by any particular individual at a particular time or place.

---

[63] Peterson et al., *Reason and Religious Belief*, pp. 168–9.
[64] Peterson et al., *Reason and Religious Belief*, p. 169.
[65] Peterson et al., *Reason and Religious Belief*, p. 169.

When considering predeterminism, it is possible to ask this question: did Jesus know the "script"?

> And going a little farther, he threw himself on the ground and prayed, "My Father, if it is possible, let this cup pass from me; yet not what I want but what you want". (Matthew 26:39)

This does not read as the actions and words of a person who knows his action will save the world. The *precise* intention of Jesus' mission also becomes questionable. Was it to reform the house of Israel in the tradition of other Hebrew and Jewish prophets? "He answered, 'I was sent only to the lost sheep of the house of Israel'" (Matthew 15:24). Jesus' death and resurrection *may* not even have been the original plan; if so, then those who believe should be even more appreciative that God's gracious response after Jesus was crucified was to resurrect Jesus. A classical god, having witnessed the cruel death of Jesus, might have simply abandoned humanity. I believe that God died for the sins of the world; I do not believe that God was compelled to raise Jesus from the dead, and to me this makes God more wonderful and worthy of thanks and praise.

According to Peterson:

> Process theists ... criticize open theism because it retains the traditional doctrines of divine omnipotence and creation *ex nihilo*, which they have rejected ... because of these doctrines, open theism has serious difficulties with the problem of evil.[66]

This book accepts open theism, and creation *ex nihilo,* although it does not accept God's omnipotence in the classical understanding of god; God's omnipotence (and omniscience) are both considered in this book to be affected, and thus limited, by God's Holiness. Put simply, the nature of God proposed in this book is not "totalitarian" and in this aspect has some accord with what process theists believe, but for a different reason.

---

[66] W. Hasker, "The Problem of Evil in Process Theism and Classical Free Will Theism", *Process Studies* 29:2 (2000), pp. 194–208, in Peterson et al., *Reason and Religious Belief,* p. 169.

Open theism may depart from theological tradition with respect to the denial of "comprehensive divine foreknowledge".[67] It is perhaps quite right that "comprehensive divine foreknowledge" should be rejected, since it is not compatible with a personal relationship with God with any meaning or integrity (from God's perspective), nor with any authentic human free will in the libertarian sense, and neither with any need for redemption; the cross and resurrection become empty gestures.

If we accept Peterson's statement that the "viability of open theism depends on the success of the philosophical arguments against Molinism" and deem for whatever reason that these arguments do succeed against Molinism, then, as Peterson suggests, there is now a "three-way contest" between process theism, theological determinism and open theism, and "many theistic believers will find open theism to be the most credible and attractive position to hold".[68] As a Christian, I reject theological determinism for reasons already given, and I see little difference in Molinism: a "Calvinist" determinism states that God wrote the script; the determinism of Molina states that God, having considered the "free choices" people will make, is able to "write the script, because God has foreknowledge of each possible outcome".[69]

I reject process theism since it has little common ground with Christian theology as expressed, for example, in the Nicene Creed. I accept and embrace the understanding of the *persons* of the Trinity, the belief that I do exercise free will, the need for salvation and the comfort that comes from belief in God who travels with me; these are contained in an understanding of God that only open theism can provide.

The *philosophy* of open theism says much about the omnipotence and omniscience of God, but Holiness is rarely mentioned; the Holiness of God is what prevented God from knowing what the consequences of human freedom would be.

God's Holiness was the reason that God was not able to foresee the moral evil that human beings would perpetrate once they had been granted free will. Another consequence of the Holiness of God is

---

[67] Peterson et al., *Reason and Religious Belief*, p. 169.
[68] Peterson et al., *Reason and Religious Belief*, p. 159.
[69] Peterson et al., *Reason and Religious Belief*, p. 160.

that God could not *create* natural evil but was only able to permit the development of natural evil by creating a cosmos with a non-determined element provided by quantum phenomena.

As mentioned previously, and discussed in more detail later, the "discovery" by God of moral evil may have occurred in the *pre-archaios*, in a temporality other than the cosmos in which humanity exists. It is also possible that God *continues* to be unable to *fore*see the specific detail of evil acts that human beings commit. If this is so then theological determinism, "Calvinism", Molinism and compatibilist free will all become untenable. That mass murderers such as Hitler and Stalin were allowed to live and rise to power suggests that God continues to be unable to foresee acts of evil. Whilst God may not be able to foresee the evil acts of particular persons, it is possible, however, that through being sufficiently distanced from God (the Father) Jesus *could* foresee evil. It is possible that the *kenosis* or self-limitation of Jesus meant that Jesus was, seemingly paradoxically, able to foresee evil through a reduction of intrinsic Holiness. Jesus is recorded as having foreseen his betrayal during the institution of the Lord's Supper; "and while they were eating, he said, 'Truly I tell you, one of you will betray me'" (Matthew 26:21).

If God is unable to foresee evil, then this makes some sense of the *three covenants* in the Hebrew Bible. In these covenants, it might be assumed that God expected each one to succeed, but God's Holiness prevented God from foreseeing how they would fail. The New Covenant may have to be the final covenant inasmuch as it confronts moral evil directly.

Verification and interpretation

However God may be present in the cosmos, whatever the evidence or otherwise that God is the Creator, however God may be continuing to create, and thus be the God who is "becoming" (Exodus 3:14), there is the question of verification, the question of how to determine if and how God acts within the cosmos. Peacocke, minded as a scientist, and quite appropriately within this constraint, seeks evidence that God has so acted.[70] As has been stated before, human free will is presumed to be a feature of humankind that is very important to God. It would not

---

[70] Peacocke, *Theology for a Scientific Age*, p. 251.

HOW MIGHT GOD ACT IN THE COSMOS? 207

therefore be expected that the acts of God would be made apparent to humankind such that the evidence of God's action provided only one interpretation: i.e. that God had indeed acted. For example, at (the first) Pentecost the outpouring of the Holy Spirit enabled some of the early followers of "the Way" to speak in other languages. Yet others were able to dismiss what was happening by claiming that the event was fuelled by wine: "all were amazed and perplexed, saying to one another, 'What does this mean'? But others sneered and said, 'They are filled with new wine'" (Acts 2:12-13).

Evidence would seem to be rarely so concrete in nature that it provides only one interpretation.[71] It is thus the interpretation that is paramount, and in the interpretation of evidence the interpreter will always bring their own hopes and prejudices. Just as in a court of law where evidence is presented, it is the interpretation of the evidence that follows that leads to conclusions rather than the "evidence" *per se*. Thus it is not the evidence that is needed to recognize if God has acted in a unique way. It is the interpretation of the evidence that requires trust and faith. The current freedom to interpret the evidence posed by the cosmos enables the preservation of human free will, for the time being, and this freedom would seem to be something that God has deemed to be in need of preservation.

Mathematics: chaos theory

Before concluding the exposition of physical and biological aspects of the cosmos, the contribution of (mathematical) chaos theory that describes the disproportionate effect of small events is worthy of note.

In his book *Chaos: A Very Short Introduction* (2007), the statistician Leonard Smith stated that small, otherwise localized (randomly produced) phenomena may, according to chaos theory, produce wide-ranging effects by two main mechanisms.[72] Firstly there is the power

---

[71] For example, the two interpretations of the experiment specifically designed to investigate the EPR (spooky action at a distance) effect.

[72] L. Smith, *Chaos: A Very Short Introduction* (Oxford: Oxford University Press, 2007), p. 42.

of exponential increase. Exponential increase[73] is the phenomenon through which both the mass media and in particular social media are efficacious. Exponential increase increases the efficacy of pathogens such as bacteria and viruses that self-replicate, for example the epidemic of "Spanish" influenza that killed more people after the First World War than had died in that war.[74] Exponential increase is also seen in the living world in genetic replication and cellular division that underpins the Creation of all forms of living matter. This may be beneficial division, as in the natural or physiological formation of a complex animal or plant, or it may be harmful, such as the development of a malignant tumour.

The second mechanism is the outcome of sensitive dependence in which small events can lead to large outcomes such as the emergence of political and religious movements. For example, there was an instance in which a British soldier could have shot Adolf Hitler during the course of the First World War but did not do so out of compassion because Adolf Hitler was already injured.[75] Thus not only did Adolf Hitler survive the war, but the episode also led Adolf Hitler to believe in his indestructibility and his having been saved for a greater purpose.

One poignant example (amongst millions) illustrates both mechanisms. Bob Marley, who was both a talented musician and an advocate of racial tolerance and interracial harmony, sadly developed a malignant melanoma in his toe. His choice not to seek conventional treatment is thought to have contributed to his early death.[76] Thus the decay of a single atomic nucleus that may have occurred billions of years ago and billions of light years away from this planet produced a particle of radiation that interacted with one atom in a strand of DNA, thus

---

[73] Exponential increase is the mechanism in which, for example, one might become two, two become four and after ten steps a thousand are created.

[74] <https://www.cdc.gov/flu/pandemic-resources/1918-commemoration/1918-pandemic-history.htm>, accessed 17 July 2023.

[75] <https://www.bbc.co.uk/news/uk-england-28593256>, accessed 17 July 2023; if Pte Tandey's account is not accepted then a myriad of other examples could be substituted to illustrate the point being made.

[76] <https://en.wikipedia.org/wiki/Bob_Marley>, accessed 17 July 2023. The text is extensively referenced.

changing the genetic code in the one cell, and rendered it malignant. The exponential increase of the resulting tumour caused death. The sensitive dependence produced by Bob Marley's achievements resulted not only in great loss on a personal level amongst his family but a great amount of deprivation in the human activities of music and interracial progress.

Whilst chaos theory, and the phenomena (non-linear complex dynamical systems) that it describes, may be seen to increase the non-determinism (randomness) in the cosmos, chaos theory may contrarily provide support to the assertion that an omnipotent God can achieve what God wants despite the cosmos being partly constituted by a random element. One such understanding comes from the intermediate placement, between deterministic and non-deterministic extremes, of the outcome of similar states that have been shown mathematically to converge in a stochastic system.[77] Stochastic systems are based on a natural (Bell-shaped) distribution of probabilities in which likely things happen more often than the less probable, for example when two six-sided dice are thrown, there is a six-fold greater probability of getting a total of 7 rather than 12. It is proposed that whilst chaotic and random processes may lead to a myriad of possibilities God can determine the eventual overall outcome of a scenario or period of history without necessarily specifying the exact sequence of events.

Peacocke has redefined the omniscient nature of God in that, whilst God does not know the future in detail as this is not knowable, God is omniscient in knowing all that is possible to know, and the probabilities of an event occurring.[78] To know what the possible outcomes are and the probability of them occurring is surely similar to not knowing. Whilst this "balance of probabilities" approach may help to explain how God holds the brush in the "broad sweep" of history, it does leave in itself the question as to whether the fate of individuals is something that is precious to God. I prefer a personal understanding of God as one who travels through time with God's creatures and who shares the future with humanity as personal histories unfold in mystery, sadness and joy.

---

[77] Smith, *Chaos*, p. 51.
[78] Peacocke, *Theology for a Scientific Age*, pp. 122–3.

Creativity

If the causal nexus of the cosmos is considered to be a hybrid economy of the predictable and the unpredictable, and thus enables the distribution of natural evil in a non-prejudicial manner and the reality of human free will, it may be appropriate to consider how such a mixed mode may provide any other benefits. In this part of the chapter, it is argued that the mixture may assist in the creative process; not only through, for example, the evolutionary benefit that comes via natural variation, but also through human creativity; and human creativity may also reflect how God may sometimes function as a Creator. The existence of creativity that results from the mixed mode of order and chaos could be seen as a contribution to the "justification" of such a mixed mode being the "fabric" of the cosmos; the ordered and chaotic do not only produce "bad things", but "good things" as well.

That the cosmos is in the process of being created is apparent from many aspects of scientific enquiry: from the cyclical emergence of stars and planets to the process and progress of evolution. The cosmos is also expanding following the "Big Bang" as it is actively drawn apart by so-called "dark" forces. When considering the creative nature of God, it is appropriate to not only consider the cosmos that God has created but to also include the creativity of the creatures made by God, indeed in particular human beings who were made in the image of God. "God thought it good to create a world containing significantly free creatures, beings who, like himself, are centres of creative activity."[79]

The artist who starts with a "blank sheet" does not create out of nothing (*creatio ex nihilo*) but starts the creative process with materials; in prehistoric times these would have been powdered materials and space on the wall of a cave, but crucially with a mind in which the creative process may commence. Creativity does not only involve what might be regarded as art in its widest definition, but also scientific theory. Einstein famously described scientific theory as being "freely invented"[80] and it almost invariably follows on from what has been created or previously

---

[79] Alvin Plantinga in Peterson et al., *Reason and Religious Belief*, p. 132.
[80] Polkinghorne, *Quantum Physics and Theology*, p. 25.

expressed, as in Newton's "standing on the shoulders of giants"; in a similar manner artistic creativity is usually related to what has gone before.

Deterministic aesthetics are rational and ordered and may include, for examples, classical music, Wedgewood pottery, Palladian architecture and the gardens at the Palace of Versailles. Non-deterministic aesthetics do not rely on rationality or order and may include romantic music, raku pottery, ruins, and the gardens in Sissinghurst. A "post-Modern" aesthetic might be irrational and focus on uncertainties.

Totally ordered or predictable music could be a perpetual monotone, or the (somewhat tedious) repetition of one short unaltered phrase.[81] Totally disordered music might have the form of white noise or a variant thereof, or a sequence of randomly generated notes.

In visual art, a "perpetual monotone" might be represented by a blank sheet of homogenous paper or a featureless block of material. The edges of the paper or the interface between the block and the surrounding air would yield some structure; this would be analogous to the music stopping and starting. In visual art, complete disorder could be represented by random dots of colour on the page or a (three-dimensional) sculpture lacking any consistency, self-referencing or external referencing and therefore with a "random" appearance. It is difficult to imagine that the human mind would not nevertheless "see" something in what the artist had created, however motivated to produce a fully "random" work.

The status of apparent randomness in creativity should not be underestimated. In 1994, I composed a piece of music, *Two Minutes for Vienna*. Here are the opening bars of the score:

---

[81] Music that is based upon repetition, such as "Trance", does exist, and for some the ability of such music to induce a trance-like state provides a satisfying aesthetic. It is debatable whether or not this relates to the manner in which music is more normally experienced.

Although the composition is two minutes long, the title actually refers to the time it took to devise a way of converting a series of random numbers into the notes that help to form a musical score.

The non-random "ordered" element is decided as the composer selects instruments and assigns a pitch range to each instrument, chooses the length of the composition and adds expression, dynamics and tempi.

The random "chaotic" element is provided by a Hewlett-Packard 11C calculator that was used to generate four-digit random numbers. These were used to generate a series of rests or notes with specified pitches formed from a discrete number of quavers. Notes were generated from the random sequence of numbers thus: if the first digit was 1–8 this gave the length of note in quavers, and then the second and third digits determined the pitch of the note selected from ranges appropriate for the instruments used; e.g. from C2–C4 for cello, C3–C5 for viola, G3–G5 for second violin and C4–C6 for first violin, from the conversion tables below.

C	C#	D	D#	E	F	F#	G	G#
00-03	04-07	08-11	12-15	16-18	20-23	24-27	28-31	32-35
G	G#	A	A#	B	C	C#	D	D#
G#	A	A#	B	C	C#	D	D#	E
32-35	36-39	40-43	44-47	48-51	52-55	56-59	60-63	64-67
D#	E	F	F#	G	G#	A	A#	B
E	F	F#	G	G#	A	A#	B	C
64-67	68-71	72-75	76-79	80-83	84-87	88-91	92-95	96-99
B	C	C#	D	D#	E	F	F#	G

The fourth digit in each number was not required, and in the examples any redundant digits are marked * for clarity. 345* for violin 1, viola or cello = dotted crotchet B in lower octave; 487* for violin 2 = minim A in upper octave; for any instrument 94** = minim rest and 0*** = rest until end of bar. If the first digit was 9, this indicated a rest, and the next digit that was not 9 or 0 gave the length of the rest in quavers. If the first digit was 0, this indicated a rest for the remainder of the bar, including a whole bar rest if the rest started at the beginning of a bar; thus there was some representation of bar structure in the composition. Orchestration such as blending, abrupt change or punctuation, and any resemblance of melody, counter-melody, harmony or counterpoint, are all generated indirectly by the sequence of randomly generated notes and rests. The open fifth of the first chord is coincidental, as indeed are any recognizable intervals or chords.

The music sounds similar to other genres of *avant garde* music.[82] For me, the music lacks pleasing aesthetics since it is lacking in structure; for others the smorgasbord of musical fragments may create a pleasing aesthetic.

Music is generally composed with the composer exercising choice in all aspects of the composition, although it is recognized that musical notation is open to interpretation and thus what is heard also has some creative input from the performer. The music composed, however, can follow a predictable path according to what is normative for the genre. A specific technique that may be used in composition that has this predictability is the inclusion of the unpredictable, a feature that is not available to music that is consistently lacking in predictability. Aesthetics therefore seem to require a blend of, or positioning between, the ordered and the random. The tension that underpins the climactic points of the greatest music may be the simultaneous experiences of the predictable and the unpredictable, for example the sudden *decrescendo* towards the end of Elgar's *Enigma Variation "Nimrod"*, when a sudden *crescendo* would normally be expected.

---

[82] <https://soundcloud.com/song-2/two-minutes-for-vienna> (accessed 17 July 2023) is a link to a computer synthesized version.

It may be argued that the most pleasing aesthetics in visual art also occur at the boundary of the determined and non-determined; for example the paintings of Vincent van Gogh and John Piper which are neither "photographic" nor "abstract", and provide an attractive blend or merger of the two forms of visual art.[83]

A genre of sculpture in which the disordered and relatively crudely hewn background contrasts with the ordered, detailed and polished figure does not detract from but can enhance the sculpture. Examples are found by Michelangelo in the Galleria dell'Accademia di Firenze. Sculptors sometimes describe their work as a process of discovering the final form of the sculpture that was hidden within the stone before they began to shape it. Composers such as Arvo Pärt describe the creative process as one in which they discover their music from within a vast array of choice; the initial "empty" page of manuscript is likened to being covered in a myriad of hidden possibilities of tempo, scoring and other musical choices that are reduced to a few choices, analogous to stone being removed to reveal a sculpture.

This boundary between the ordered and the "disordered" seems to be important not only in artistic creation but in the creation of life itself; Al-Khalili has argued that "Life lives on the quantum edge", the boundary between the classical ordered world and the "peculiar depths" of the quantum world.[84]

If the random element is important in creativity, there is the possibility that such an element, that of surprise, may even mean that God can have greater enjoyment of what has been created by Godself, and also that which is created by God's creatures such as human beings. "The heavens are telling the glory of God; and the firmament proclaims his handiwork" (Psalm 19:1): God may also be enjoying "the show". The cosmos was not

---

[83] For example, "Red Vineyards near Arles" by Vincent van Gogh, Pushkin State Museum of Fine Arts, Moscow at <https://upload.wikimedia.org/wikipedia/commons/3/35/Red_vineyards.jpg> and "St Mary le Port" by John Piper, Tate Gallery London at <https://commons.wikimedia.org/wiki/File:St_Mary_le_Port,_Bristol_by_John_Piper_(1940)_(Tate_N05718).jpg>, accessed 17 July 2023.

[84] Al-Khalili and McFadden, *Life on the Edge*, p. 46.

created only for the purpose that human beings might praise God; all of creation praises God as in Psalm 148 and verses 5 and 13 explain why:

> Let them praise the name of the Lord, for he
> commanded and they were created.
> Let them praise the name of the Lord, for his name alone
> is exalted; his glory is above earth and heaven.[85]

This is another reason why the cosmos is important to God and hence another reason why the cosmos exists. The cosmos was not simply created so that God could have relationships with free beings, but also so that God would have enjoyment of the cosmos, a cosmos that could surprise God.

Thus the random element in Creation, through which natural evil becomes manifest, is also an essential part of the process through which "good" things become manifest, and may not only give pleasure and enjoyment to humankind but also to God who created such a cosmos.

---

[85] Bauckham, *Bible and Ecology*, pp. 76–8.

5

Some implications of the proposed theodicy

The Parousia

It is not possible to speak of the justice element of Christian theodicy without speaking about resurrection and eternal life, for it is in the heavenly realm that it is believed that the full and final justice of God will be meted out. Such eschatology is an integral part of the Christian story that is needed for a complete theodicy and also to tell the Christian story in full. The Gospel writers and those who contributed to the New Testament wrote of a triumphant return of Jesus Christ, the *Parousia* that would be the beginning of the process in which a new Heaven and a new Earth would be formed. The judgement of Christ, rather than the love of God, is not so much to the fore in contemporary theological understanding, particularly in contemporary worship, and so I wish to redress this balance by quoting from St Luke (based on the writing of St Mark), St John and St Paul:

> There will be signs in the sun, the moon, and the stars, and on the earth distress among nations confused by the roaring of the sea and the waves. People will faint from fear and foreboding of what is coming upon the world, for the powers of the heavens will be shaken. Then they will see the Son of Man coming in a cloud with power and great glory. Now when these things begin to take place, stand up and raise your heads, because your redemption is drawing near. (Luke 21:25–8)

> Very truly, I tell you, the hour is coming, and is now here, when the dead will hear the voice of the Son of God, and those who hear will live. For just as the Father has life in himself, so he has granted the Son also to have life in himself; and he has given him authority to execute judgement, because he is the Son of Man. Do not be astonished at this; for the hour is coming when all who are in their graves will hear his voice and will come out—those who have done good, to the resurrection of life, and those who have done evil, to the resurrection of condemnation. (John 5:25–9)

> For all of us must appear before the judgement seat of Christ, so that each may receive recompense for what has been done in the body, whether good or evil. (2 Corinthians 5:10)

For those who suffer now, the prospect of the *Parousia* occurring in the very near or immediate future must be an attractive prospect, except that it would mean that all life as mortal beings would come to an end, including those dear to them. In times of suffering on a massive scale, such as during times of plague, famine, war and, most poignantly, the *Shoah* of the last century, it would be expected that the question of how God could permit this level of suffering or tolerate such a repugnant exercise of human free will would be widespread. The despair from unanswered prayer was and is distressing. This feeling of abandonment is nothing new within the Hebrew tradition:[1]

> How long, O Lord? Will you forget me for ever?
> How long will you hide your face from me? (Psalm 13:1)

In the Christian tradition during the time that the New Testament was written, the *Parousia* was expected imminently and so the questioning of why the wait was so long did not arise. The feeling of abandonment was, however, very present and experienced most acutely by Jesus as he was crucified. Since those very early times the suffering of Christians

---

[1] Eleven of the Psalms have the phrase "How long?" that is used to protest against God.

has led and still leads Christians, and possibly those of other faiths, to question why God does not "call time" on Earth and commence the new Creation now.

What is termed the delay of the *Parousia* is an enigma in itself, but it does point to one quality of mortal life; there is within it an implication that a characteristic or characteristics that have arisen through living this mortal life will be present or somehow represented in eternal life; such characteristics may include memories, physical attributes or relationships, for if nothing is "carried forward", then there seems little point in God continuing to sustain the cosmos which for many creatures means an experience of living that is short, brutal and painful. Jesus spoke about heavenly reward, and spoke of an upside-down economy in which those who had been poor would be wealthy, and vice versa. This points to inter-dependence: the earthly realm is incomplete without some form of justice in eternal life, and the heavenly realm is incomplete without the memories, physical attributes or relationships of the earthly realm being carried forward into the heavenly realm.

The delay of the *Parousia* is evidence that God, for whatever reason, *values* the cosmos: the delay enables those who are alive to seek the promise of an eternal life and the forgiveness of God through repentance and faith in Jesus Christ during mortal life; Hick's concept of the maturation of souls can be enhanced by the concept of the harvest of souls.

The *pre-archaios*

One of the objections to ascribing all suffering to the rebellious nature of humanity is the animal suffering that occurred on this planet (and continues to occur) prior to the evolution of (human) beings capable of moral choices. The relevance to this theodicy is that it is necessary to postulate the *pre-archaios* to explain what would otherwise be the pre-existence of animal suffering prior to the Fall. It is to be emphasized that the Fall forms part of my preferred explanation. If the Fall is not accepted, then the alternative step in this theodicy is that God had known in advance that human beings, once they had evolved to the status of the possession of free will and the ability to choose between good and evil, would commit acts of moral evil. Human beings were thus (fittingly) placed in a world in which natural evil pre-existed. Despite moral evil being repugnant to God, God nevertheless granted free will to human beings because human free will was sufficiently important to God.

The Russian cosmonaut, Yuri Gagarin, declared in 1961 that God did not exist because he had orbited the Earth and had not found God to be there.[2] John Robinson, in *Honest to God* (1963), developed Tillich's idea that God was not separated by distance but permeated the whole of Creation, and used Tillich's phrase to describe God as the "ground of our being";[3] and in so doing undermined the traditional view that God was somehow "up there" that had persisted despite the Earth no longer being conceived as flat but as spherical. If the eternal domain is separate but within the cosmos (i.e. the time-space continuum in which we exist), then such a Heaven could be separated by distance and be at the far end of the physical cosmos as we know it. Heaven might exist in a different time and will not exist until Earth itself has passed away. Heaven might exist in a parallel continuum that is cotemporal and colocated with our Earth; yet generally completely imperceptible to us, separated by an undiscovered dimension. It is proposed by Moltmann (q.v.) that Heaven may exist in both the present and the future.

The concept of a transcendental plane that is not part of our "terrestrial" temporality was part of Origen's theodicy: "Origen is a firm exponent of the theory of the pre-existence of all individual souls."[4] For Origen, souls are created in the transcendental plane, and for those that rebel "God therefore made the present world, binding the body to the soul as a punishment".[5] Whether souls pre-exist or are formed as the body is formed is not questioned in this book; however, if our temporality ("the terrestrial") and the *pre-archaios* are *both* separated in time *and*

---

[2] M. Peterson et al., *Reason and Religious Belief*, 3rd edn (Oxford: Oxford University Press, 2003), p. 77.
[3] J. Robinson, *Honest to God* (London: SCM Press, 1963), pp. 44–63.
[4] J. N. D. Kelly, *Early Christian Doctrines*, 5th edn (London: Continuum, 1977), p. 180.
[5] Kelly, *Early Christian Doctrines*, p. 181.

not separated in time, in a manner analogous to Moltmann's *futurum* and *adventus*, then the question becomes invalid. We commonly speak about Jesus as a person who was born into our temporality, yet who has eternally coexisted, i.e. beyond temporality with the other persons of the Holy Trinity, namely God the Father and God the Holy Spirit.

Regarding Origen's idea of the body being a punishment device for a corrupted soul, there is no reason to suppose that God would willingly allow the continued creation of intrinsically sinful or corrupt beings; the "lump of sin" as per Augustine's description of his fellow human beings.[6] It is proposed that human beings are born without being tainted with original sin but they are born with a soul and free will, and the latter enables moral evil to exist.

For Origen, "the soul pre-existed the body to which it was assigned as a penalty for its sins". The notion of the body being a prison for the soul was rejected, preferring the Greek theory of creationism that "each individual soul was created independently by God at the moment of its infusion into the body".[7] Origen's contemporary critics depended upon a literal acceptance of the Genesis narrative and regarding Adam and Eve to be actual persons from whom humanity sprung.[8] It is perhaps to be regretted that Origen's ideas were not reappreciated as the foundation of a literal Adam and Eve was no longer widely held.

Although Origen's "soul-trap" was rejected this did not preclude acceptance that the soul may have had a pre-existence for an unspecified reason. The soul was considered to be immortal, but is there any reason to suppose that the eternal existence can only start when the body exists; could not such an eternal existence pre-date the body? There is no reason to suppose that a future eternal form could not also have an eternal existence prior to the temporality that we experience; put another way we do not know, and we cannot know, where we have come from, and so it is not possible to reject the idea of an eternally pre-existent soul on logical grounds.

---

[6] Kelly, *Early Christian Doctrines*, p. 357.
[7] Kelly, *Early Christian Doctrines*, p. 345.
[8] Kelly, *Early Christian Doctrines*, p. 183.

According to Anselm of Canterbury (1033–1109) God is considered to be "outside" of time: "Indeed You exist neither yesterday nor today nor tomorrow but are absolutely outside all time."[9] If God is *fully* outside of the time in which we exist, and therefore not present in any manner within the four dimensions of the cosmos in which humankind exists, then this denies the belief that God either became, or always was, incarnate within God's Creation as we know it. If God is fully outside of earthly time, this also denies God's ability to interact with the causal nexus of the cosmos, or arguably even to be aware of it. If God is outside of time and it is believed that those who have died are with God now, then this may also lead to the question—of personal, emotional and pastoral significance—as to whether those who have died are beyond our ability to have a (transcendental) relationship with now.

The mathematics of Einstein's theory of relativity included the concept of time existing as a dimension distinct from the three dimensions of space (height, length and width), but placed time at right angles to the three dimensions of space. It was possible to develop the mathematics of a four-dimensional continuum even though the four-dimensional continuum could not be satisfactorily drawn on (two-dimensional) paper or even constructed as a three-dimensional model. As discussed before, quantum physical experiments have clearly demonstrated spatial superposition, that an object can exist in two places at the same time. Given the quasi-equivalence of time as one of the four dimensions (the other dimensions being spatial), it is not a great conceptual leap to consider temporal super-temporality, in that an object, person or Godself might coexist both now and at some point in the future or past within the same temporality, or exist in two separate timelines.

It is also possible that the continuum of eternity ("Heaven") is not the same as the time-space continuum of the world "temporality" in which we live as mortals and that they both exist now. Moltmann speaks of two kinds of future.[10] The first is the *futurum*, and this occurs as time passes

---

[9] St Anselm, Prosologion Ch. 19, in J. H. Hick, *Philosophy of Religion*, 2nd edn (Hoboken, NJ: Prentice-Hall, 1973), p. 8.

[10] J. Moltmann, *The Coming of God: Christian Eschatology*, tr. Margaret Kohl (London: SCM Press, 1996), pp. 25–6.

with the myriad of possibilities being reduced to the irrevocable past that is fixed or frozen in time as we move towards a future that is imagined conventionally. The second future for Moltmann is the *adventus*, a future in which the past can be "carried forward" without the passage of time itself as in the diagram below; the thick arrows indicate the passage of time that is experienced normally and the lines indicate a *post-mortem* transfer that will be experienced instantaneously after death, as in waking after sleep.

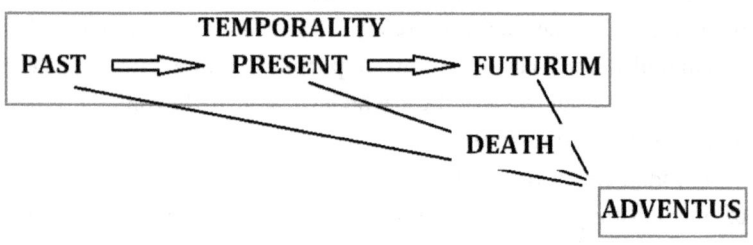

Moltmann (1967) in *Theology of Hope* stated that eschatology was not the future itself but of Jesus Christ and *His* future. Since Jesus was also "identified with this world's reality", Jesus' resurrection means the transformation of this reality, and not the promise of another world.[11] The *adventus*, therefore, has its origin in mortal existence; the *adventus* is the transformation of the cosmos. For Moltmann, it is within this eternal future that the resolution of all ills present and past occurs.

If God is considered to be present in both the eternal and the worldly continua, this might explain why transcendental experiences that are mediated through God are sometimes described as having a "timeless" quality. If God is considered to be immanent in both the eternal and the worldly continua, this means that we can, through prayer, commune with those who have already died despite the *Parousia* still being awaited as an event on Earth. Existing permanently in both continua, God may pass through time with us, and experience the unfolding of history as we do; for example, God may have experienced the effectiveness (or otherwise)

---

[11] J. Moltmann, *Theology of Hope: On the Ground and the Implications of a Christian Eschatology*, tr. James W. Leitch (London: SCM Press, 1967), p. xiv.

of the three covenants in the Hebrew Bible before initiating the New Covenant whilst God was and is fully present in the eternal continuum.

Just as the *adventus* may exist both currently in our timeline and in our future, then it is also possible that such an "eternal" continuum may exist that pre-dates the worldly one. John's Gospel takes "the beginning" in Genesis to refer to the divine eternity "before" creation.[12] For such a "pre-existence", I have used the term the *pre-archaios*. The standard definition of the word *archaios* is "that has been from the beginning, original, primal, old, ancient",[13] and this has been prefixed to convey the sense that this temporality predates our own—it is a time actually before our time. It is possible that the *pre-archaios* and *adventus* are parts of the same continuum or else may become continuous once the worldly "temporality" ceases to exist.

If it can be accepted that the *adventus* exists, a place which is both in our distant future and in our immediate future, then why should there not also be a *pre-archaios*, a place which is both in our distant past and also in our immediate past, a place where "souls" are created?

Patristic theology, e.g. Origen and St Augustine, had the Greek idea that souls existed separately "pre-birth" in a primordial place. Peacocke stated: "Somehow, biology has produced a being of infinite restlessness, and this certainly raises the question of whether human beings have properly conceived of what their true 'environment' is."[14] How could such an environment be *properly* conceived, unless it had some reference to a place in the past?

There is an indication of such a *pre-archaios* in Genesis. I am not proposing a literal acceptance of Genesis, and such rejection of the literal acceptance of the Genesis mythologies dates back to the second-century

---

[12] R. Bauckham, *Bible and Ecology: Rediscovering the Community of Creation* (London: Darton, Longman & Todd, 2010), p. 162.

[13] <https://www.biblestudytools.com/lexicons/greek/kjv/archaios.html>, accessed 4 August 2023.

[14] S. Conway Morris, *Life's Solution: Inevitable Humans in a Lonely Universe* (Cambridge: Cambridge University Press, 2003), p. 314, quoting A. Peacocke in J. Durant (ed.), *Darwinism and Divinity: Essays on Evolution and Religious Belief* (Oxford: Blackwell, 1985), pp. 101–30.

theologian Origen.[15] Whilst the challenge of contemporary (and earlier) science has correctly diminished the authority of the Bible as an exact scientific account, the order in which the constituents of Creation were formed that appear in the two Genesis narratives shows remarkable insight for a work written in antiquity. The writer of Genesis could have been describing an enclosed primordial world in which humans, untouched by sin, did live alongside their Creator. The Garden of Eden might originate from a memory of a time when humans were hunter-gatherers and did not have to compete with each other for land as they were required to as a matter of survival once they were settled in stationary communities. After the expulsion, Adam was told: "cursed is the ground because of you; in toil you shall eat of it all the days of your life" (Genesis 3:17). The collective human memory can be impressive; the indigenous people of what is now Australia have an oral tradition that contains an accurate description of a mountain range that has been submerged under the sea for thousands of years.[16] If those people had recorded in their oral tradition something of their ancestors' existence c.8,000 years previously, then it is not unimaginable that the early Hebrew may have been aware of a Mesolithic existence c.3,000 years in their past,[17] when their ancestors had lived as hunter-gatherers who did not have to toil to grow crops. Presumably those represented by Adam became farmers and this mythology may relate to the increase in the cultural and social awareness of humans and their evolutionary ancestors that had started c.30,000 years ago that was associated with the beginnings of agriculture.

If Genesis contains a reference to such prehistory, then could the notion of a *pre-archaios*, a better place from which we have come, be a possibility for the origin of such collective human imagination? C. S.

---

[15] Hick, *Philosophy of Religion*, p. 9.

[16] R. M. W. Dixon, "Origin legends and linguistic relationships", *Oceania* 67:2 (1996), 127–140 at <https://en.wikipedia.org/wiki/Australian_Aboriginal_religion_and_mythology>, accessed 17 July 2023.

[17] The Mesolithic period was the "final period of hunter-gatherer cultures in Europe and Western Asia" and persisted as late as 3,000 BC. Cf. <https://en.wikipedia.org/wiki/Mesolithic>, accessed 17 July 2023.

Lewis, in *Mere Christianity,* argues a case for an innate sense of right and wrong;[18] could such an innate sense have been formed in a *pre-archaios*? Augustine of Hippo had pondered how God created time, that the world was created *with* time rather than *in* time, stating:

> Nor dost Thou by time, precede time: else shouldest Thou not precede all times. But Thou precedest all things past, by the sublimity of an ever-present eternity; and surpassest all future because they are future, and when they come, they shall be past; but Thou art the Same, and Thy years fail not.[19]

The timelessness of God or otherwise is contentious in philosophical theology.[20] Is this approach too binary? It is proposed that God is present in both the *pre-archaios–adventus* and in "our" temporality; and perhaps in a myriad of temporalities known only to God, sentient creatures being only aware of the temporality in which they are placed. For if God can create and sustain without physical connection, then such super-temporality becomes possible for God; for without physical connection God is disconnected from the *pre-archaios–adventus* and the separate temporalities, but yet able to create and sustain them all, with interventions imperceptible to sentient creatures in each temporality.

It is not unreasonable to assume that God may first have existed "within" the eternal or heavenly *pre-archaios* and from this the earthly temporal continuum was created. This would still represent *creatio ex nihilo* as a new continuum was created where none had previously existed in "our" temporality. The *pre-archaios* may have connected with the worldly continuum only in past times (i.e. when what is now the past was the present), or may continue to do so. As previously stated, it is even possible that the *pre-archaios* is where human souls are created.

---

[18] C. S. Lewis, *Mere Christianity* (Glasgow: Collins Fontana Religious, 1952), p. 16.

[19] Peterson et al., *Reason and Religious Belief,* p. 70, quoting St Augustine, *The Confessions of St Augustine,* tr. Edward B. Pusey (New York: Random House Book, 1949), pp. 252–3.

[20] Peterson et al., *Reason and Religious Belief,* p. 72.

Events such as the Fall may have occurred in the *pre-archaios*; yet the transference of humankind into the earthly continuum may have occurred *without any delay apparent* to humankind as a "fallen" Earth was created that was fit for inhabitation by a fallen humankind. The *pre-archaios* is depicted in the diagram below; as before, the thick arrows indicate the passage of time that is experienced normally,[21] and the lines indicate an instantaneous *pre-vitam* transfer at the time of birth.

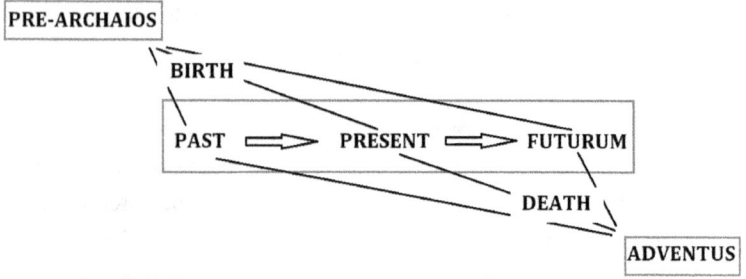

Should the notion of the *pre-archaios* be rejected, then we might need to pose this question with Bauckham: "Is there something wrong in the natural world itself, irrespective of our human presence in it, something that was wrong long before there were humans at all?" Bauckham suggests this may be a consequence of malign spiritual powers.[22] If malign spiritual powers are responsible then we have a dualist approach in that God is no longer omnipotent, and either God has abandoned the cosmos or else it has gone into shared ownership. I prefer the explanation that a natural world that is "wrong" was the deliberate act of the one true God, the wrongness being necessary to mitigate against the moral capabilities of the human beings placed within it.

The Incarnation may be imagined as a time when eternal time and temporal time—"temporality"—fused when the dual nature of Jesus Christ was formed. John Macquarrie states that "the Incarnation is a

---

[21] Although I have drawn time in a "forward" direction, there is the question of whether God is actually pushing us through time when God could equally be pulling us to our final destination within the futurum.

[22] Bauckham, *Bible and Ecology*, p. 160.

process which began with the Creation".[23] Was, however, the Incarnation inevitable? God could have left humankind bereft as a failed experiment, yet chose to redeem this Creation starting with the Incarnation. There is an interesting point: was the Incarnation there from the beginning? If so the birth of Jesus was presumably inevitable since it is problematic to consider an Incarnation with no Christ. Alternatively was earthly humankind cut off from Heaven before the birth of Christ? In the former, if the coming of Jesus was inevitable, then what was the function of the three Old Testament covenants (Noahide, Abrahamic and Mosaic) apart from setting a cultural context into which Jesus was to be born? It does not seem likely that God would have made promises for an indirect purpose. If there was no connection between Earth and Heaven prior to the birth of Christ, then was all transcendental experience, including for example that of the Psalmist, an illusion; and if so, how and by what means was this illusion created? This enigma is potentially soluble if it is accepted that God can interact with the past simultaneously with the present.

Perhaps the cross is atemporal: the salvific effect moving back in time as well as forwards, and this might represent a schism in the time-space continuum:

> And it was about the sixth hour (i.e. noon), and there was a darkness over all the earth until the ninth hour. And the sun was darkened, and the veil of the temple was rent in the midst.
> (Luke 23:44–5, KJV)

Thus the effect of the cross may not be confined and restricted to any particular time but exist as an event of cosmic proportion that affects the created world from its beginning to its end. Consequences of such cosmic impact, such as the darkened sun and torn veil of the temple, could properly be expected were God, the crucified God, to suffer and die.

If at the crucifixion the timelines split, then it is possible that the eternal Jesus is still being crucified. If it is considered that an eternal Jesus

---

[23] J. Macquarrie, *Jesus Christ in Modern Thought* (London: SCM Press, 1990), p. 392, cited in Peacocke, *Theology for a Scientific Age*, p. 314.

is being crucified today and will go on being crucified until God calls the end times, then the proclamation of "Christ crucified" (1 Corinthians 1:23) is no longer just as an historical event, but also as an ongoing reality. It could be stated that Christ *is dying* for the sins of the world and to atone for the suffering in God's Creation. In Cox is a contrasting sentiment from Unamuno, who pointed out in the *Tragic Sense of Life* that those who believe that they believe in God and yet have no passion in their hearts or anguish in their minds—"no uncertainty, no doubt, no element of despair, such people believe not in God but in a god-idea".[24] On a personal note, I can only imagine the heart of God being filled with empathetic grief for the immense suffering on this planet.

If God is full of joy, it can only be because God either already exists in the time beyond the end-times of this Earth, or else can enjoy the certainty that this will occur. In other words, God knows what will exist and such a future is what humanity can only hope for. To rejoice in God today we must commune with the *adventus*, with the eternal God, so that we might celebrate the hope of things that are to come, for even if there are joys in life presently, they are nevertheless temporary, a fleeting illusion of permanence:

> As for mortals, their days are like grass; they
>   flourish like a flower of the field;
> for the wind passes over it, and it is gone, and its place
>   knows it no more. (Psalm 103:15–16)

A new creation

> If anyone is in Christ, there is a new creation: everything old has passed away; see, everything has become new! (2 Corinthians 5:17)

---

[24] D. Cox, *Man's Anger and God's Silence: The Book of Job* (Slough: St Paul Publications, 1990), p. 84.

SOME IMPLICATIONS OF THE PROPOSED THEODICY 229

> Since all these things are to be dissolved in this way, what sort of people ought you to be in leading lives of holiness and godliness, waiting for and hastening the coming of the day of God, because of which the heavens will be set ablaze and dissolved, and the elements will melt with fire? But, in accordance with his promise, we wait for new heavens and a new earth, where righteousness is at home. (2 Peter 3:11–13)

> Then I saw a new heaven and a new earth; for the first heaven and the first earth had passed away, and the sea was no more. And I saw the holy city, the new Jerusalem, coming down out of heaven from God, prepared as a bride adorned for her husband. And I heard a loud voice from the throne saying, "See, the home of God is among mortals. He will dwell with them as their God; they will be his peoples, and God himself will be with them; he will wipe every tear from their eyes. Death will be no more; mourning and crying and pain will be no more, for the first things have passed away." (Revelation 21:1–4)

Earlier in this book, in "Philosophy of creation", it was stated that it is possible to believe that God limits natural suffering in the world to the lowest possible level, by reasoning that a benevolent God would not be expected to have allowed the level of suffering to be higher than that necessary for God's purposes. This does beg the question of how can we expect a new creation to be better than the cosmos as it is?

Barth described the Roman Catholic view of the Church as one in which human activity is a prime mover, of a created order that was incomplete without a Church, and contrasts this with Protestant theology that does not speak of a God as one who is incomplete without a Church.[25] The Protestant view seems to be more feasible since it is conceptually difficult to accept that God would be obliged to do anything. A created order without a "Church", i.e. a created order without a population of people from whom a Church could be called out (the *ekklesia*), would appear to be the pattern of the entire cosmos apart from planet Earth. It is

---

[25] Barth, *Church Dogmatics* I.1, p. 52

accepted that humankind has only explored an infinitesimally small part of the cosmos, but there is indirect evidence that, so far, no beings have travelled to Earth from the hitherto unexplored parts or sent intelligible information to planet Earth. It would seem that human beings were not necessary for God and therefore the existence of human beings suggests that they and the cosmos in which they live are important to God. It is to be noted that God's purposes appear to include the provision of abundant life on planet Earth in greater profusion than is necessary for the existence of human beings, and this suggests that the cosmos is important to God for reasons other than the provision of the conditions for human beings to exist.

Tooley poses "the question of whether God would be morally blameworthy if he failed to create the best world that he could".[26] If it is assumed that God is not morally blameworthy then the implication of Tooley's question is that God *has* created the best world possible. If it is accepted that humankind was created freely out of God's love, and that, to put it rather disrespectfully, we are living today in the best world that God is able to make for us, then this does pose a question regarding a new creation: "If this is how things have to be, how can we have confidence or hope that Heaven will be a place where there is no more suffering, pain or death?"

In order for evil to be absent in a new creation, or heavenly realm, there are a number of distressing scenarios. Humankind might lose its free will and people will function the same way that angels do and praise God, even mindlessly, in perpetuity. Humankind might become like animals that simply "live": to be born, live and die with no concern other than to eat and breed. Humankind might sustain a loss of physicality such that people, whilst promoted to a state of timeless transcendental bliss, are yet immobile and unable to initiate or create in what might seem, both subjectively and objectively, to be an illusory existence. Moltmann alludes to a timeless eternity: "faith and love are timeless acts which remove us out of time, because they make us wholly present (with

---

[26] M. Tooley, "Theodicy and the Problem of Evil", <http://plato.stanford.edu/entries/evil>, accessed 11 July 2023, p. 8.

God)".[27] Humankind might have a limitation on intellect such that people can happily accept a created order in which the lack of evil, tension and other negativity that is important in our current enjoyment of literature, music and other forms of art is not missed.

It has to be a matter of faith that God can and will create a better world for human beings (with free will) to inhabit; perhaps the inhabitants of this new creation will form a mixed economy in which the "moral average" has been raised sufficiently through soul-maturing processes that occur in some during mortal life.

Christian hope is founded upon belief in the resurrection of Jesus Christ. There are no historical witnesses to the actual resurrection event as it happened, for in order for this to have been observed, then such witnesses would have needed to have been placed within the sealed tomb. There is, however, evidence in seismological form as those who met or observed the resurrected Jesus witnessed to what they had seen, and this impacted upon human history. The "missionary" writing that occurred afterwards was possibly delayed on account of the expectation of the imminent *Parousia*. For example, there are indications in the New Testament that the people in the first community of those who believed in the resurrection of Jesus did not expect to die, and those who did die were regarded as having "fallen asleep":

> After that, he was seen of above five hundred brethren at once; of whom the greater part remain unto this present, but some are fallen asleep. (1 Corinthians 15:6, KJV)[28]

The Gospel accounts of the resurrection point to an unknown future; for Moltmann, "they [the resurrection narratives] stand directly within the special horizon of prophetic and apocalyptic expectations, hopes and questions about that which is according to the promises of God

---

[27] Moltmann, *Theology of Hope*, p. 15.

[28] ἐκοιμήθησαν (*ekoimethesan*) literally "were put to repose" translated as "fallen asleep" in the KJV quoted from <https://www.scripture4all.org/OnlineInterlinear/NTpdf/1co15.pdf>, accessed 18 July 2023.

to come".[29] Furthermore, interpretations of the resurrection are neither Docetist, in which Jesus was "purely divine" but had a human appearance, nor Ebionitist, in which Jesus is a "purely human figure", nor Modalist, in which the three persons of the Trinity are different "modes" of the Godhead that may therefore exist independently.[30] A resurrection that combines the fully dual nature of Jesus, as in the Incarnation, points to a re-Creation in which the cosmos is not abandoned by God but is incorporated into it.[31]

> For God so loved the world that he gave his only Son, so that everyone who believes in him may not perish but may have eternal life. Indeed, God did not send the Son into the world to condemn the world, but in order that the world might be saved through him. (John 3:16–17)

Verse 17 above suggests that it is not "only" human beings that are saved, but the world itself. In this verse, the word translated as "world" is κόσμον (*kosmon*) which may be translated as "system".[32]

Our present reality, so full of the miraculous that such phenomena have become ordinary experience, might be a premonition of what is to be. Yet Christian hope of a better Creation is based upon the resurrection appearances of Jesus, being minded of Jesus' mastery over the natural world.

For Moltmann, eschatology *is* the doctrine of Christian hope.[33] According to Moltmann:

---

[29] Moltmann, *Theology of Hope*, p. 178.
[30] Definitions of Docetist, Ebionitist and Modalist from A. E. McGrath, *The Christian Theology Reader*, 2nd edn (Oxford: Blackwell, 2001), pp. 696 and 699.
[31] Moltmann, *Theology of Hope*, pp. 185–6.
[32] <https://www.scripture4all.org/OnlineInterlinear/NTpdf/joh3.pdf>, accessed 18 July 2023.
[33] Moltmann, *Theology of Hope*, p. 2.

> Jesus in his death was identified with the godless, the godforsaken and the dead; it is his resurrection that promises that God will provide a new future for the godless, the godforsaken and even the dead.[34]

Therefore this new Creation is something in which humankind might live in a similar manner in which life is experienced now, for the resurrected Jesus, according to the Gospel accounts, acquired supernatural attributes yet retained characteristics of his pre-death form. The different forms in which the resurrected Jesus was "seen" suggest that the heavenly and eternal worlds have a different physics, and if Eternity has a different physics, then the intervention of God in "our" world does not have to be explained with a description that is compatible with the description of "our" physics. Jesus, however, did not appear to be deprived of a normal "human" personality, physicality, mobility or the ability to initiate or create, nor was there any intellectual blunting. Jesus' resurrection body was reported to be neither ghostly nor ethereal: Jesus ate with his disciples after he was resurrected (Luke 24:39–43). According to Bauckham, the descriptions in Revelation and Ezekiel of the New Jerusalem give hope that the new city is an improvement on the former Garden of Eden as it includes that which is good in human culture,[35] all of the aforementioned "distressing scenarios" may be allayed.

The resurrection appearances looked forward to the coming glory of the Kingdom of God and also back to the past with the marks of crucifixion,[36] and this suggests that mortal existence will somehow continue in, or affect, heavenly existence. For Moltmann, the promise of a new Creation created an interval of tension between the declaration of the promise *via* the resurrected Jesus, and its redemption or fulfilment in the *eschaton*. This interval allows humankind to "obey or disobey, to be hopeful or resigned".[37]

---

[34] Moltmann, *Theology of Hope*, p. xiv.
[35] Bauckham, *Bible and Ecology*, p. 176.
[36] Moltmann, *Crucified God*, p. 172.
[37] Moltmann, *Theology of Hope*, p. 91.

For Bauckham, the connection between Christ and the new Creation is through "the universal solidarity of the risen Christ". In this, it is recognized that mortal humans have solidarity with material creation, and also that in the Incarnation Jesus has solidarity with material creation, and in dying Jesus has solidarity with material creation. In rising, it is therefore not unreasonable to assume that Jesus has solidarity with material creation. Jesus' resurrection was bodily and not (only) spiritual.[38]

Thus mortal life may be there to prepare humankind for something greater. Moral evil exists as a consequence of the freedom of choice that humankind can exercise. Natural "evil", with the associated finitude, mitigates the effect of death by murder that is perpetrated by deliberate human choice. If there are qualities or experiences that are transferred from mortal life into an eternal existence, then such transfers are perhaps the reason why mortal life, with its suffering and finitude, is presently necessary to both God and to humankind. It will not be knowable during mortal life whether the eternal future may be of such a quality that complaint regarding mortal existence becomes irrelevant. I believe that I will be with Jesus Christ, and this will suffice for me.

---

[38] Bauckham, *Bible and Ecology*, p. 171.

Epilogue

But am I better off being able to share God's perspective on such matters, and was I not happier when I could simply feel angry about suffering and then only have to accept that God is mysterious? This book may provide a degree of intellectual satisfaction but may offer little emotional or spiritual comfort. As Rowan Williams has been quoted, the problem of theodicy will not go away even if "some genius does work it all out".[1] The book, however, provides an alternative to the pastoral justification for personal tragedy, as "I do not understand why this has happened to me (or you) but I trust that it is part of a greater plan" is substituted by "I do not understand why the *cosmos* exists, but I trust that it is part of a greater plan", and the latter may be easier to accept.

I have described why God created the cosmos and creatures to live in it with free will. I have explained why there is moral evil in the world despite God being both omniscient and omnipotent. I have demonstrated how the necessary random element within the "fabric" of the cosmos is a capable means through which the harm of natural evil may be distributed in a non-prejudicial manner. I have proposed that natural evil is necessary in a world in which human beings live who commit acts of evil. I have described how God can act in God's creation. I have described how there is a hope of a heavenly eternal life in which questioning or resentment about suffering during mortal life becomes an irrelevance.

Since writing this book, I have come to see the cosmos differently, not the neat description of A-level science or even that of my bachelor's degree. I now see the cosmos as something that is miraculous, described but not yet properly explained. Have you noted how the ripples on a pond from several sources collide and make the picture unintelligible? Yet, if

---

[1] T. Honey, "How could God have allowed the tsunami" (2007), at <https://www.youtube.com/watch?v=2wdkxdiOFJA>.

you are blessed with sight, every atom in the place that can be seen from where you are is emitting radiation, in tiny quantities and in two planes at right angles to each other, with different frequencies or wavelengths, yet your eye and brain can create a wonderful picture for you to enjoy.

In my personal journey, I have, at my better moments, finally come to no longer fear my own death. Indeed I now welcome it. Recently I found this line in the liturgy to distress me: "Dying you destroyed our death." I know that I need to die in order that I too might be resurrected.

If God travels with us, we can have some empathy with God and in our own way "stand alongside" Jesus who wept when He saw how sad the bereaved were after Lazarus had died. God must surely weep greatly in our times as human wickedness, greed and disrespect for creation and the creatures within it seem to grow exponentially. How long Lord do we have to wait for a new creation, how long?

Eminent scientists who are agnostic have stated that we have a choice whether to accept that the cosmos is the work of a Creator God, or that the cosmos somehow created itself out of nothing. One objection to accepting that the cosmos is the work of a benevolent and all-powerful Creator is the presence of suffering—I believe that I have answered this objection. We may do well to let God reveal Godself to ourselves and seek to commence a relationship with Almighty God whilst we are free to exercise choices.

APPENDIX

Further comparison with some other theodicies

Ancient[1]

One of the early theodicies was formulated by the Christian theologian and philosopher Augustine of Hippo (354–430). According to this Augustinian theodicy, the universe is good for God only creates that which is good. Evil is the privation of goodness.[2] Augustine's "conception of mankind" was "as a 'lump of sin', unable to make any move to save itself and wholly dependent on God's grace".[3] There appears to be a description of two creative processes in Augustine's theodicy: God creating the good, and human beings somehow creating themselves since God only creates that which is good. It is true that human beings reproduce; however, the need for God to sustain the cosmos must create tension between God only being able to create the good, and yet somehow being able to sustain the human race consisting of "lumps of sin".

For Augustine, God is good and unchangeable, whereas the cosmos was created *ex nihilo* and so is mutable or changeable. The misuse of free will allows evil into human experience. Augustine accepts the Fall,

---

[1] I have used J. N. D. Kelly, *Early Christian Doctrines*, 5th edn (London: Continuum, 1977), almost exclusively as the principal source for this brief review of Ancient theodicies and thus may not have represented the breadth of current opinion.

[2] M. Peterson et al., *Reason and Religious Belief*, 3rd edn (Oxford: Oxford University Press, 2003), p. 144, quoting Augustine, *Enchiridion* i, 8, 7.

[3] Augustine (396), *Ad Simplicianum*, in Kelly, *Early Christian Doctrines*, p. 357.

an account in which an "originally perfect creation ... rebelled against God". The rebellion brought sin and death, and some will be redeemed by God, and God's kingdom will be established.[4]

Central figures in Augustine's theology are Adam and Jesus: through Adam, human beings became mortal and immortality was restored through the death and resurrection of Jesus Christ. Augustine's prayer, "Give what Thou commandest, and command what Thou wilt",[5] suggested to the moralist Pelagius "that men were puppets wholly determined by the movements of divine grace".[6] Augustine, however, appears ambivalent on the matter of free will; Augustine's "normal doctrine is that ... we retain our free will intact, the sole use to which in our unregenerate state we put it is to do wrong",[7] the unregenerate state having been inherited from Adam.[8]

For Augustine, Adam exists with the ability not to sin, *posse non peccare*, whereas the "liberty enjoyed in heaven by the blessed" is the state of being unable to sin; *non posse peccare*.[9] Adam's ability not to sin was, however, combined with "a settled inclination to virtue".[10] Augustine lays the blame for the Fall solely with Adam, Adam's "creatureliness ... meant he was changeable by nature and so able to turn away from the transcendent good".[11]

God could, however, have denied Adam the freedom to sin, and granted Adam the inability to sin that according to Augustine immortal mankind would acquire in the future Paradise, namely Heaven. God, however, according to Augustine, granted Adam the ability not to sin *and* the creatureliness that enabled Adam to commit sin. Is not such

---

[4] Peterson et al., *Reason and Religious Belief*, p. 144, quoting Augustine, *Confessions, City of God, Enchiridion*.
[5] Augustine, *Confess.* 10, 40 in Kelly, *Early Christian Doctrines*, p. 357.
[6] Kelly, *Early Christian Doctrines*, p. 357.
[7] Augustine in e.g. *Enchiridion* 30: esp. 145, 2, in Kelly, *Early Christian Doctrines*, p. 365.
[8] Kelly, *Early Christian Doctrines*, p. 365.
[9] Augustine, *De corrept. et grat.* 33 in Kelly, *Early Christian Doctrines*, p. 362.
[10] Augustine, *De civ. dei* 14, 11 in Kelly, *Early Christian Doctrines*, p. 362.
[11] Augustine, *De civ. dei* 14, 12 in Kelly, *Early Christian Doctrines*, p. 362.

creatureliness, the ability to "turn away from the transcendent good", indicative of the ability to exercise free will? Augustine deals with any ambivalence in his view of Adam's descendants with the explanation that the will that Adam possessed was "uniquely free".[12]

If it is considered that God *was* able to foresee the evil that Adam (and his descendants) would perpetrate on account of the state of creatureliness in which Adam and humanity were and are created, then God *cannot* place the blame for acts of evil solely on humanity, since God created the conditions sufficient for such evil acts to occur. If it is considered that God could not foresee the consequent evil then God cannot be blamed, although God can be held responsible for the continuing existence of humanity. This begs the question of whether God is in a state of perpetual optimism and, like empathetic human beings, is distressed by the manner in which human beings often abuse their liberty to do evil rather than good.

The influence of Augustine was immense. Augustine's "special role (a posthumous accreditation) was to sum up the theological insights of the West and pass them on . . . to the Middle Ages".[13] The Council of Carthage (418, i.e. held during Augustine's lifetime) insisted that "death . . . was a penalty imposed in view of Adam's sin", that "original sin inherited from Adam is present in every man and even newly born children need baptism if they are to be cleansed from this taint of sin" and that grace was "absolutely indispensable since the Lord said, 'Without Me you can do nothing'" (John 15:5):[14]

> God's judgement, he [Augustine] affirms, is a permanent feature of history, but since the fact of it is not always obvious [to us] God must have a day on which His combined wisdom and righteousness will be vindicated before every eye.[15]

---

[12] Augustine, *Op. imperf. c. Iul.* 6, 22: 3, 57, in Kelly, *Early Christian Doctrines*, p. 363.
[13] Kelly, *Early Christian Doctrines*, p. 390.
[14] Kelly, *Early Christian Doctrines*, p. 369.
[15] Augustine, *De civ. dei* 20, 1–3, in Kelly, *Early Christian Doctrines*, p. 481.

The theodicy of Augustine may be summarized thus: that humans are born sinful and no treatment is too harsh for them, they should be grateful for God's grace; and secondly that God will one day explain why all the evils in the cosmos had to happen. This view dominated the theology of the Church into the Middle Ages and persists today.

I see no possible vindication for almost all of the natural and moral evil in the cosmos and to even suggest that some overall good may result in all cases is either a delusion or indicative of a perverted idea of what is good. I do accept, of course, that the means by which some people who experience suffering and disabilities are nevertheless able to "cope" and be of good cheer can be inspirational and encouraging to others. This book proposes that in the experience of our future eternal life, the questions of why bad things were allowed will become irrelevant. This is not because the sufferings of the past and the "good" that they produced will be revealed to us with a satisfactory explanation, but because the experience of eternal life will be so wonderful that any previous resentment carried into future eternal life will be overwhelmed and seem insignificant.

The Augustinian theodicy does beg the question of *why* would God create a cosmos that reverted to evil if goodness was rejected. This almost suggests that God did not create the cosmos *ex nihilo* but added a layer upon that which had already been created by an evil deity. As noted by Peterson, this undermines the "power and unquestionable sovereignty of God"[16] but also insinuates a dual nature of the cosmos in which the good and the evil were created by a pair of demi-gods. This resonates, for example, with the Babylonian creation mythology of Marduk in which order was drawn out of pre-existing chaos.

The theodicy in this book proposes that God's Holiness prevents God from purposefully creating that which is evil. God tolerates moral evil since it is a consequence of human free will. Natural evil is required to mitigate against the effects of moral evil, and the random element within the physical creation leads to natural evil with a non-prejudicial distribution.

Is it more plausible that God created a cosmos with the potential for natural evil because God either (a) foresaw that humanity would

---

[16] Peterson et al., *Reason and Religious Belief*, p. 144.

perpetrate acts of moral evil once free will was granted and that a cosmos with natural evil was necessary to mitigate the effects of moral evil or (b) discovered evil only after human beings, created in "God's image", had chosen to commit acts of evil once they had been granted free will? I favour the latter and cite God's Holiness as the reason that God did not foresee the full consequences of granting humanity free will.

Augustine proposes a "golden" age in which there was no evil, and it is questioned "how is it that they would ever choose to do evil"? The answer given in Genesis is that human curiosity and the desire to be independent, to break the parent–child relationship between Creator and creature, were too powerful for sentient beings.

Bishop Irenaeus of Lyon (c.AD130—c.202) was a "Christian thinker", who proposed a theodicy that was later developed by Hick in which the development of "morally mature persons"[17] was required since God was not deemed able to create "morally mature persons" because part of the process involves dealing with, or actual "participation" in, evil.[18] According to Irenaeus, human beings were created "in the image and likeness of God"; however, in Paradise Adam was "morally, spiritually and intellectually a child".[19] Furthermore, Irenaeus states that Adam "fell an easy prey to Satan's wiles and disobeyed God",[20] although this does beg the question of why would God empower Satan to corrupt Adam.

The inability of God to create morally mature persons resonates with the idea that evil, being *anathema* to God, is such that God is not able to voluntarily create evil by a direct means, and that God has only been able to achieve this by creating a cosmos in which natural evil is generated by chaotic and random "non-ordered" processes, and the allowance of human beings to express their free will in thoughts, words and actions.

If we are to accept that there is evidence of God's love for the cosmos then this should presumably mean the entire cosmos, and not just "Holy" or otherwise sanctified parts of the cosmos. Therefore if it is considered that God "loves" the evil within the cosmos, then God, being thought

---

[17] Peterson et al., *Reason and Religious Belief*, p. 144.
[18] Peterson et al., *Reason and Religious Belief*, p. 145.
[19] Irenaeus, *Dem.* 12, in Kelly, *Early Christian Doctrines*, p. 171.
[20] Irenaeus, *Dem.* 16, in Kelly, *Early Christian Doctrines*, p. 171.

to be both Holy and benevolent, must surely love the evil in the cosmos not for the benefit of evil, or in some gratuitous manner, but because evil serves some purpose.

The maturation of human souls could, as Hick promotes, be that purpose. It has to be recognized that many are not able to progress the maturation of their souls, for example those who are stillborn, those who are restricted in thought or action by personal factors or else restricted through societal factors such as lack of education or those living under crushing oppression that prevents the free transmission of ideas. It is therefore suggested that the purpose of evil may be to provide those who enter eternal life with a mixed degree of moral maturation. It would seem inappropriate and plain unfair if those who entered eternity with low degrees of spiritual, emotional and intellectual maturation *persisted* eternally in a disadvantaged status in such a mixed economy. It would seem "fairer" and more in accord with a new creation that all of humanity attains some uniformity; yet the truth is that those who die attain before death differing degrees of spiritual, emotional and intellectual maturation. This differentiation may be how things are in the cosmos as we experience it now, but such differentiation may not, and instinctively one feels should not, carry forwards into eternal life.

Modern

An important element of Irenaean theodicy is that though the process of living, maturation occurs not only as a moral being but also as a spiritual being, and spiritual development occurs as faith and trust in God grows. For Hick, there is an "epistemic distance between creature and Creator".[21] The presence of evil is an important factor in creating this distance, and for Hick the cosmos is configured to appear as if God did not exist.[22] Hick states that this distance is important: "the silence of God" as described in Job. In Dermot Cox's book *Man's Anger and God's Silence*, the Book of

---

[21] Peterson et al., *Reason and Religious Belief*, p. 145.
[22] This book proposes that the cosmos provides evidence for both unbelief *and* belief in God.

Job asks whether negative reactions to human suffering are in any form of dialogue with God when God seems to be silent. Certainly such silence creates epistemic distance.

G. Stanley Kane has critiqued Hick, claiming that the "epistemic distance" Hick wants to postulate between humanity and God to make room for faith "can be maintained at much less cost".[23] This is surely a matter of judgement, bearing in mind the fact that whatever the level of suffering and evil in the world this would always seem unacceptably too high.

Soul-making has also been critiqued on the grounds of the collateral damage, those whose lives are ruined whilst others learn. Hick's response is that it is for each person to "ultimately decide whether the soul-making process is worth it".[24] For some, accepting that God has shown evidence of God's love in the cosmos may be considered to be a sufficient reason for the cosmos to exist, and for those it may similarly be appropriate to view soul-making not from our perspective but from that of God and accept that if God has ordained the cosmos so to be, it is not for us to decide otherwise.

Process theodicy is derived from process thought that is "a view of reality as becoming rather than being". Process thinkers regard god as possessing a consequent nature (that) changes in response to events in the creaturely world; god may also be said to change or to be "in process". Process theodicy grants that god has some power, but not all of it, and this permits creatures to exercise freedom that god cannot restrict. Process thinkers would regard god as being "persuasive" rather than "coercive". The process exponent David Ray Griffin (b.1939) goes further to deny god any persuasive ability with the statement "god cannot unilaterally affect any state of affairs".[25]

Process theism is similar to Deism: god in primordial nature creates the cosmos, but then allows the creatures to behave as they wish, to

---

[23] Peterson et al., *Reason and Religious Belief*, p. 145, quoting G. S. Kane, "The Failure of Soul-Making Theodicy", *International Journal for the Philosophy of Religion* 6 (1975), pp. 1–22.

[24] Peterson et al., *Reason and Religious Belief*, p. 146.

[25] D. R. Griffin, *God, Power and Evil* (Philadelphia, PA: Westminster, 1976), p. 280, quoted in Peterson et al., *Reason and Religious Belief*, p. 146.

exercise complete freedom, and thus evil occurs in which god is powerless to intervene. Somehow, through a mechanism not detailed in Peterson's account, "all positive and negative experiences in the creaturely realm are ultimately conserved and reconciled in god's own conscious life".[26] This form of Deism, however, does not include any of the defining characteristics of the Christian understanding of God, the need for salvation and the eschatological hope of a new Creation. Process thinkers are left with the hope that "experiences in God's own conscious life are the basic hope for the triumph of good and the redemption of the world".[27] But for whom will this redeemed world exist?

For those to whom god is a metaphysical concept, there may be some attraction in process theodicy as a description of god who has some investment in the wellbeing of creatures, however limited. For those to whom God is a person, with moral qualities, the lack of "divine goodness" with an "orientation that is essentially *aesthetic* rather than *moral*",[28] will find that this attempt to explain the occurrence of evil in the world is not compatible with a Christian understanding of a loving God who is the Creator, sustainer and *redeemer* of the cosmos. It would seem that the essential task of process theology is to limit the description of god to fit with what is observed and experienced; this is a normal "scientific" endeavour and of course has much to commend it, but process theology, as with much of the theological understandings of many faiths and belief systems, does not progress an attempt to inform a *Christian* understanding of the problem of theodicy.

When considering suffering, and in particular "Horrendous Evils", the philosopher Marilyn Adams (b.1943) has suggested that the argument should "migrate from a global level to an individual level".[29] As a theist, Adams argues that an individual may regard "infinite and eternal goods" to be part of the benefit that outweighs evil, even if non-theists will not

---

[26] Peterson et al., *Reason and Religious Belief*, p. 147. This part of the account seems to relate to moral evil but omits natural evil.

[27] Peterson et al., *Reason and Religious Belief*, p. 147.

[28] Peterson et al., *Reason and Religious Belief*, p. 147.

[29] M. Adams, *Horrendous Evils and the Goodness of God* (Ithaca, NY: Cornell University Press, 1999).

accept these. Such infinite goods must surely refer to some form of eternal recompense, and this is in accord with the Hebrew understanding that Heaven or some form of post-death existence is required so that God can mete out eternal justice. This is also in accord with Paul's expectation of Heaven: "I consider that the sufferings of this present time are not worth comparing with the glory about to be revealed to us" (Romans 8:18). Adams' view appears to be Deist in nature; suggesting that the evil in the world is of no account since God will make amends in the next life.[30]

Adams' consideration of the individual is pastorally appropriate; those who are suffering are likely to be unaffected by any probabilistic or sociological approach. The consideration of individual suffering is brought into sharp focus in Dostoevsky's *The Brothers Karamazov* where the question is posed: "What kind of a God would permit the torture of small children?"

If we are to suspend the *omniscience* of God then this could be rephrased: "what kind of a God would *knowingly* permit the torture of small children?" In this book, I have proposed two paths. The first is that God foreknew the evil consequences that would be the result of granting free will to human beings, and therefore created a cosmos with a fitting level of natural evil to balance human moral evil. The level of horrendous evils that exists leads me to reject this proposition; a benevolent God would not have knowingly created such beings capable of such evil acts.

A second possibility is that humans evolved into what was actually a fitting environment even though God did not foreknow how evil human beings would become. This proposition is to be rejected since it is tautological and self-providential: why would God have ever created the conditions so that such a cosmic "coincidence" would occur?

My preferred explanation is that God, being Holy, *could not* foreknow the extent of the depravity of human beings once free will was granted. This has some accord with the Genesis account in which God's discovery

---

[30] Adams is also a Universalist, stating that "any created persons who experienced horrendous evils will be able at some point to affirm the value of their own lives". Cf. Peterson et al., *Reason and Religious Belief*, p. 149. How God will deal with individuals according to how they have lived their lives or expressed any faith in God, or otherwise, is outside the remit of this book.

of how bad human beings would become once free will was granted occurred at the beginning of the human "race": the allegorical Adam and Eve.[31] "And the Lord was sorry that he had made humankind on the earth, and it grieved him to his heart" (Genesis 6:6). How could the Lord be sorry for what the Lord had done if the Lord had foreknown the consequences? This does in effect absolve God from responsibility for moral evil, and perhaps the ancient acceptance of this absolution or dissociation is why there is such an unabashed exposition of human depravity described in the Hebrew Bible with both detail and repetition.

This last and preferred explanation does undermine the doctrine of the omniscience of God in that God is proposed to lack fully predictive abilities. The scale of such a task has already been described, and it is almost possible to believe that even God could not have fully predictive abilities having created a cosmos that would proceed in a non-deterministic manner. Without such predictive abilities, however, this describes a more personal God who travels with us through our time, a God who achieves God's purposes not through the following of a predetermined script (that effectively excludes any real human freedom), but a God who achieves God's purposes through a myriad of possibilities in which the exact detail is not known to God.[32] If the cosmos is not deterministic, there is "room" for God to alter the course of future events, and it is possible that prayer can alter the outcome of events; the seemingly random pattern of future events could even make such interventions less overt. This does beg the question of why prayers are not always answered. My best answer would be that if all prayer was answered this would effectively hand control of the cosmos over to human beings. Prayer can also act importantly in a non-physical manner by strengthening the spiritual link between the people who pray with the God to whom they pray, connected by a non-physical consciousness and soul.

---

[31] It is suggested that the "Garden of Eden", in which God's discovery was made, will not ever be discovered as a geographical location or archaeological site on planet Earth, but that these events occurred in another temporality, the *pre-archaios* that is proposed in this book.

[32] Peterson et al., *Reason and Religious Belief*, p. 154.

Bibliography

Adams, M., *Horrendous Evils and the Goodness of God* (Ithaca, NY: Cornell University Press, 1999).

Al-Khalili, J., *The Secrets of Quantum Physics* (Furnace Ltd., 2014), at <https://www.dailymotion.com/video/x37sq23>, accessed 19 July 2023.

Al-Khalili, J. and McFadden, J., *Life on the Edge: A Coming of Age of Quantum Biology* (London: Black Swan, 2014).

Arndt, M. et al., "Wave–particle duality of C_{60} molecules" *Nature* 401 (1999), pp. 680–2.

Atkinson, D., *Renewing the Face of the Earth: A Theological and Pastoral Response to Climate Change* (Norwich: Canterbury Press, 2008).

Barth, K., *Church Dogmatics* I.1, tr. Geoffrey Bromiley (Edinburgh: T & T Clark, 1975).

Bauckham, R., "'Only the Suffering God Can help'. Divine passibility in modern theology", *Themelios* 9:3 (1984), pp. 6–12.

Bauckham, R., *Bible and Ecology: Rediscovering the Community of Creation* (London: Darton, Longman & Todd, 2010).

Brooks, M., "The conflict between science and Christianity; artefact or real?", Essay submitted in part fulfilment for the requirements for the Degree of Bachelor of Science of the University of London, 1978.

Brooks, M., "The Mechanics of Breathing", *The Trombonist* 1 (1996), pp. 28–9.

Brooks, M., "The Church's One Foundation: 'Why Christians in the Church of England may disagree on matters of faith with each other and others, and an approach to resolving such disagreements'", Dissertation submitted in part fulfilment of the requirements for the Degree of Master of Arts in Ministerial Theology of the University of Canterbury Christ Church, 2013.

Campling, M., *Theological Papers* (London: Marcel Music, 2022).

Conway Morris, S., *Life's Solution: Inevitable Humans in a Lonely Universe* (Cambridge: Cambridge University Press, 2003).

Cox, D., *Man's Anger and God's Silence: The Book of Job* (Slough: St Paul Publications, 1990).

Davies, P. C. W. and Brown, J. R., *The Ghost in the Atom: A Discussion of the Mysteries of Quantum Physics* (Cambridge: Cambridge University Press, 1986/1993).

Davis, S. T. (ed.), *Encountering Evil: Live Options in Theodicy*, 1st edn (Edinburgh: T & T Clark, 1981).

Douglas-Klotz, N., *Prayers of the Cosmos: Reflections on the Original Meaning of Jesus's Words* (San Francisco: Harper, 1990).

Fein, Y. et al., "Quantum superposition of molecules beyond 25kDa", *Nature Physics* 15:12 (2019), pp. 1242–5.

Green, J. B., *The Gospel of Luke*, The New International Commentary on the New Testament (Grand Rapids, MI: Eerdmans, 1997).

Gribbin, J., *In Search of Schrödinger's Cat* (London: Transworld Publishers, 1984).

Griffin, D. R., "A Critique of John H. Hick's Theodicy", at <http://www.anthonyflood.com/griffincritiquehicktheodicy.htm>, accessed 15 July 2023.

Gutiérrez, G., *On Job: God-Talk and the Suffering of the Innocent* (Maryknoll, NY: Orbis Books, 1986).

Hawking, S., *A Brief History of Time* (London: Bantam Books, 1988).

Hawking, S. and Mlodinow, L., *The Grand Design* (London: Bantam Books, 2010).

Heschel, A. J., *The Prophets* (New York: Harper Classics, 1962).

Hick, J. H., *Philosophy of Religion*, 2nd edn (Hoboken, NJ: Prentice-Hall, 1973).

Hick, J. H., "An Irenaean Theodicy" and "Response to Critiques", in S. T. Davis (ed.), *Encountering Evil: Live Options in Theodicy*, 1st edn (Edinburgh: T & T Clark, 1981), pp. 39–52 and 63–8.

Honey, T., "How could God have allowed the tsunami" (2007), at <https://www.youtube.com/watch?v=2wdkxdiOFJA>.

Kelly, J. N. D., *Early Christian Doctrines*, 5th edn (London: Continuum, 1977).

Kropf, R. W., *Evil and Evolution: A Theodicy* (Eugene, OR: Wipf & Stock, 1984).

Kroto, H. W. et al., "C_{60}: Buckminsterfullerene", *Nature* 318 (1985), pp. 162–3.

Lewis, C. S., *Mere Christianity* (Glasgow: Collins Fontana Religious, 1952).

McFague, S., *Metaphorical Theology: Models of God in Religious Language* (Philadelphia, PA: Fortress Press, 1982).

McGrath, A. E., *Christian Theology: An Introduction*, 3rd edn (Oxford: Blackwell, 2001).

McGrath, A. E., *The Christian Theology Reader*, 2nd edn (Oxford: Blackwell, 2001).

Moltmann, J., *Theology of Hope: On the Ground and the Implications of a Christian Eschatology*, tr. James W. Leitch (London: SCM Press, 1967).

Moltmann, J., *The Crucified God: The Cross of Christ as the Foundation and Criticism of Christian Theology*, tr. R. A. Wilson and John Bowden (London: SCM Press, 1974).

Moltmann, J., *God in Creation*, tr. Margaret Kohl (London: SCM Press, 1985).

Moltmann, J., *The Coming of God: Christian Eschatology*, tr. Margaret Kohl (London: SCM Press, 1996).

Morris, L., *Luke*, Tyndale New Testament Commentaries (Leicester: InterVarsity Press, 1988).

Pannenberg, W., *An Introduction to Systematic Theology* (Grand Rapids, MI: Eerdmans, 1991).

Peacocke, A., *Theology for a Scientific Age: Being and Becoming—Natural, Divine, and Human* (Minneapolis, MN: Fortress Press, 1993).

Peterson, E., *Eat this Book: The Art of Spiritual Reading* (London: Hodder & Stoughton, 2006).
Peterson, M., Hasker, W., Reichenbach, B. and Basinger, D., *Reason and Religious Belief*, 3rd edn (Oxford: Oxford University Press, 2003).
Pirani, F. and Roche, C., *The Universe for Beginners* (Cambridge: Icon Books, 1993).
Polkinghorne, J., *Quantum Theory: A Very Short Introduction* (Oxford: Oxford University Press, 2002).
Polkinghorne, J., *Quantum Physics and Theology: An Unexpected Kinship* (London: SPCK, 2007).
Ramsey, M., *The Christian Priest Today* (London: SPCK, 1972).
Robinson, J. A. T., *Honest to God* (London: SCM Press, 1963).
Romer, J., *Testament: the Bible and History* (London: Michael O'Mara Books, 1988).
Rovelli, C., *Reality is not what it seems* (London: Allen Lane, 2014).
Schwartz, J. and McGuinness, M., *Introducing Einstein* (Cambridge: Icon Books, 1992).
Smith, L., *Chaos: A Very Short Introduction* (Oxford: Oxford University Press, 2007).
Southgate, C., *The Groaning of Creation* (Louisville, KY: Westminster John Knox Press, 2008).
Talbert, C. H., *Reading Luke: A Literary and Theological Commentary on the Third Gospel* (Macon, GA: Smyth & Helwys, 2002).
Tooley, M. "Theodicy and the Problem of Evil", <http://plato.stanford.edu/entries/evil>, accessed 11 July 2023.
Tremblay, P. and Dick, A. S., "Broca and Wernicke are dead, or moving past the classic model of language neurobiology", *Brain and Language* 162 (2016), pp. 60–71.
Watts, F., Nye, R. and Savage, S., *Psychology for Christian Ministry* (London: Routledge, 2002).
Williams, R., *On Christian Theology* (Oxford: Blackwell, 2000).
Wright, N. T., *The Resurrection of the Son of God* (London: SPCK, 2002).

EU GPSR Authorized Representative:

LOGOS EUROPE, 9 rue Nicolas Poussin, 17000 La Rochelle, France

contact@logoseurope.eu

www.ingramcontent.com/pod-product-compliance
Lightning Source LLC
Chambersburg PA
CBHW071621170426
43195CB00038B/1598